Twelfth Night
Webster's Spanish Thesaurus Edition

for ESL, EFL, ELP, TOEFL®, TOEIC®, and AP® Test Preparation

William Shakespeare

D1360195

ICON CLASSICS

Published by ICON Group International, Inc.
7404 Trade Street
San Diego, CA 92121 USA

www.icongrouponline.com

Twelfth Night: Webster's Spanish Thesaurus Edition for ESL, EFL, ELP, TOEFL®, TOEIC®, and AP®
Test Preparation

This edition published by ICON Classics in 2005
Printed in the United States of America.

ISBN 0-497-26212-6

Contents

PREFACE FROM THE EDITOR

Webster's paperbacks take advantage of the fact that classics are frequently assigned readings in English courses. By using a running English-to-Spanish thesaurus at the bottom of each page, this edition of *Twelfth Night* by William Shakespeare was edited for three audiences. The first includes Spanish-speaking students enrolled in an English Language Program (ELP), an English as a Foreign Language (EFL) program, an English as a Second Language Program (ESL), or in a TOEFL® or TOEIC® preparation program. The second audience includes English-speaking students enrolled in bilingual education programs or Spanish speakers enrolled in English speaking schools. The third audience consists of students who are actively building their vocabularies in Spanish in order to take foreign service, translation certification, Advanced Placement® (AP®)[1] or similar examinations. By using the Webster's Spanish Thesaurus Edition when assigned for an English course, the reader can enrich their vocabulary in anticipation of an examination in Spanish or English.

Webster's edition of this classic is organized to expose the reader to a maximum number of difficult and potentially ambiguous English words. Rare or idiosyncratic words and expressions are given lower priority compared to "difficult, yet commonly used" words. Rather than supply a single translation, many words are translated for a variety of meanings in Spanish, allowing readers to better grasp the ambiguity of English, and avoid them using the notes as a pure translation crutch. Having the reader decipher a word's meaning within context serves to improve vocabulary retention and understanding. Each page covers words not already highlighted on previous pages. If a difficult word is not translated on a page, chances are that it has been translated on a previous page. A more complete glossary of translations is supplied at the end of the book; translations are extracted from Webster's Online Dictionary.

Definitions of remaining terms as well as translations can be found at www.websters-online-dictionary.org. Please send suggestions to websters@icongroupbooks.com

The Editor
Webster's Online Dictionary
www.websters-online-dictionary.org

---

[1] TOEFL®, TOEIC®, AP® and Advanced Placement® are trademarks of the Educational Testing Service which has neither reviewed nor endorsed this book. All rights reserved.

PERSONS REPRESENTED

ORSINO, Duke of Illyria.
SEBASTIAN, a young Gentleman, **brother** to Viola.
ANTONIO, a Sea Captain, **friend** to Sebastian.
A SEA CAPTAIN, friend to Viola
VALENTINE,
CURIO, } gentleman **attending** on the Duke.
SIR TOBY BELCH, Uncle of Olivia.
SIR ANDREW AGUE-CHEEK.
MALVOLIO, Steward to Olivia.
FABIAN,
CLOWN, } servants to Olivia.
OLIVIA, a **rich** Countess.
VIOLA, in love with the Duke.
MARIA, Olivia's Woman.
LORDS, PRIESTS, SAILORS, OFFICERS, MUSICIANS, and OTHER
ATTENDANTS.

Spanish

attending: asistiendo.
brother: hermano, el hermano,
  cofrade.
fabian: fabianista.
friend: amigo, amiga, el amigo.
maria: María.
rich: rico.
sir: señor.
viola: la viola.

ACT I

SCENE I. AN APARTMENT IN THE DUKE'S PALACE.

[Enter DUKE, CURIO, LORDS; MUSICIANS attending.]
DUKE.
If **music** be the food of love, play on,
Give me **excess** of it; that, surfeiting,
The **appetite** may **sicken** and so die.--
That **strain** again;--it had a **dying** fall;
O, it came **o'er** my **ear** like the **sweet** south,
That **breathes** upon a bank of violets,
Stealing and **giving** odour.--Enough; no more;
'Tis not so sweet now as it was before.
O **spirit** of love, how **quick** and **fresh art** thou!
That, **notwithstanding thy** capacity
Receiveth as the **sea**, **nought enters** there,
Of what **validity** and **pitch** soever,
But **falls** into **abatement** and **low** price
Even in a **minute**! so full of **shapes** is fancy,
That it **alone** is high-fantastical.

Spanish

abatement: descuento, rebaja, reducción, disminución, supresión, baja, Abolición.
alone: solo, único, solamente, sólo.
appetite: apetito, el apetito.
art: arte, el arte.
breathes: respira.
dying: muriendo, agonizante.
ear: oreja, espiga, la oreja, oído.
enters: entra, inscribe, monta.
excess: exceso, excedente.
falls: se cae, decrece, derriba.

fresh: fresco.
giving: dando.
low: bajo, depresión.
minute: minuto, el minuto, minuta, menudo.
music: música.
notwithstanding: sin embargo, a pesar de, no obstante.
nought: cero, nada.
o'er: sobre.
pitch: paso, pez, grado de inclinación, tono, cabeceo, diapasón, altura, brea,

pendiente.
quick: rápido, pronto.
sea: mar, el mar.
shapes: las formas, formas, aspectos.
sicken: enfermar.
spirit: espíritu.
strain: colar, esfuerzo, deformación, cepa, tensión, torcedura.
sweet: dulce, caramelo, postre.
thy: tu.
validity: validez, vigencia.

CURIO.
   Will you go **hunt**, my lord?

DUKE.
                              What, Curio?

CURIO.
   The hart.

DUKE.
   Why, so I do, the noblest that I have:
   O, when **mine** eyes did see Olivia first,
   Methought she purg'd the air of pestilence;
   That **instant** was I turn'd into a hart;
   And my desires, like **fell** and **cruel** hounds,
   E'er since **pursue** me.--How now! what news from her?
   [Enter VALENTINE.]

VALENTINE.
   So please my lord, I might not be admitted,
   But from her **handmaid** do return this answer:
   The **element** itself, **till** seven years' heat,
   Shall not **behold** her face at **ample** view;
   But like a **cloistress** she will **veiled** walk,
   And water once **a-day** her **chamber** round
   With eye-offending **brine**: all this to season
   A brother's **dead** love, which she would keep fresh
   And **lasting** in her **sad remembrance**.

DUKE.
   O, she that hath a heart of that **fine** frame
   To pay this **debt** of love but to a brother,
   How will she love when the rich **golden** shaft
   Hath kill'd the **flock** of all affections else
   That live in her; when **liver**, **brain**, and heart,
   These **sovereign** thrones, are all **supplied** and fill'd,--

Spanish

a-day: día de llegada.
ample: amplio, abundante.
behold: tenga.
brain: cerebro, seso.
brine: salmuera, escabeche.
chamber: cámara, habitación, cuarto.
cloistress: monja.
cruel: cruel.
dead: muerto.
debt: deuda.
element: elemento, ingrediente.
fell: talar, derribar.

fine: multa, fino, multar, excelente, bonito, delgado, bien, estupendo, bueno.
flock: bandada, rebaño, manada.
golden: dorado, áureo, de oro.
handmaid: sirvienta, criada, peón.
hunt: cazar, cazo, caza, cazáis, cazas, cazamos, cazad, cacen, cace, cazan, acosar.
instant: momento, instante, momentito, instantáneo.
lasting: continuo, duradero.

liver: hígado.
mine: mina, mío, minar.
pursue: perseguir, perseguid, persiguen, persigue, persigo, persigan, persiga, perseguís, perseguimos, persigues.
remembrance: recuerdo.
sad: triste, afligido.
sovereign: soberano.
supplied: suministrado.
till: caja, hasta que, hasta, a que.
veiled: rebozado, velado.

Her **sweet** perfections,--with one **self** king!--
Away before me to sweet **beds** of flowers:
Love-thoughts **lie rich** when **canopied** with bowers.
[Exeunt.]

SCENE II. THE SEA-COAST.

[Enter VIOLA, CAPTAIN, and SAILORS.]

VIOLA.
What country, **friends**, is this?

CAPTAIN.
This is Illyria, **lady**.

VIOLA.
And what should I do in Illyria?
My **brother** he is in Elysium.
Perchance he is not drown'd--What think you, **sailors**?

CAPTAIN.
It is **perchance** that you **yourself** were sav'd.

VIOLA.
O my **poor** brother! and so perchance may he be.

CAPTAIN.
True, madam; and, to **comfort** you with chance,
Assure yourself, after our **ship** did split,
When you, and those poor number sav'd with you,
Hung on our **driving boat**, I saw your brother,
Most **provident** in **peril**, **bind** himself,---
Courage and **hope** both **teaching** him the practice,--
To a **strong mast** that liv'd upon the sea;

Spanish

beds: las camas.
bind: liar, ligar, encuadernar, enlazar, obligar, comprometer, lazo.
boat: barco, bote, barca, el barco.
brother: hermano, el hermano, cofrade.
canopied: doselado, endoselado.
comfort: comodidad, consolar, anchas, consuelo, confort.
driving: conduciendo, manejando, conducción, conducir.
friends: amigos, los amigos.

hope: esperanza, esperar, espera, espere, esperen, esperas, esperan, esperamos, esperáis, esperad, espero.
lady: dama, señora.
lie: mentir, mentira, yacer, estar tendido, embuste, echarse.
mast: mástil.
perchance: quizás, tal vez.
peril: peligro.
poor: pobre, malo, deplorable, indigente, miserable.
provident: previsor, providente,

prudente.
rich: rico.
sailors: marinería.
self: mismo.
ship: barco, enviar, enviad, envía, envíen, envíe, envías, envían, enviamos, enviáis, envío.
strong: fuerte, intenso, marcado.
sweet: dulce, caramelo, postre.
teaching: enseñando, enseñanza, instruyendo, desacostumbrando.
yourself: tú mismo, se.

Where, like Arion on the dolphin's back,
I saw him **hold acquaintance** with the waves
So long as I could see.

VIOLA.
For **saying** so, there's gold!
Mine own **escape** unfoldeth to my hope,
Whereto thy **speech serves** for authority,
The like of him. Know'st **thou** this country?

CAPTAIN.
Ay, madam, well; for I was **bred** and born
Not three **hours' travel** from this very place.

VIOLA.
Who **governs** here?

CAPTAIN.
A **noble duke**, in **nature** as in name.

VIOLA.
What is his name?

CAPTAIN.
Orsino.

VIOLA.
Orsino! I have **heard** my father name him.
He was a **bachelor** then.

CAPTAIN.
And so is now, or was so very **late**;
For but a **month** ago I went from **hence**;
And then 'twas fresh in murmur,--as, you know,
What great **ones** do, the less will **prattle** of,--
That he did **seek** the love of **fair** Olivia.

VIOLA.
What's she?

Spanish

acquaintance: conocido, conocimiento, notoriedad.
bachelor: bachiller, soltero, solterón.
bred: pret y pp de breed, Criado.
duke: duque.
escape: escaparse, escapar, huida, fuga, escape, evadir, escapada, huir.
fair: justo, rubio, mercado, feria, verbena, bazar, equitativo, hermoso.
governs: gobierna, capitanea, rige, reprime.
heard: oído.

hence: de aquí a, por tanto.
hold: tener, sujetar, continuar, retención, sostener, contener, mantener, retenido, presa, bodega.
hours: horas, las horas.
late: tarde, tardío, tardo.
month: mes, el mes.
nature: naturaleza, índole, carácter.
noble: hidalgo, noble.
ones: unos.
prattle: cháchara, balbuceo, charlar, parlotear, parloteo, balbucear.

saying: diciendo, dicho, decir, refrán.
seek: buscar, busque, busca, buscan, buscamos, busquen, buscas, buscáis, buscad, busco.
serves: sirve.
speech: discurso, habla, lenguaje, oración, conversación, dialecto, idioma.
thou: tú, usted, vosotros, ustedes, vos.
travel: viajar, viaje, viajo, viaja, viajas, viajan, viajamos, viajen, viajad, viajáis, conducir.

CAPTAIN.
A **virtuous maid**, the daughter of a count
That died some **twelvemonth** since; then leaving her
In the protection of his son, her brother,
Who **shortly** also died; for whose dear love,
They say, she hath **abjured** the company
And sight of men.

VIOLA.
O that I **served** that lady!
And might not be **delivered** to the world,
Till I had made mine own **occasion** mellow,
What my estate is.

CAPTAIN.
That were hard to compass:
Because she will **admit** no kind of suit,
No, not the duke's.

VIOLA.
There is a fair behaviour in **thee**, captain;
And though that nature with a **beauteous** wall
Doth **oft** close in **pollution**, yet of thee
I will believe thou **hast** a mind that suits
With this thy fair and **outward** character.
I **pray** thee, and I'll pay thee bounteously,
Conceal me what I am; and be my aid
For such **disguise** as, **haply**, shall become
The form of my **intent**. I'll serve this duke;
Thou **shalt** present me as an **eunuch** to him;
It may be worth thy **pains**, for I can sing,
And speak to him in many sorts of music,
That will allow me very worth his service.

Spanish

abjured: abjurado, renunciado, contramandado.
admit: confesar, confesad, confesáis, confieso, confiesen, confiese, confiesas, confiesan, confiesa, confesamos, admitir.
beauteous: bello, bonito, hermoso.
delivered: entregado.
disguise: disfraz, disfrazar.
eunuch: eunuco.
haply: posiblemente.
hast: haya.

intent: intento, intención, propósito.
maid: criada, sirvienta, doncella, la criada.
occasion: motivo, ocasión, lugar, oportunidad.
oft: a menudo, mucho, con frecuencia, muchas veces.
outward: exterior.
pains: dolores del parto, esfuerzos, desvelos.
pollution: contaminación, polución.
pray: rezar, rezáis, rezas, rezamos,

rezad, reza, recen, rece, rezan, rezo, rogar.
serve: servir, sirva, sirvo, servimos, servid, servís, sirvan, sirve, sirven, sirves.
served: servido.
shalt: irá, verbo auxiliar inglés para especificar futuro.
shortly: brevemente.
thee: ustedes, te, vosotros, usted, tú.
twelvemonth: mes doce.
virtuous: virtuoso.

What else may **hap to** time I **will** commit;
Only **shape** thou **silence** to my wit.

CAPTAIN.

Be you his eunuch and your **mute** I'll be;
When my **tongue** blabs, then let mine eyes not see.

VIOLA.

I thank thee. Lead me on.

[Exeunt.]

SCENE III. A ROOM IN OLIVIA'S HOUSE.

[Enter SIR TOBY BELCH and MARIA.]

SIR TOBY.

What a **plague** means my **niece**, to take the death of her brother thus? I am
sure care's an **enemy** to life.

MARIA.

By my **troth**, Sir Toby, you must come in earlier o' nights; your **cousin**, my
lady, **takes** great **exceptions** to your ill hours.

SIR TOBY.

Why, let her except, before **excepted**.

MARIA.

Ay, but you must **confine** yourself within the **modest limits** of order.

SIR TOBY.

Confine? I'll confine **myself** no finer than I am: these **clothes** are good enough
to **drink** in, and so be these **boots** too; an they be not, let them **hang**
themselves in their own **straps**.

MARIA.

That **quaffing** and **drinking** will **undo** you: I heard my lady talk of it

Spanish

boots: botas.
clothes: ropa, viste, la ropa, ropaje.
confine: limitar, confín.
cousin: primo, prima, el primo.
drink: beber, bebida, tomar, el refresco, trago, copa.
drinking: potable, el beber, bebida, beber.
enemy: enemigo.
except: excepto, menos, exceptuar, además de, amén de.
excepted: excepto, exceptuando.

exceptions: excepciones.
hang: colgar.
hap: destino, pase, tener suerte.
ill: enfermo, malo, doliente.
limits: límites.
modest: modesto.
mute: mudo, muda, sordina.
myself: yo mismo.
niece: sobrina, la sobrina.
o: oxígeno.
plague: plaga, peste, atormentar.
quaffing: zampar.

shape: forma, formar, figura, amoldar, horma, la forma, perfil, conformar.
silence: silencio, acallar, hacer callar, el silencio.
straps: abrazaderas, cintas.
takes: toma, desempeña.
tongue: lengua, la lengua, lengüeta.
troth: fidelidad, fe.
undo: deshacer, deshaga, deshagan, deshago, deshaces, deshacen, deshacemos, deshacéis, deshaced, deshace, deshaz.

yesterday; and of a **foolish knight** that you **brought** in one night here to be her wooer.

SIR TOBY.
Who? Sir Andrew Ague-cheek?

MARIA.
Ay, he.

SIR TOBY.
He's as **tall** a man as any's in Illyria.

MARIA.
What's that to the **purpose**?

SIR TOBY.
Why, he has three **thousand** ducats a year.

MARIA.
Ay, but he'll have but a year in all these ducats; he's a very fool, and a **prodigal**.

SIR TOBY.
Fye that you'll say so! he **plays** o' the viol-de-gambo, and **speaks** three or four **languages word** for word without book, and hath all the good **gifts** of nature.

MARIA.
He hath indeed,--almost **natural**: for, **besides** that he's a fool, he's a great **quarreller**; and, but that he hath the gift of a **coward** to **allay** the **gust** he hath in **quarrelling**, 'tis thought among the **prudent** he would **quickly** have the gift of a **grave**.

SIR TOBY.
By this hand, they are **scoundrels** and subtractors that say so of him. Who are they?

MARIA.
They that **add**, **moreover**, he's **drunk nightly** in your company.

Spanish

add: sumar, sumad, sumáis, sumamos, suman, sumas, sume, sumen, suma, sumo, agregar.
allay: calmar, aliviar.
besides: además, demás, además de, amén de.
brought: Traído.
coward: cobarde, el cobarde.
drunk: borracho, bebido, ebrio.
fool: engañar, necio, tonto.
foolish: zote, tonto, necio, bobo.
gift: regalo, donación, el regalo, don,
talento.
gifts: regalos.
grave: tumba, grave, crítico, sepulcro.
gust: ráfaga, racha.
knight: caballero, caballo.
languages: las lenguas.
moreover: además, demás.
natural: natural.
nightly: nocturno.
plays: juega, toca.
prodigal: pródigo.
prudent: prudente.
purpose: fin, objeto, finalidad, propósito, intención.
quarreller: pendenciero.
quarrelling: disputas, peleón, pelear.
quickly: rápidamente, de prisa, aprisa, pronto.
scoundrels: sinvergüenzas.
speaks: habla.
tall: alto.
thousand: mil.
word: palabra, la palabra, vocablo, término, formular.

SIR TOBY.
With **drinking healths** to my **niece**; I'll drink to her as long as there is a **passage** in my **throat** and drink in Illyria. He's a **coward** and a coystril that will not drink to my niece till his **brains** turn o' the **toe** like a parish-top. What, **wench**! Castiliano-vulgo! for here **comes** Sir Andrew Ague-face.
[Enter SIR ANDREW AGUE-CHEEK.]
AGUE-CHEEK.
Sir Toby Belch! how now, Sir Toby Belch!
SIR TOBY.
Sweet Sir Andrew?
SIR ANDREW.
Bless you, fair **shrew**.
MARIA.
And you too, sir.
SIR TOBY.
Accost, Sir Andrew, **accost**.
SIR ANDREW.
What's that?
SIR TOBY.
My niece's chamber-maid.
SIR ANDREW.
Good Mistress Accost, I **desire** better **acquaintance**.
MARIA.
My name is Mary, sir.
SIR ANDREW.
Good Mistress Mary Accost,--
SIR TOBY.
You **mistake**, **knight**: accost is, **front** her, **board** her, **woo** her, **assail** her.

Spanish

accost: abordar, dirigirse a, abordamos, abordo, aborden, aborde, abordan, abordáis, abordad, aborda, abordas.
acquaintance: conocido, conocimiento, notoriedad.
assail: asaltar, asalto, asalta, asaltáis, asaltad, asaltamos, asaltan, asaltas, asalten, asalte.
board: tabla, tablero, bordo, cartón, placa, panel, abordar, junta, tablón, cuadro, consejo.
brains: sesos, inteligencia.
comes: Viene.
coward: cobarde, el cobarde.
desire: desear, deseo, tener, querer, gana, codiciar.
drinking: potable, el beber, bebida, beber.
front: frente, fachada, delantero, el frente, frontón, delantera.
healths: sanidad.
knight: caballero, caballo.
mistake: error, equivocación, yerro, la falta.
niece: sobrina, la sobrina.
passage: paso, pasillo, pasaje.
shrew: arpía, musaraña.
throat: garganta, la garganta.
toe: dedo del pie, dedo de pie, el dedo del pie.
wench: muchacha.
woo: cortejar, corteje, cortejamos, cortejo, cortejen, cortejan, cortejáis, cortejad, corteja, cortejas.

SIR ANDREW.
By my **troth**, I would not **undertake** her in this company.
Is that the **meaning** of **accost**?

MARIA.
Fare you well, gentlemen.

SIR TOBY.
An **thou** let part so, Sir Andrew, would thou mightst never **draw sword** again.

SIR ANDREW.
An you part so, **mistress**, I would I might never draw sword again. **Fair lady**, do you think you have fools in hand?

MARIA.
Sir, I have not you by the hand.

SIR ANDREW.
Marry, but you shall have; and here's my hand.

MARIA.
Now, sir, thought is free. I **pray** you, **bring** your hand to the buttery-bar and let it **drink**.

SIR ANDREW.
Wherefore, **sweetheart**? what's your **metaphor**?

MARIA.
It's **dry**, sir.

SIR ANDREW.
Why, I think so; I am not such an **ass** but I can keep my hand dry. But what's your **jest**?

MARIA.
A dry jest, sir.

SIR ANDREW.
Are you full of them?

Spanish

accost: abordar, dirigirse a, abordamos, abordo, aborden, aborde, abordan, abordáis, abordad, aborda, abordas.
ass: burro, asno, culo.
bring: traer, traigan, trae, traed, traéis, traemos, traen, traigo, traes, traiga, llevar.
draw: dibujar, dibujáis, dibujad, dibujen, dibuje, dibujas, dibujamos, dibuja, dibujan, dibujo, tirar.
drink: beber, bebida, tomar, el refresco, trago, copa.
dry: seco, secar, enjugar.
fair: justo, rubio, mercado, feria, verbena, bazar, equitativo, hermoso.
jest: bromear, broma.
lady: dama, señora.
meaning: intención, significado, sentido, significación.
metaphor: metáfora, lenguaje figurado.
mistress: señora.
pray: rezar, rezáis, rezas, rezamos, rezad, reza, recen, rece, rezan, rezo, rogar.
sir: señor.
sweetheart: novio, querido.
sword: espada.
thou: tú, usted, vosotros, ustedes, vos.
troth: fidelidad, fe.
undertake: emprender, emprenda, emprenden, emprended, emprendo, emprendes, emprendéis, emprendan, emprende, emprendemos, encargarse de.

MARIA.
Ay, sir, I have them at my **fingers'** ends: **marry**, now I let go your hand I am barren.

[Exit MARIA.]

SIR TOBY.
O knight, **thou** lack'st a **cup** of **canary**: When did I see **thee** so put down?

SIR ANDREW.
Never in your life, I think; **unless** you see canary put me down. Methinks sometimes I have no more **wit** than a Christian or an **ordinary** man has; but I am great **eater** of **beef**, and, I believe, that does **harm** to my wit.

SIR TOBY.
No question.

SIR ANDREW.
An I thought that, I'd **forswear** it. I'll **ride** home **to-morrow**, Sir Toby.

SIR TOBY.
Pourquoy, my **dear** knight?

SIR ANDREW.
What is pourquoy? do or not do? I would I had **bestowed** that time in the **tongues** that I have in **fencing**, **dancing**, and bear-baiting. Oh, had I but **followed** the **arts**!

SIR TOBY.
Then hadst thou had an **excellent** head of **hair**.

SIR ANDREW.
Why, would that have **mended** my hair?

SIR TOBY.
Past question; for thou seest it will not **curl** by nature.

SIR ANDREW.
But it **becomes** me well enough, does't not?

Spanish

arts: letras, artes.
becomes: acontece.
beef: carne de vaca.
bestowed: conferido, otorgado, concedido.
canary: canario.
cup: taza, la taza, copa.
curl: rizo, bucle, rizar, rizarse, rotacional, encrespar.
dancing: bailando, baile.
dear: caro, querido, estimado.
eater: tener siempre buen apetito,

comedero, comedor, manzana, agua.
excellent: excelente.
fencing: esgrima.
fingers: los dedos.
followed: seguido.
forswear: abjurar, abjuráis, abjuro, abjuren, abjure, abjuras, abjuramos, abjurad, abjura, abjuran.
hair: pelo, cabello, el pelo, vello.
harm: daño, dañar, perjudicar a, detrimento, dañar a, perjuicio, mal.
marry: casarse, casar, cásese, se casan,

se casa, nos casamos, me caso, te casas, cásense, cásate, cásados.
mended: Mejorado.
ordinary: ordinario, común.
ride: montar, conducir, paseo, cabalgar, cabalgata.
thee: ustedes, te, vosotros, usted, tú.
thou: tú, usted, vosotros, ustedes, vos.
to-morrow: mañana.
tongues: lenguas.
unless: a menos que, a no ser que.
wit: ingenio.

SIR TOBY.
Excellent; it **hangs** like **flax** on a **distaff**; and I hope to see a houswife take thee between her **legs** and **spin** it off.

SIR ANDREW.
Faith, I'll home to-morrow, Sir Toby; your niece will not be seen; or, if she be, it's four to one she'll none of me; the **count** himself here hard by **woos** her.

SIR TOBY.
She'll none o' the Count; she'll not match above her degree, neither in **estate**, years, nor wit; I have heard her swear't. **Tut**, there's life in't, man.

SIR ANDREW.
I'll stay a month **longer**. I am a **fellow** o' the strangest mind i' the world; I **delight** in masques and **revels** sometimes **altogether**.

SIR TOBY.
Art thou good at these kick-shaws, knight?

SIR ANDREW.
As any man in Illyria, **whatsoever** he be, under the degree of my **betters**; and yet I will not **compare** with an old man.

SIR TOBY.
What is thy **excellence** in a galliard, knight?

SIR ANDREW.
Faith, I can cut a **caper**.

SIR TOBY.
And I can cut the **mutton** to't.

SIR ANDREW.
And, I think, I have the back-trick simply as strong as any man in Illyria.

SIR TOBY.
Wherefore are these things **hid**? **wherefore** have these gifts a **curtain** before them? are they like to take **dust**, like Mistress Mall's picture? why dost thou not go to church in a galliard and come home in a coranto? My very walk

Spanish

altogether: todo, en conjunto.
betters: mejor.
caper: cabriola, alcaparra.
compare: comparar, comparas, comparen, comparo, compare, comparan, comparamos, comparáis, compara, comparad, cotejar.
count: contar, recuento, cuenta, conde, calcular, entrar en cuenta, computar, unidad de cuenta, cargo.
curtain: cortina, la cortina.
delight: deleitar, delicia, encantar.

distaff: tareas femeninas, rueca.
dust: polvo, quitar el polvo, quitar el polvo a.
estate: finca, granja, propiedad, herencia, hacienda, patrimonio.
excellence: excelencia.
fellow: compañero, hombre, socio, tipo, becario.
flax: lino.
hangs: continúa, cuelga.
hid: escondió, pret de hide.
legs: las piernas.

longer: más, más tiempo.
mutton: carnero, carne de carnero.
revels: jarana, jolgorio, fiestas.
spin: giro, girar, hilar.
tut: eso no, vamos, pche, hacer un gesto de desaprobación, gesto de desaprobación, qué horror, Vaya.
whatsoever: lo que, en absoluto, todo lo que, cualquier cosa, cualquier.
wherefore: por qué, por eso, por consiguiente.
woos: corteja.

should be a **jig**; I would not so much as make water but in a sink-a-pace. **What** dost thou mean? is it a world to **hide** virtues in? I did think, by the excellent **constitution** of thy **leg**, it was **formed** under the **star** of a galliard.

SIR ANDREW.

Ay, 'tis strong, and it does **indifferent** well in flame-colour'd **stock**. Shall we set about some revels?

SIR TOBY.

What shall we do else? were we not **born** under Taurus?

SIR ANDREW.

Taurus? that's **sides** and **heart**.

SIR TOBY.

No, sir; it is legs and **thighs**. Let me see thee **caper**: ha, **higher**: ha, ha!-- excellent!

[Exeunt.]

SCENE IV. A ROOM IN THE DUKE'S PALACE.

[Enter VALENTINE, and VIOLA in man's attire.]

VALENTINE.

If the duke **continue** these favours towards you, Cesario, you are like to be much **advanced**; he hath known you but three days, and already you are no **stranger**.

VIOLA.

You either **fear** his **humour** or my **negligence**, that you **call** in question the **continuance** of his love. Is he **inconstant**, sir, in his favours?

VALENTINE.

No, believe me.

[Enter DUKE, CURIO, and ATTENDANTS.]

Spanish

advanced: avanzado, adelantado.
born: nacido, nato.
call: llamada, llamar, llaman, llamen, llamad, llamas, llamo, llamamos, llamáis, llame, llama.
caper: cabriola, alcaparra.
constitution: constitución, complexión.
continuance: persistencia.
continue: continuar, continúe, continuad, continuáis, continuamos, continúan, continúas, continúen,

continúo, continúa, durar.
fear: temer, miedo, temor, angustia, recelar.
formed: formó, formado.
ha: ah, decir ah, ja.
heart: corazón, cogollo.
hide: ocultar, oculto, oculta, oculte, ocultas, ocultan, ocultamos, ocultáis, ocultad, oculten, piel.
higher: superior.
humour: humor.
inconstant: inconstante, voluble.

indifferent: indiferente.
jig: giga.
leg: pierna, la pierna, pata, tramo.
negligence: negligencia, descuido.
sides: costados, Lados.
star: estrella, la estrella, astro.
stock: acciones, existencias, existencia, almacenar, acción, mango, proveer, reserva, ganado, valores.
stranger: forastero, extraño, desconocido.
thighs: muslos.

VIOLA.
I thank you. Here comes the count.

DUKE.
Who saw Cesario, ho?

VIOLA.
On your **attendance**, my lord; here.

DUKE.
Stand you **awhile** aloof.--Cesario,
Thou know'st no less but all; I have unclasp'd
To thee the book even of my **secret** soul:
Therefore, good **youth**, **address** thy **gait unto** her;
Be not **denied** access, stand at her doors,
And tell them there thy **fixed foot** shall grow
Till thou have **audience**.

VIOLA.
                  Sure, my noble lord,
If she be so abandon'd to her sorrow
As it is **spoke**, she never will admit me.

DUKE.
Be **clamorous** and **leap** all **civil** bounds,
Rather than make unprofited return.

VIOLA.
Say I do **speak** with her, my lord. What then?

DUKE.
O, then **unfold** the **passion** of my love,
Surprise her with **discourse** of my dear faith:
It shall become thee well to act my woes;
She will attend it better in thy youth
Than in a **nuncio** of more grave **aspect**.

Spanish

address: dirección, dirigir, discurso, señas, dirigirse a, alocución, dirigirse, domicilio, dirigir la palabra a.
aspect: aspecto, vista.
attend: asistir, asistan, asisto, asistís, asistimos, asistid, asistes, asisten, asiste, asista, visitar.
attendance: asistencia, servicio.
audience: audiencia, público.
awhile: durante un rato, por un rato, un momento, un rato.
civil: civil.

clamorous: clamoroso.
denied: negado, desmentido.
discourse: discurso.
fixed: fijo, fijado, reparado.
foot: pie, pata, el pie, pujamen.
gait: paso.
leap: saltar, salto, brincar, el salto.
nuncio: nuncio apostólico.
passion: pasión.
secret: secreto, el secreto, arcano, clandestino.
speak: hablar, hablamos, hablo,

hablas, habláis, hablad, hablen, habla, hablan, hable.
spoke: decir, radio, rayo, raya, radioactivo, rayo de rueda, hablar, pret de speak, expresar.
unfold: desplegar, despliegue, desplegáis, desplegamos, despliega, desplegan, despliegas, desplieguen, desplegad, despliego, desdoblar.
unto: hacia.
youth: juventud, joven, jóvenes, adolescencia.

VIOLA.
I think not so, my lord.

DUKE.
Dear **lad, believe** it,
For they shall yet belie **thy happy** years
That say thou art a man: Diana's lip
Is not more **smooth** and **rubious**; thy small pipe
Is as the maiden's **organ, shrill** and sound,
And all is semblative a woman's part.
I know thy **constellation** is right apt
For this affair:--some four or five attend him:
All, if you will; for I myself am best
When **least** in company:--prosper well in this,
And thou **shalt live** as **freely** as thy lord,
To call his fortunes **thine**.

VIOLA.
I'll do my best
To **woo** your lady. [**Aside**] Yet, a barful strife!
Whoe'er I woo, myself would be his **wife**.

SCENE V. A ROOM IN OLIVIA'S HOUSE.

[Enter MARIA and CLOWN.]

MARIA.
Nay; either tell me where thou **hast** been, or I will not open my **lips** so **wide** as a **bristle** may **enter** in way of thy **excuse**: my lady will hang **thee** for thy **absence**.

CLOWN.
Let her hang me: he that is well hanged in this world needs to fear no colours.

Spanish

absence: ausencia, falta.
aside: aparte, al lado.
belie: desmentir, desmientes, desmentid, desmiento, desmienten, desmiente, desmientan, desmienta, desmentís, desmentimos.
bristle: cerda, erizarse.
constellation: constelación.
enter: entrar, entro, entra, entrad, entráis, entramos, entran, entras, entren, entre, inscribir.
excuse: excusa, excusar, disculpa, disculpar.
freely: libremente.
happy: feliz, alegre, contento.
hast: haya.
lad: muchacho, chico.
least: menos, mínimo, menor.
lips: labios, los labios.
live: vivir, viven, vive, vivo, vivan, vivís, vivimos, vives, viva, vivid, habitar.
organ: órgano.
rubious: de color rubí.
shalt: irá, verbo auxiliar inglés para especificar futuro.
shrill: chillón.
smooth: liso, plano, alisar, suavizar, suave.
thee: ustedes, te, vosotros, usted, tú.
thine: tuyo, tuyos, tuyas, tuya, tus.
thy: tu.
wide: ancho, amplio, vasto, lejos.
woo: cortejar, corteje, cortejamos, cortejo, cortejen, cortejan, cortejáis, cortejad, corteja, cortejas.

MARIA.
Make that good.

CLOWN.
He shall see **none** to fear.

MARIA.
A good **lenten** answer: I can tell thee where that saying was born, of, I fear no **colours**.

CLOWN.
Where, good Mistress Mary?

MARIA.
In the wars; and that may you be **bold** to say in your **foolery**.

CLOWN.
Well, God give them **wisdom** that have it; and those that are fools, let them use their **talents**.

MARIA.
Yet you will be **hanged** for being so long **absent**: or to be turned away; is not that as good as a **hanging** to you?

CLOWN.
Many a good hanging **prevents** a **bad marriage**; and for **turning** away, let **summer bear** it out.

MARIA.
You are **resolute**, then?

CLOWN.
Not so, **neither**: but I am **resolved** on two **points**.

MARIA.
That if one **break**, the other will hold; or if both break, your gaskins **fall**.

CLOWN.
Apt, in good **faith**, very **apt**! Well, go thy way; if Sir Toby would leave drinking, thou wert as **witty** a **piece** of Eve's **flesh** as any in Illyria.

Spanish

absent: ausente.
apt: apropiado.
bad: malo, mal, podrido.
bear: oso, llevar, el oso, bajista, producir, dar a luz, parir, portar, soportar.
bold: grueso, negrita, audaz.
break: romper, descanso, interrupción, rotura, quebrar, corte, pausa, adiestrar, fractura, interrumpir.
colours: bandera.
faith: fe, la fe.

fall: caer, os caéis, cáedos, se caen, se cae, te caes, caígase, cáete, caíganse, me caigo, nos caemos.
flesh: carne, pulpa.
foolery: tontería.
hanged: colgar, ahorcado, continuar, caída, colgó.
hanging: ahorcamiento, pendiente.
lenten: cuaresmal.
marriage: matrimonio, casamiento, enlace.
neither: tampoco, ninguno, nadie, ni.

none: ninguno, nadie, nada.
piece: pieza, pedazo, parte, trozo, tela.
points: puntos, aguja.
prevents: impide, previene.
resolute: resuelto.
resolved: resuelto.
summer: verano, el verano, estival.
talents: talentos.
turning: girando, volviendo, trastornando.
wisdom: sabiduría, sapiencia.
witty: ingenioso.

MARIA.
Peace, you **rogue**; no more o' that; here comes my lady: make your excuse **wisely**; you were best.
[Exit.]
[Enter OLIVIA and MALVOLIO.]

CLOWN.
Wit, and't be thy will, put me into good **fooling**! Those wits that think they have thee do very oft prove fools; and I, that am sure I lack thee, may pass for a wise man. For what says Quinapalus? Better a witty fool than a foolish wit.--God **bless** thee, lady!

OLIVIA.
Take the fool away.

CLOWN.
Do you not hear, fellows? Take away the lady.

OLIVIA.
Go to, you're a dry fool; I'll no more of you: besides, you grow **dishonest**.

CLOWN.
Two **faults**, **madonna**, that drink and good **counsel** will **amend**: for give the dry fool drink, then is the fool not dry; **bid** the dishonest man mend himself: if he mend, he is no longer dishonest; if he **cannot**, let the botcher mend him. Anything that's mended is but **patched**; **virtue** that **transgresses** is but patched with **sin**, and sin that **amends** is but patched with virtue. If that this simple **syllogism** will serve, so; if it will not, what **remedy**? As there is no true **cuckold** but **calamity**, so beauty's a flower:--the lady **bade** take away the fool; therefore, I say again, take her away.

OLIVIA.
Sir, I bade them take away you.

CLOWN.
Misprision in the highest degree!--Lady, Cucullus **non** facit monachum; that's

Spanish

amend: enmendar, enmienden, enmiendas, enmiendan, enmendamos, enmendáis, enmendad, enmiendo, enmiende, enmienda, corregir.
amends: enmienda, corrige, compensación.
bade: pret de bid, Mandó.
bid: ofrecer, licitación, postura, oferta, solicitar, licitar, pedir, demandar, rogar, puja.
bless: bendecir, bendecimos, bendigo, bendigan, bendices, bendicen, bendecís, bendecid, bendice, bendiga.
calamity: calamidad.
cannot: presente de no poder.
counsel: consejo, aconsejar, abogado, anunciar.
cuckold: cornudo.
dishonest: improbo, deshonesto.
faults: desperfecto, fallas.
fooling: engañar.
madonna: Madona.
mend: remendar, enmendar, reparar,
zurcir.
non: in, fattening, des, no.
patched: remendado.
remedy: curar, remedio, recurso, medio, remediar.
rogue: pícaro.
sin: pecado, pecar.
syllogism: silogismo.
transgresses: transgrede.
virtue: virtud.
wise: sabio, sensato, guisa.
wisely: sabiamente.

as much to say, I **wear** not **motley** in my brain. Good **madonna**, give me **leave** to **prove** you a fool.

OLIVIA.
Can you do it?

CLOWN.
Dexteriously, good madonna.

OLIVIA.
Make your **proof**.

CLOWN.
I must **catechize** you for it, madonna.
Good my **mouse** of virtue, **answer** me.

OLIVIA.
Well, sir, for want of other **idleness**, I'll 'bide your proof.

CLOWN.
Good madonna, why **mourn'st** thou?

OLIVIA.
Good fool, for my brother's death.

CLOWN.
I think his **soul** is in **hell**, madonna.

OLIVIA.
I know his soul is in **heaven**, fool.

CLOWN.
The more fool you, madonna, to mourn for your brother's soul being in heaven.--Take away the fool, **gentlemen**.

OLIVIA.
What think you of this fool, Malvolio? doth he not **mend**?

MALVOLIO.
Yes; and shall do, till the pangs of death **shake** him.   Infirmity, that decays the wise, doth ever make the better fool.

Spanish

answer: respuesta, responder, contestar, contestación, responder a, corresponder al, contestar a, la respuesta, réplica.
catechize: catequizar, catequizáis, catequizo, catequizas, catequizamos, catequizad, catequiza, catequicen, catequice, catequizan.
gentlemen: señores.
heaven: cielo.
hell: infierno.
idleness: ociosidad.

leave: salir, sal, sale, salís, salimos, salgo, salgan, salga, sales, salen, saled.
madonna: Madona.
mend: remendar, enmendar, reparar, zurcir.
motley: abigarramiento, abigarrado, multicolor.
mourn: deplorar, deploro, deplora, deplorad, deploráis, deploramos, deploran, deploras, deplore, deploren, llorar.

mouse: ratón, laucha.
proof: prueba, demostración, probanza.
prove: probar, probad, prueban, pruebas, pruebo, probamos, probáis, prueben, prueba, pruebe, verificar.
shake: sacudir, sacuda, sacudimos, sacudís, sacudid, sacudes, sacuden, sacude, sacudan, sacudo, sacudida.
soul: alma, espíritu, ánimo.
wear: llevar, desgaste, usar, tener puesto, vestir, uso, llevar puesto.

CLOWN.

God send you, sir, a **speedy infirmity**, for the better increasing your **folly**! Sir Toby will be **sworn** that I am no **fox**; but he will not pass his word for twopence that you are no fool.

OLIVIA.

How say you to that, Malvolio?

MALVOLIO.

I **marvel** your **ladyship** takes delight in such a **barren rascal**; I saw him put down the other day with an ordinary fool that has no more brain than a stone. Look you now, he's out of his guard already; unless you laugh and minister occasion to him, he is **gagged**. I protest I take these wise men that **crow** so at these set kind of fools, no better than the fools' **zanies**.

OLIVIA.

O, you are sick of **self**-love, Malvolio, and taste with a **distempered** appetite. To be **generous, guiltless**, and of free **disposition**, is to take those things for bird-bolts that you **deem cannon bullets**. There is no **slander** in an allowed fool, though he do nothing but rail; nor no **railing** in known **discreet** man, though he do nothing but **reprove**.

CLOWN.

Now Mercury **endue** thee with **leasing**, for thou speakest well of fools!

[Re-enter MARIA.]

MARIA.

Madam, there is at the gate a young gentleman much desires to speak with you.

OLIVIA.

From the Count Orsino, is it?

MARIA.

I know not, madam; 'tis a fair young man, and well attended.

OLIVIA.

Who of my people hold him in delay?

Spanish

barren: árido, estéril, yermo.
bullets: balas, destacadores.
cannon: cañón.
crow: el cuervo, corneja, cuervo.
deem: creer, crea, creemos, crees, creo, creen, creéis, creed, crean, cree, contemplar.
discreet: discreto.
disposition: disposición, talento, capacidad.
distempered: destemplado.
endue: dotar.

folly: tontería.
fox: zorro, el zorro.
gagged: amordazado.
generous: generoso, dadivoso.
guiltless: inocente.
infirmity: enfermedad, debilidad.
ladyship: señora, señoría.
leasing: arrendamiento, alquiler, arriendo.
marvel: maravilla, asombrarse.
railing: barandilla, balaustrada, pasamano, baranda.

rascal: bribón.
reprove: reprobar, reprobad, reprueba, repruebo, reprueben, repruebe, reprueban, reprobamos, reprobáis, repruebas, reprender.
self-love: narcisismo, egolatría, egoísmo.
slander: calumniar, calumnia, infamar, difamación.
speedy: rápido.
sworn: jurado.
zanies: Estrafalario.

MARIA.
Sir Toby, madam, your **kinsman**.

OLIVIA.
Fetch him off, I pray you; he speaks nothing but **madman**. Fie on him!
[Exit MARIA]
Go you, Malvolio: if it be a **suit** from the count, I am **sick**, or not at home;
what you will to **dismiss** it.
[Exit MALVOLIO.]
Now you see, sir, how your **fooling grows** old, and people **dislike** it.

CLOWN.
Thou **hast** spoke for us, madonna, as if thy **eldest son** should be a fool:
whose skull Jove **cram** with brains, for here he comes-- one of thy kin, has a
most **weak** pia mater.
[Enter SIR TOBY BELCH.]

OLIVIA.
By mine **honour**, half drunk!--What is he at the **gate**, cousin?

SIR TOBY.
A **gentleman**.

OLIVIA.
A gentleman? What gentleman?

SIR TOBY.
'Tis a gentleman here.--A plague o' these pickle-herrings!--How now, **sot**?

CLOWN.
Good Sir Toby,--

OLIVIA.
Cousin, cousin, how have you come so early by this **lethargy**?

SIR TOBY.
Lechery! I **defy lechery**. There's one at the gate.

Spanish

cram: atestar, empollar, apretura, abarrotado, repaso de última hora, rellenar con, hartarse de comer, emborrar, cebar, atiborrar, atiborramiento.
defy: desafiar, desafiáis, desafío, desafíen, desafías, desafiamos, desafiad, desafía, desafían, desafíe.
dislike: aversión, repugnancia, detestar, detesto, detesten, deteste, detestas, detestan, detesta, detestamos, detestáis.
dismiss: despedir, despedimos, despido, despiden, despide, despides, despedís, despedid, despidan, despida, expedir.
eldest: mayor.
fooling: engañar.
gate: puerta, paso, verja, compuerta, barrera.
gentleman: caballero, señor, gentilhombre.
grows: crece, aumenta.
hast: haya.
honour: honor, homenaje.
kin: parientes.
lechery: libertinaje, lascivia.
lethargy: letargo.
madman: loco.
sick: enfermo.
skull: cráneo, calavera.
son: hijo, el hijo.
sot: beodo, borrachín, borracho.
suit: traje, convenir, el traje, pleito.
weak: débil, flojo.
whose: cuyo, cuya.

OLIVIA.
Ay, marry; what is he?

SIR TOBY.
Let him be the **devil** an he will, I care not: give me faith, say I. Well, it's all one.
[Exit.]

OLIVIA.
What's a **drunken** man like, fool?

CLOWN.
Like a **drowned** man, a fool, and a **madman**: one **draught** above **heat makes** him a fool; the second **mads** him; and a third **drowns** him.

OLIVIA.
Go **thou** and seek the **coroner**, and let him **sit** o' my coz; for he's in the third **degree** of drink; he's drowned: go, look after him.

CLOWN.
He is but mad yet, **madonna**; and the fool shall look to the madman.
[Exit.]
[Re-enter MALVOLIO.]

MALVOLIO.
Madam, yond young fellow **swears** he will speak with you. I told him you were sick; he takes on him to **understand** so much, and therefore comes to speak with you; I told him you were **asleep**; he seems to have a **foreknowledge** of that too, and therefore comes to speak with you. What is to be said to him, lady? he's **fortified** against any **denial**.

OLIVIA.
Tell him, he shall not speak with me.

MALVOLIO.
Has been told so; and he says he'll stand at your door like a sheriff's **post**, and be the **supporter** of a **bench**, but he'll speak with you.

Spanish

asleep: dormido.
bench: banco, estrado, banquillo, escaño.
coroner: médico forense.
degree: grado, título, licencia.
denial: negación, denegación.
devil: diablo, el diablo.
draught: calado, trago.
drowned: se ahogado, ahogado.
drowns: se ahoga.
drunken: borracho, ebrio.
foreknowledge: presciencia.

fortified: fortificado.
heat: calor, calentar, el calor, hornada, carga de fusión.
mad: loco, enojado, chiflado, majara, majareta, demente, enfadado.
madman: loco.
madonna: Madona.
mads: loco.
makes: hace, comete, confecciona.
post: poste, correo, empleo, cargo, puesto, oficio, apostar, posta, función, fijar, estaca.

sit: sentarse, estar sentado, sentar.
stand: estar de pie, puesto, levantarse, granero, posición, cabina, soporte, base, estante, caseta, pararse.
supporter: partidario, hincha, seguidor.
swears: jura.
thou: tú, usted, vosotros, ustedes, vos.
understand: entender, entiendes, entienda, entiendan, entendemos, entendéis, entended, entienden, entiendo, entiende, comprender.

OLIVIA.
What kind of man is he?

MALVOLIO.
Why, of mankind.

OLIVIA.
What **manner** of man?

MALVOLIO.
Of very **ill** manner; he'll **speak** with you, will you or no.

OLIVIA.
Of what **personage** and years is he?

MALVOLIO.
Not yet old enough for a man, **nor** young enough for a **boy**; as a **squash** is before 'tis a peascod, or a **codling**, when 'tis almost an **apple**: 'tis with him e'en **standing** water, between boy and man. He is very well-favoured, and he **speaks** very **shrewishly**; one would think his mother's **milk** were **scarce** out of him.

OLIVIA.
Let him **approach**. **Call** in my **gentlewoman**.

MALVOLIO.
Gentlewoman, my **lady** calls.
[Exit.]
[Re-enter MARIA.]

OLIVIA.
Give me my **veil**; come, **throw** it **o'er** my face;
We'll once more **hear** Orsino's **embassy**.
[Enter VIOLA.]

VIOLA.
The **honourable** lady of the house, which is she?

Spanish

apple: manzana, la manzana.
approach: aproximación, enfoque, aproximarse, acercarse, acercar, acercamiento, método, planteamiento.
boy: chico, muchacho, niño, el muchacho, criado, chamaco.
call: llamada, llamar, llaman, llamen, llamad, llamas, llamo, llamamos, llamáis, llame, llama.
codling: bacalao, bacalao pequeño.
embassy: embajada.
gentlewoman: dama.
hear: oír, oigan, oyes, oyen, oye, oís, oigo, oíd, oímos, oiga.
honourable: honorable.
ill: enfermo, malo, doliente.
lady: dama, señora.
manner: manera.
milk: leche, ordeñar, la leche.
nor: ni, tampoco.
o'er: sobre.
personage: personaje.
scarce: escaso.
shrewishly: regañonamente, regañónmente.
speak: hablar, hablamos, hablo, hablas, habláis, hablad, hablen, habla, hablan, hable.
speaks: habla.
squash: aplastar, calabaza.
standing: permanente, posición.
throw: lanzar, echar, tirar, tirada, arrojar, lanzamiento.
veil: velo.

OLIVIA.
Speak to me; I shall answer for her. Your will?

VIOLA.
Most **radiant**, **exquisite**, and **unmatchable** beauty,--I pray you, tell me if this
be the lady of the house, for I never saw her: I would be **loath** to cast away
my speech; for, besides that it is **excellently** well **penned**, I have taken great
pains to **con** it. Good beauties, let me **sustain** no **scorn**; I am very comptible,
even to the least **sinister** usage.

OLIVIA.
Whence came you, sir?

VIOLA.
I can say little more than I have studied, and that question's out of my part.
Good gentle one, give me modest assurance, if you be the lady of the house,
that I may proceed in my speech.

OLIVIA.
Are you a **comedian**?

VIOLA.
No, my **profound** heart: and yet, by the very fangs of malice
I **swear**, I am not that I play. Are you the lady of the house?

OLIVIA.
If I do not **usurp** myself, I am.

VIOLA.
Most certain, if you are she, you do usurp yourself; for what is yours to
bestow is not yours to reserve. But this is from my commission: I will on with
my speech in your **praise**, and then show you the heart of my message.

OLIVIA.
Come to what is important in't: I **forgive** you the praise.

VIOLA.
Alas, I took great pains to study it, and 'tis **poetical**.

Spanish

bestow: conferir, otorgar.
comedian: cómico, comediante.
con: estafas, estudien, estudie,
estudias, estudian, estudiamos,
estudiáis, estudiad, estudia, estafo,
estudio.
excellently: magníficamente,
relevantemente, excelentemente, muy
bien, sobresalientemente.
exquisite: exquisito.
forgive: perdonar, perdona, perdonad,
perdono, perdonen, perdonas,

perdonan, perdonamos, perdonáis,
perdone.
loath: renuente.
penned: escrito.
poetical: poético.
praise: alabar, alabanza, elogio,
elogiar.
profound: profundo.
radiant: resplandeciente, radiante,
brillante.
scorn: desdén, desdeñar.
sinister: siniestro.

sustain: sostener, sosten, sostengan,
sostiene, sostenemos, sostenéis,
sostened, sostienes, sostienen,
sostengo, sostenga.
swear: jurar, jura, jurad, juráis,
juramos, juran, juras, juren, juro, jure,
maldecir.
unmatchable: incomparable.
usurp: usurpar, usurpe, usurpo,
usurpa, usurpad, usurpáis,
usurpamos, usurpan, usurpas,
usurpen.

OLIVIA.
It is the more like to be **feigned**; I pray you keep it in. I heard you were **saucy** at my gates; and allowed your approach, rather to wonder at you than to hear you. If you be not mad, be gone; if you have reason, be brief: 'tis not that time of **moon** with me to make one in so **skipping** a dialogue.

MARIA.
Will you **hoist sail**, sir? here lies your way.

VIOLA.
No, good **swabber**; I am to **hull** here a little longer.--
Some **mollification** for your **giant**, sweet lady. Tell me your mind. I am a **messenger**.

OLIVIA.
Sure, you have some **hideous** matter to **deliver**, when the **courtesy** of it is so **fearful**. Speak your office.

VIOLA.
It alone concerns your ear. I bring no **overture** of war, no **taxation** of **homage**; I hold the **olive** in my hand: my words are as full of peace as matter.

OLIVIA.
Yet you began **rudely**. What are you? what would you?

VIOLA.
The **rudeness** that hath appeared in me have I learned from my **entertainment**. What I am and what I would are as secret as **maidenhead**: to your ears, **divinity**; to any **other's**, **profanation**.

OLIVIA.
Give us the place alone: we will hear this divinity.
[Exit MARIA.]
Now, sir, what is your text?

VIOLA.
Most sweet lady,--

Spanish

courtesy: cortesía.
deliver: entregar, entregas, entrego, entregan, entregamos, entregáis, entregad, entreguen, entrega, entregue.
divinity: divinidad.
entertainment: recreación, entretenimiento, diversión, función.
fearful: temeroso, medroso, angustioso.
feigned: fingido, aparentado.
giant: gigante.

hideous: horroroso, abominable, horrible.
hoist: montacargas, enarbolar, izar, polipasto.
homage: homenaje.
hull: casco, cáscara.
maidenhead: virginidad, himen.
messenger: mensajero, embajador, ordenanza.
mollification: apaciguamiento, molificación, tranquilización.
moon: luna, la luna.

olive: aceituna, oliva, la aceituna.
other's: otro.
overture: proposición.
profanation: profanación.
rudely: grosero, groseramente, bastamente, rudamente.
rudeness: rudeza.
sail: vela, navegar, la vela.
saucy: descarado.
skipping: saltar, salto a la comba.
swabber: mozo de la limpieza.
taxation: tributación, fiscalidad.

OLIVIA.
A **comfortable doctrine**, and much may be said of it.
Where lies your **text**?

VIOLA.
In Orsino's **bosom**.

OLIVIA.
In his bosom? In what chapter of his bosom?

VIOLA.
To answer by the **method**, in the first of his heart.

OLIVIA.
O, I have read it; it is **heresy**. Have you no more to say?

VIOLA.
Good madam, let me see your face.

OLIVIA.
Have you any **commission** from your lord to **negotiate** with my face? you are
now out of your text: but we will draw the curtain and show you the **picture**.
Look you, sir, such a one I was this present. Is't not well done?
[Unveiling.]

VIOLA.
Excellently done, if God did all.

OLIVIA.
'Tis in **grain**, sir; 'twill **endure wind** and **weather**.

VIOLA.
'Tis **beauty truly blent**, whose **red** and white
Nature's own sweet and **cunning** hand **laid** on:
Lady, you are the cruel'st she alive,
If you will **lead** these **graces** to the grave,
And leave the world no **copy**.

Spanish

beauty: belleza, la belleza.
blent: pret y pp de blend.
bosom: pecho, seno.
comfortable: cómodo, agradable.
commission: comisión, encargar,
    encargo, comisionar.
copy: copiar, copia, traslado, trasladar,
    la copia.
cunning: astucia, astuto, hábil.
doctrine: doctrina.
endure: durar, duráis, duro, duren,
    dure, duras, duran, duramos, dura,

durad, tolerar.
graces: Gracias.
grain: grano, cereal, veta, fibra.
heresy: herejía.
laid: puesto, colocado, recostado,
    acostado.
lead: plomo, guiar, guía, conducir,
    guiáis, guiamos, guian, guías, guíe,
    guíen, guío.
method: método, procedimiento.
negotiate: negociar, negocías,
    negocien, negocia, negocian,

negociamos, negociáis, negociad,
negocie, negocio.
picture: imagen, cuadro, grabado,
    pintura, retrato, el cuadro,
    reproducción, ilustración, foto.
red: rojo, tinto, encarnado.
text: texto.
truly: verdaderamente, de veras, en
    realidad, en efecto, realmente.
weather: tiempo, el tiempo, clima.
wind: viento, serpentear, el viento,
    enrollar, devanar.

OLIVIA.
O, sir, I will not be so **hard**-hearted; I will give out **divers schedules** of my beauty. It shall be **inventoried**; and every **particle** and **utensil labelled** to my will: as, **item**, two lips indifferent red; item, two **grey** eyes with **lids** to them; item, one **neck**, one **chin**, and so **forth**. Were you **sent hither** to praise me?

VIOLA.
I see you what you are: you are too proud;
But, if you were the devil, you are fair.
My **lord** and **master loves** you. O, such love
Could be but recompens'd though you were crown'd
The **nonpareil** of beauty!

OLIVIA.
How does he love me?

VIOLA.
With adorations, **fertile** tears,
With groans that **thunder** love, with sighs of fire.

OLIVIA.
Your lord does know my mind; I cannot love him:
Yet I suppose him virtuous, know him noble,
Of great estate, of fresh and **stainless** youth;
In voices well **divulged**, free, learn'd, and valiant,
And, in **dimension** and the shape of nature,
A **gracious** person: but yet I cannot love him;
He might have took his answer long ago.

VIOLA.
If I did love you in my master's flame,
With such a **suffering**, such a **deadly** life,
In your denial I would find no sense,
I would not understand it.

Spanish

chin: barba, barbilla, la barbilla, mentón.
deadly: mortal.
dimension: dimensión, tamaño.
divers: varios, diversos.
divulged: divulgado.
fertile: fértil, fecundo.
forth: adelante.
gracious: cortés.
grey: gris, pardo.
hard-hearted: corazón duro, duro, duro de corazón, empedernido,

insensible.
hither: acá.
inventoried: inventariado.
item: artículo, elemento, partida, ítem, rubro.
labelled: etiquetado, marcado.
lids: cubiertas.
lord: señor, caballero.
loves: amor.
master: maestro, amo, dueño, patrón, principal, magister.
neck: cuello, el cuello, garganta,

pescuezo, cerviz.
nonpareil: sin igual, cosa sin par, persona sin pareja, sin par, persona sin par.
particle: partícula.
schedules: programas.
sent: enviado, mandado, despachado.
stainless: inoxidable.
suffering: sufriendo, padeciendo, sufrimiento.
thunder: trueno, tronar, el trueno.
utensil: utensilio.

OLIVIA.

                         Why, what would you?

VIOLA.

Make me a **willow cabin** at your gate,
And call upon my soul within the house;
Write **loyal** cantons of contemned love,
And **sing** them **loud**, even in the dead of night;
Holla your name to the **reverberate** hills,
And make the **babbling gossip** of the **air**
Cry out Olivia! O, you should not rest
Between the **elements** of air and earth,
But you should **pity** me.

OLIVIA.

You might do much. What is your **parentage**?

VIOLA.

Above my fortunes, yet my state is well:
I am a gentleman.

OLIVIA.

                         Get you to your lord;
I cannot love him: let him **send** no more;
Unless, perchance, you come to me again,
To tell me how he takes it. **Fare** you well:
I **thank** you for your pains: **spend** this for me.

VIOLA.

I am no fee'd post, lady; keep your purse;
My master, not myself, **lacks** recompense.
Love make his heart of **flint** that you shall love;
And let your **fervour**, like my master's, be
Placed in **contempt**! **Farewell**, fair cruelty.
[Exit.]

Spanish

air: aire, airear, el aire, aéreo, orear.
babbling: balbuceando, balbuceo.
cabin: cabaña, camarote, cabina, litera.
contempt: desprecio, menosprecio.
elements: elementos, abecé, alfabeto.
fare: tarifa, pasaje.
farewell: adiós, despedida.
fervour: celo.
flint: pedernal.
gossip: cotillear, cotilleo, chismear, chismes, los chismes, chismorreo.
lacks: le falta.

loud: alto, fuerte, ruidoso, chillón.
loyal: fiel, leal.
parentage: linaje.
pity: dolerse por, piedad, compadecer a, lástima, compasión.
reverberate: reverberar, reverbere, reverbero, reverbera, reverberen, reverberas, reverberan, reverberamos, reverberáis, reverberad.
send: enviar, envío, envía, envíe, enviad, enviáis, enviamos, envían, envías, envíen, mandar.
sing: cantar, cantan, cantas, canten, cantamos, cantáis, canta, cantad, canto, cante.
spend: gastar, gastáis, gastas, gasten, gastad, gasta, gastamos, gastan, gasto, gaste, pasar.
thank: agradecer, agradezco, agradeces, agradezcan, agradece, agradezca, agradecemos, agradeced, agradecen, agradecéis, dar gracias.
willow: sauce.

OLIVIA.
   * What is your parentage?
   'Above my fortunes, yet my state is well:
   I am a gentleman.'--I'll be **sworn thou** art;
   Thy **tongue, thy** face, thy **limbs, actions,** and spirit,
   Do give **thee five**-fold **blazon.** Not too fast:--soft, soft!
   Unless the master were the man.--How now?
   Even so quickly may one **catch** the plague?
   Methinks I feel this **youth's** perfections
   With an **invisible** and **subtle** stealth
   To **creep** in at mine **eyes.** Well, let it be.--
   What, ho, Malvolio!--
   [Re-enter MALVOLIO.]

MALVOLIO.
               Here, madam, at your service.

OLIVIA.
   Run after that same **peevish** messenger,
   The county's man: he left this **ring** behind him,
   Would I or not; tell him I'll none of it.
   Desire him not to **flatter** with his lord,
   Nor hold him up with **hopes**; I am not for him:
   If that the youth will come this way to-morrow,
   I'll give him **reasons** for't. **Hie** thee, Malvolio.

MALVOLIO.
   Madam, I will.
   [Exit.]

OLIVIA.
   I do I know not what: and fear to find
   Mine eye too great a **flatterer** for my mind.
   Fate, show thy **force. Ourselves** we do not owe:

Spanish

actions: acciones.
blazon: blasón.
catch: coger, cogéis, cojan, coged, cogemos, cogen, coges, coja, coge, cojo, asir.
creep: arrastrarse, arrastrar, deslizamiento, arrastre, fluencia, arrastras, arrastren, arrastran, arrastramos, arrastráis, arrastrad.
eye: ojo, el ojo, ojear, mirar.
five-fold: quíntuplo.
flatter: adular, adula, adulo, adulen,

adule, adulas, adulan, adulamos, aduláis, adulad, halagar.
flatterer: lisonjero, adulador.
force: fuerza, forzar, obligar, virtud.
hie: ir caminando, apresurar, caminar, correr, pasear, ir con pasos, ir paseando, ir volando.
hopes: espera.
invisible: invisible.
limbs: extremidades.
ourselves: nosotros mismos.
peevish: malhumorado.

reasons: razona.
ring: anillo, el anillo, llamar, aro, anilla, argolla, tocar la campanilla, sonar, sortija, corro.
subtle: sutil.
sworn: jurado.
thee: ustedes, te, vosotros, usted, tú.
thou: tú, usted, vosotros, ustedes, vos.
thy: tu.
tongue: lengua, la lengua, lengüeta.
youth: juventud, joven, jóvenes, adolescencia.

What   is **decreed** must be; and be this so!
[Exit.]

Spanish

decreed: decretado.

ACT II

SCENE I. THE SEA-COAST.

[Enter ANTONIO and SEBASTIAN.]

ANTONIO.
Will you stay no longer; nor will you not that I go with you?

SEBASTIAN.
By your **patience**, no; my **stars shine darkly** over me; the **malignancy** of my **fate** might, perhaps, **distemper yours**; therefore I shall **crave** of you your leave that I may bear my evils alone. It were a bad **recompense** for your love, to lay any of them on you.

ANTONIO.
Let me know of you **whither** you are **bound**.

SEBASTIAN.
No, 'sooth, sir; my **determinate voyage** is **mere extravagancy**. But I **perceive** in you so excellent a touch of **modesty**, that you will not **extort** from me what I am **willing** to keep in; therefore it charges me in **manners** the rather to **express** myself. You must know of me then, Antonio, my name is Sebastian, which I called Rodorigo; my father was that Sebastian of Messaline whom I

Spanish

bound: encuadernado, saltar, salto, ligado, límite, obligado.
crave: ansiar, pedir, ansía, ansío, ansíen, ansíe, ansías, ansían, ansiad, ansiáis, ansiamos.
darkly: cetrinamente, misteriosamente, oscuramente, tristemente.
determinate: determinado.
distemper: moquillo, pintura al temple.
express: expresar, expresa, expresas,

expresen, expresan, expresamos, expresáis, expresad, expreso, exprese.
extort: arrancar, arrancáis, arranquen, arranco, arrancas, arrancamos, arrancad, arranca, arrancan, arranque, extorsionar.
extravagancy: extravagancia, gasto excesivo, gastos excesivos.
fate: destino, suerte, sino, hado.
malignancy: malignidad.
manners: modales, educación.
mere: mero.

modesty: modestia, pudor.
patience: paciencia.
perceive: percibir, perciben, percibes, percibe, perciban, percibid, percibimos, percibís, percibo, perciba.
recompense: recompensa.
shine: brillar, brillo, lucir.
stars: estrellas.
voyage: viaje.
whither: adónde, adonde.
willing: dispuesto, deseoso.
yours: vuestro, suyo, el tuyo.

know you have heard of: he left behind him myself and a **sister**, both born in an hour; if the **heavens** had been **pleased**, would we had so **ended**! but you, sir, **altered** that; for some hours before you took me from the **breach** of the sea was my sister **drowned**.

ANTONIO.

Alas the day!

SEBASTIAN.

A lady, sir, though it was said she much **resembled** me, was **yet** of many **accounted** beautiful: but though I could not, with such **estimable** wonder, overfar believe that, yet thus far I will **boldly publish** her,--she **bore** mind that **envy** could not but call fair. She is drowned already, sir, with **salt** water, though I seem to drown her remembrance again with more.

ANTONIO.

Pardon me, sir, your bad entertainment.

SEBASTIAN.

O, good Antonio, forgive me your trouble.

ANTONIO.

If you will not murder me for my love, let me be your **servant**.

SEBASTIAN.

If you will not undo what you have done--that is, **kill** him whom you have recovered--desire it not. Fare ye well at once; my bosom is full of **kindness**; and I am yet so near the manners of my mother that, upon the least occasion more, mine eyes will tell **tales** of me. I am bound to the Count Orsino's court: farewell.

[Exit.]

ANTONIO.

The **gentleness** of all the **gods** go with thee!
I have many cnemies in Orsino's court,
Else would I very shortly see thee there:
But come what may, I do **adore** thee so

Spanish

accounted: contabilizados, contabilizo.
adore: adorar, adoran, adoren, adore, adoro, adoras, adoramos, adoráis, adora, adorad.
altered: cambiado, alterado, mudado.
boldly: audazmente.
bore: aburrir, barrena, taladrar, calibre, perforar, barrenar, barreno, perforación.
breach: brecha, infracción, contravención, incumplimiento, violación, violar.

drown: ahogarse, ahogar.
ended: finalizó, terminado.
envy: envidiar, envidiad, envidiáis, envidiamos, envidian, envidias, envidie, envidien, envidio, envidia.
estimable: apreciable, estimable.
gentleness: apacibilidad, suavidad.
gods: paraíso, gallinero.
heavens: cielo, cielos.
kill: matar.
kindness: amabilidad, la bondad.
pleased: contento.

publish: publicar, publicáis, publiquen, publico, publicas, publican, publicad, publica, publicamos, publique, editar.
resembled: Parecido.
salt: sal, la sal, salar, salado.
servant: criado, criada, sirviente, servidor.
sister: hermana, la hermana, cuñada.
tales: cuentos.
ye: usted, vosotros, ustedes, vosotras, tú, los, lo, las, la, el, vos.

That **danger** shall seem **sport**, and I will go.
[Exit.]

SCENE II. A STREET.

[Enter VIOLA; MALVOLIO following.]

MALVOLIO.
Were you not even now with the Countess Olivia?

VIOLA.
Even now, sir; on a **moderate pace** I have since **arrived** but hither.

MALVOLIO.
She **returns** this ring to you, sir; you might have **saved** me my pains, to have taken it away yourself. She **adds** moreover, that you should put your lord into a **desperate assurance** she will none of him: and one thing more: that you be never so **hardy** to come again in his **affairs**, unless it be to report your lord's taking of this. **Receive** it so.

VIOLA.
She took the ring of me: I'll none of it.

MALVOLIO.
Come, sir, you **peevishly threw** it to her; and her will is it should be so **returned**. If it be worth **stooping** for, there it lies in your eye; if not, be it his that **finds** it.
[Exit.]

VIOLA.
I left no ring with her; what means this lady?
Fortune **forbid** my outside have not charm'd her!
She made good view of me; indeed, so much,
That methought her eyes had lost her tongue,

Spanish

adds: suma, agrega, añade.
affairs: asuntos.
arrived: llegado.
assurance: garantía, convicción, aseguramiento.
danger: peligro, el peligro.
desperate: desesperado.
finds: funda, funde.
forbid: prohibir, prohibid, prohiban, prohibo, prohibimos, prohibes, prohiben, prohibe, prohibís, prohiba.
hardy: robusto, fuerte, resistente,

audaz.
moderate: moderado, módico, moderar.
pace: paso.
peevishly: tercamente, enojadizamente, obstinadamente, quejándose, con mal humor.
receive: recibir, reciben, recibís, recibimos, recibes, recibe, reciban, recibid, reciba, recibo, tomar.
returned: devuelto.
returns: devolver, reembolso,

ganancias, devoluciones, cheques y letras devueltos, retorno, rendimiento, remuneración, regreso, ingresos, volver.
saved: guardado, salvado, ahorrado.
sport: deporte.
stooping: inclinar, inclinarse, rebajamiento, rebajar, rebajarse, cargado de espaldas, agachado, agacharse, inclinación, humillarse, encorvado.
threw: pret de throw, Tiró, tiro.

For she did speak in starts distractedly.
She **loves** me, **sure**: the **cunning** of her passion
Invites me in this **churlish** messenger.
None of my lord's ring! why, he sent her none.
I am the man; --if it be so,--as 'tis,--
Poor lady, she were better love a dream.
Disguise, I see **thou** art a wickedness
Wherein the **pregnant enemy** does much.
How **easy** is it for the proper-false
In women's **waxen hearts** to set their forms!
Alas, our **frailty** is the **cause**, not we;
For such as we are made of, such we be.
How will this fadge? My master loves her dearly,
And I, poor **monster**, **fond** as much on him;
And she, **mistaken**, seems to **dote** on me.
What will become of this? As I am man,
My state is **desperate** for my master's love;
As I am woman, now **alas** the day!
What **thriftless** sighs shall poor Olivia breathe!
O time, thou must **untangle** this, not I;
It is too **hard** a **knot** for me to untie!
[Exit.]

SCENE III. A ROOM IN OLIVIA'S HOUSE.

[Enter SIR TOBY BELCH and SIR ANDREW AGUE-CHEEK.]
SIR TOBY.
 Approach, Sir Andrew; not to be a-bed after **midnight** is to be up **betimes**; and *diluculo surgere*, thou know'st.

Spanish

alas: ay, es una lástima.
betimes: al alba, a tiempo.
cause: causa, causar, ocasionar, dar lugar a, instigar, producir, maquinar, provocar.
churlish: rústico.
cunning: astucia, astuto, hábil.
desperate: desesperado.
dote: chochear, chochean, chochee, chocheen, chocheas, chocheáis, chochea, chochead, chocheo, chocheamos.

easy: fácil.
enemy: enemigo.
fond: aficionado.
frailty: debilidad, flaqueza, cosa débil, fragilidad.
hard: duro, difícil, tieso.
hearts: corazones, copas.
knot: nudo, correlimos gordo, lazo.
loves: amor.
midnight: medianoche, media noche, la medianoche.
mistaken: malo, equivocado.

monster: monstruo.
pregnant: embarazada, en estado, encinta, preñada.
sure: seguro, cierto.
thou: tú, usted, vosotros, ustedes, vos.
thriftless: gastoso, malgastador.
untangle: desenredar, desenmarañe, desenredáis, desenredo, desenreden, desenrede, desenredas, desenredamos, desenredad, desenreda, desenredan.
waxen: ceroso.

SIR ANDREW.
Nay; by my **troth**, I know not; but I know to be up late is to be up late.
SIR TOBY.
A **false conclusion**; I **hate** it as an **unfilled** can. To be up after midnight, and to go to **bed** then is early: so that to go to bed after midnight is to go to bed **betimes**. Do not our **lives consist** of the four elements?
SIR ANDREW.
Faith, so they say; but I think it rather **consists** of **eating** and drinking.
SIR TOBY.
Thou art a **scholar**; let us therefore eat and drink.--
Marian, I say!--a **stoup** of **wine**.
[Enter CLOWN.]
SIR ANDREW.
Here comes the fool, i' faith.
CLOWN.
How now, my hearts? Did you never see the picture of we three?
SIR TOBY.
Welcome, **ass**. Now **let's** have a catch.
SIR ANDREW.
By my troth, the fool has an excellent **breast**. I had rather than **forty** shillings I had such a leg; and so sweet a **breath** to sing, as the fool has. In **sooth, thou** wast in very **gracious fooling** last night when thou spokest of Pigrogromitus, of the Vapians **passing** the **equinoctial** of Queubus; 'twas very good, i' faith. I sent **thee sixpence** for **thy** leman. Hadst it?
CLOWN.
I did impeticos thy gratillity; for Malvolio's **nose** is no whipstock. My lady has a white hand, and the Myrmidons are no bottle-ale **houses**.
SIR ANDREW.
Excellent! Why, this is the best fooling, when all is done. Now, a **song**.

Spanish

ass: burro, asno, culo.
bed: cama, lecho, cauce, la cama, bancada, cuadro, madre.
betimes: al alba, a tiempo.
breast: pecho, seno, pechuga, mama.
breath: aliento, respiración, hálito.
conclusion: conclusión.
consist: consistir, consista, consiste, consisten, consistan.
consists: consiste.
eat: comer, comemos, comes, coméis, comed, coman, como, comen, coma,
Come.
eating: comiendo.
equinoctial: equinoccial.
false: falso.
fooling: engañar.
forty: cuarenta.
gracious: cortés.
hate: odiar, odio, aborrecer, detestar.
houses: casas.
let's: permítanos.
lives: Vive, habita.
nose: nariz, la nariz, proa.
passing: paso.
scholar: erudito, estudiante, escolar.
sixpence: seis peniques.
song: canción, canto.
sooth: verdad, realidad.
stoup: pila de agua bendita.
thee: ustedes, te, vosotros, usted, tú.
thou: tú, usted, vosotros, ustedes, vos.
thy: tu.
troth: fidelidad, fe.
unfilled: vacío.
wine: vino, el vino.

SIR TOBY.
Come on; there is **sixpence** for you: **let's** have a **song**.

SIR ANDREW.
There's a testril of me too: if one **knight** give a--

CLOWN.
Would you have a love-song, or a song of good life?

SIR TOBY.
A love-song, a love-song.

SIR ANDREW.
Ay, **ay**; I care not for good life.

CLOWN.
[Sings.]
O, **mistress mine**, where are you roaming?
O, **stay** and **hear**; your **true** love's coming,
That can **sing** both high and low:
Trip no further, **pretty sweeting**;
Journeys end in **lovers** meeting,
Every **wise** man's son doth know.

SIR ANDREW.
Excellent good, i' **faith**.

SIR TOBY.
Good, good.

CLOWN.
What is love? 'tis not hereafter;
Present **mirth** hath **present** laughter;
What's to come is still unsure.
In **delay** there lies no plenty;
Then come **kiss** me, sweet and twenty;
Youth's a **stuff** will not **endure**.

Spanish

ay: sí.
delay: retraso, retardo, demora, retrasar, demorar, retardar.
endure: durar, duráis, duro, duren, dure, duras, duran, duramos, dura, durad, tolerar.
faith: fe, la fe.
hear: oír, oigan, oyes, oyen, oye, oís, oigo, oid, oímos, oiga.
kiss: besar, beso, besarse.
knight: caballero, caballo.
let's: permitanos.

lovers: amantes.
mine: mina, mío, minar.
mirth: alegría.
mistress: señora.
present: presente, actual, presentar, regalo, contemporáneo, ofrecer, reproducir, retratar.
pretty: bonito, lindo, majo, amable, guapo, bastante, guapa.
sing: cantar, cantan, cantas, canten, cantamos, cantáis, canta, cantad, canto, cante.

sir: señor.
sixpence: seis peniques.
son: hijo, el hijo.
song: canción, canto.
stay: quedarse, quedar, queden, quede, quedas, quedan, quedamos, quedáis, quedad, queda, quedo.
stuff: rellenar, cosas, material, llenar.
sweet: dulce, caramelo, postre.
true: verdadero, cierto.
wise: sabio, sensato, guisa.

SIR ANDREW.
A **mellifluous** voice, as I am true **knight**.
SIR TOBY.
A **contagious** breath.
SIR ANDREW.
Very **sweet** and contagious, i' faith.
SIR TOBY.
To hear by the **nose**, it is **dulcet** in **contagion**. But shall we make the welkin **dance indeed**? Shall we **rouse** the night-owl in a **catch** that will draw three souls out of one **weaver**? shall we do that?
SIR ANDREW.
An you love me, let's do't: I am **dog** at a catch.
CLOWN.
By'r lady, sir, and some **dogs** will catch well.
SIR ANDREW.
Most certain: let our catch be, 'Thou **knave**.'
CLOWN.
'Hold **thy peace, thou** knave' knight? I shall be constrain'd in't to call **thee** knave, knight.
SIR ANDREW.
'Tis not the first time I have **constrained** one to call me knave. **Begin, fool**; it **begins** 'Hold thy peace.'
CLOWN.
I shall never begin if I hold my peace.
SIR ANDREW.
Good, i' faith! Come, begin.
[They **sing** a catch.]
[Enter MARIA.]

Spanish

begin: empezar, empiecen, empezad, empezáis, empiece, empieza, empiezan, empiezas, empiezo, empezamos, comenzar.
begins: empieza, principia.
catch: coger, cogéis, cojan, coged, cogemos, cogen, coges, coja, coge, cojo, asir.
constrained: encogido.
contagion: contagio.
contagious: contagioso.
dance: bailar, baile, danza, danzar, el baile.
dog: perro, el perro, la perra, can.
dogs: los perros, las perras.
dulcet: dulce.
fool: engañar, necio, tonto.
indeed: verdaderamente, en efecto, de veras, en realidad, efectivamente.
knave: bribón.
knight: caballero, caballo.
mellifluous: melifluo.
nose: nariz, la nariz, proa.
peace: paz, la paz.
rouse: animar, instigar, espolear, incitar, despertar, estimular, espoleen, espoleo, espolead, espoleamos, espolean.
sing: cantar, cantan, cantas, canten, cantamos, cantáis, canta, cantad, canto, cante.
sweet: dulce, caramelo, postre.
thee: ustedes, te, vosotros, usted, tú.
thou: tú, usted, vosotros, ustedes, vos.
thy: tu.
weaver: tejedor.

MARIA.
What a **caterwauling** do you keep here! If my lady have not called up her **steward** Malvolio, and bid him **turn** you out of **doors**, never **trust** me.

SIR TOBY.
My lady's a Cataian, we are politicians; Malvolio's a Peg-a-Ramsey, and [Singing.] 'Three **merry** men be we.' Am not I **consanguineous**? am I not of her **blood**? Tilly-valley, lady. 'There **dwelt** a man in Babylon, lady, lady.'

CLOWN.
Beshrew me, the knight's in **admirable** fooling.

SIR ANDREW.
Ay, he does well enough if he be **disposed**, and so do I too; he does it with a better **grace**, but I do it more natural.

SIR TOBY.
[Singing]
O, the **twelfth** day of December,--

MARIA.
For the love o' God, peace!

[Enter MALVOLIO]

MALVOLIO.
My masters, are you mad? or what are you? Have you no wit, manners, nor **honesty**, but to **gabble** like **tinkers** at this time of night? Do ye make an ale-house of my lady's house, that ye **squeak** out your coziers' **catches** without any **mitigation** or **remorse** of voice? Is there no **respect** of place, persons, nor time, in you?

SIR TOBY.
We did keep time, sir, in our catches. Sneck up!

MALVOLIO.
Sir Toby, I must be round with you. My lady bade me tell you that, though she harbours you as her **kinsman** she's nothing **allied** to your disorders. If you can **separate** yourself and your misdemeanours, you are **welcome** to the

Spanish

admirable: admirable, estupendo.
allied: aliado.
blood: sangre, la sangre.
catches: coge, ase, acierta.
caterwauling: maullidos, aullidos, maullido, maullar, chillidos.
consanguineous: consanguíneo.
disposed: dispuesto.
doors: las puertas.
dwelt: pret de dwell, pp de dwell.
gabble: charla.
grace: gracia, garbo, honrar.

honesty: honestidad, honradez.
kinsman: pariente.
merry: alegre.
mitigation: mitigación.
remorse: remordimiento.
respect: respetar, respeto, estima, estimación.
separate: separado, separar, apartar, aparte, particular, dividir, separarse, segregar, independiente, compartir.
squeak: rechinar.
steward: camarero, administrador,

mayordomo.
tinkers: arregla, remienda, manosea, estropea, compone, caldereros.
trust: confiar, fideicomiso, confianza, fiduciario.
turn: girar, gira, giro, giráis, giramos, giran, giras, gire, giren, girad, vuelta.
twelfth: duodécimo.
welcome: dar la bienvenida, bienvenida, bienvenido, acoger, grato, agradable, acogida, acogen, acojan, acojo, acoges.

house; if not, an it would **please** you to take **leave** of her, she is very **willing** to **bid** you farewell.

SIR TOBY.
'Farewell, **dear heart**, since I must **needs** be gone.'

MARIA.
Nay, good Sir Toby.

CLOWN.
'His **eyes** do show his days are almost done.'

MALVOLIO.
Is't even so?

SIR TOBY.
'But I will never die.'

CLOWN.
Sir Toby, there you **lie**.

MALVOLIO.
This is much **credit** to you.

SIR TOBY.
[Singing]
'Shall I bid him go?'

CLOWN.
'What an if you do?'

SIR TOBY.
'Shall I bid him go, and **spare** not?'

CLOWN.
'O, no, no, no, no, you **dare** not.'

SIR TOBY.
Out o' **tune**? sir, ye lie. **Art** any more than a **steward**? Dost **thou** think, because thou art **virtuous**, there shall be no more **cakes** and ale?

Spanish

ale: cerveza.
art: arte, el arte.
bid: ofrecer, licitación, postura, oferta, solicitar, licitar, pedir, demandar, rogar, puja.
cakes: pasteles, tortas, tarta.
credit: crédito, haber, acreditar.
dare: atreverse, reto, cariño.
dear: caro, querido, estimado.
heart: corazón, cogollo.
leave: salir, sal, sale, salís, salimos, salgo, salgan, salga, sales, salen,

saled.
lie: mentir, mentira, yacer, estar tendido, embuste, echarse.
needs: necesidades.
o: oxígeno.
please: por favor, agradar, gustar, complacer, haz el favor, contentar, haz favor.
sir: señor.
spare: sobrante, ahorrar, recambio, perdonar.
steward: camarero, administrador,

mayordomo.
thou: tú, usted, vosotros, ustedes, vos.
tune: melodía, acomodar, adaptar.
virtuous: virtuoso.
willing: dispuesto, deseoso.
ye: usted, vosotros, ustedes, vosotras, tú, los, lo, las, la, el, vos.

CLOWN.
Yes, by Saint Anne; and **ginger** shall be **hot** i' the **mouth** too.

SIR TOBY.
Thou'art i' the right.--Go, sir, **rub** your **chain** with crumbs:
A stoup of wine, Maria!

MALVOLIO.
Mistress Mary, if you **prized** my lady's **favour** at anything more than contempt, you would not give means for this **uncivil rule**; she shall know of it, by this hand.
[Exit.]

MARIA.
Go shake your **ears**.

SIR ANDREW.
'Twere as good a **deed** as to drink when a man's a-hungry, to **challenge** him the field, and then to break **promise** with him and make a fool of him.

SIR TOBY.
Do't, knight; I'll **write** thee a challenge; or I'll deliver thy **indignation** to him by word of mouth.

MARIA.
Sweet Sir Toby, be **patient** for to-night; since the youth of the count's was **to-day** with my lady, she is much out of **quiet**. For Monsieur Malvolio, let me alone with him: if I do not **gull** him into a nayword, and make him a common **recreation**, do not think I have wit enough to lie **straight** in my bed. I know I can do it.

SIR TOBY.
Possess us, **possess** us; tell us something of him.

MARIA.
Marry, sir, sometimes he is a kind of Puritan.

SIR ANDREW.
O, if I thought that, I'd **beat** him like a dog.

Spanish

beat: golpear, batido, batir, pegar, apalear, pulsación, latido, batimiento.
chain: cadena, la cadena, encadenar.
challenge: reto, desafiar, desafío, retar, recusación, impugnar.
deed: escritura, acto, hecho, hazaña.
ears: orejas, las orejas, oídos.
favour: favor, favorecer.
ginger: jengibre.
gull: gaviota.
hot: caliente, picante, caluroso.
indignation: indignación.

mouth: boca, desembocadura, la boca.
patient: paciente.
possess: poseer, poseen, posees, poseo, posean, poseéis, posee, poseed, poseemos, posea, tener.
prized: apreciado.
promise: prometer, prometéis, prometemos, prometen, prometo, promete, prometan, prometa, prometes, prometed, promesa.
quiet: quieto, silencio, tranquilo, calmar, silencioso, sosegar, callado.

recreation: recreación, recreo.
rub: frotar, refregar, friccionar.
rule: regla, gobernar, la regla, norma, fallar, refrenar, dominio, subyugar, reprimir, regir, contener.
straight: derecho, recto, directamente, recta.
to-day: hoy.
uncivil: descortés, incivil.
write: escribir, escriba, escriban, escribo, escribís, escribimos, escribid, escribes, escribe, escriben.

SIR TOBY.
What, for being a Puritan? thy exquisite reason, dear knight?
SIR ANDREW.
I have no exquisite reason for't, but I have reason good enough.
MARIA.
The devil a Puritan that he is, or anything **constantly** but a time-pleaser: an affectioned ass that cons state without book and **utters** it by great swarths; the best **persuaded** of himself, so **crammed**, as he **thinks**, with excellences, that it is his **grounds** of faith that all that look on him love him; and on that **vice** in him will my **revenge** find **notable** cause to work.
SIR TOBY.
What **wilt** thou do?
MARIA.
I will **drop** in his way some **obscure** epistles of love; **wherein**, by the colour of his **beard**, the shape of his leg, the manner of his gait, the expressure of his eye, **forehead**, and **complexion**, he shall find himself most **feelingly** personated. I can write very like my lady, your niece; on a **forgotten** matter we can **hardly** make **distinction** of our hands.
SIR TOBY.
Excellent! I **smell** a **device**.
SIR ANDREW.
I have't in my nose too.
SIR TOBY.
He shall think, by the **letters** that thou wilt drop, that they come from my niece, and that she is in love with him.
MARIA.
My purpose is, indeed, a **horse** of that colour.
SIR ANDREW.
And your horse now would make him an ass.

Spanish

beard: barba, la barba, arista.
complexion: cutis, tez.
cons: estafa, estudia, engaña, CONTRA.
constantly: constantemente, siempre, continuamente.
crammed: Atracado, hasta los topes.
device: aparato, dispositivo, artefacto, mecanismo.
distinction: distinción.
drop: gota, caer, disminuir, amainar, decrecer, menguar, caída, descenso,

dejar caer.
feelingly: con sentimiento.
forehead: frente, la frente.
forgotten: olvidado.
grounds: terreno.
hardly: apenas.
horse: caballo, el caballo, potro, cabio.
letters: letras.
notable: señalado, memorable, excelente, personaje, notabilidad, insigne.
obscure: oscuro, disimular, disimulan,

disimulas, disímulo, disimule, disimula, disimuláis, disimulamos, disimulad, disimulen.
persuaded: convencido, persuadido.
revenge: venganza, revancha.
smell: oler, olor, apestar, oler mal, olfatear, olfato.
thinks: piensa, reflexiona.
utters: pronuncia.
vice: vicio, virtud, tornillo de banco.
wherein: en qué.
wilt: marchitarse, marchitar.

MARIA.
Ass, I **doubt** not.

SIR ANDREW.
O 'twill be **admirable**!

MARIA.
Sport **royal**, I **warrant** you. I know my **physic** will work with him. I will **plant** you two, and let the fool make a third, where he shall find the **letter**; **observe** his **construction** of it. For this night, to bed, and **dream** on the **event**. Farewell.
[Exit.]

SIR TOBY.
Good night, Penthesilea.

SIR ANDREW.
Before me, she's a good **wench**.

SIR TOBY.
She's a **beagle** true **bred**, and one that **adores** me. What o' that?

SIR ANDREW.
I was **adored** once too.

SIR TOBY.
Let's to bed, knight.--Thou hadst need send for more money.

SIR ANDREW.
If I **cannot recover** your **niece** I am a **foul** way out.

SIR TOBY.
Send for money, knight; if thou **hast** her not i' the end, call me **cut**.

SIR ANDREW.
If I do not, never trust me; take it how you will.

SIR TOBY.
Come, come; I'll go **burn** some **sack**; 'tis too late to go to bed now: come, knight; come, knight.

Spanish

admirable: admirable, estupendo.
adored: adorado.
adores: adora.
beagle: sabueso.
bred: pret y pp de breed, Criado.
burn: arder, quemar, quemadura, quemarse, encender, la quemadura, abrasar.
cannot: presente de no poder.
construction: construcción.
cut: cortar, corte, cortado, cortadura.
doubt: dudar, duda.

dream: soñar, sueño, ensueño.
event: acontecimiento, evento, suceso, acaecimiento, ocurrencia.
foul: falta, asqueroso, sucio.
hast: haya.
letter: carta, letra, la carta.
niece: sobrina, la sobrina.
observe: observar, observa, observen, observe, observas, observan, observad, observáis, observo, observamos, hacer.
physic: medicamento, remedio.

plant: planta, plantar, cultivar, fábrica, instalación.
recover: recuperar, sanar, recupere, sanad, recuperad, recuperáis, recuperamos, recuperan, recuperas, recuperen, recupero.
royal: real.
sack: saco, despedir, bolso.
warrant: garantía, orden, orden por escrito, certificado, autorizar, autorización.
wench: muchacha.

[Exeunt.]

SCENE IV. A ROOM IN THE DUKE'S PALACE.

[Enter DUKE, VIOLA, CURIO, and others.]

DUKE.
Give me some music:--Now, good **morrow**, friends:--
Now, good Cesario, but that piece of song,
That old and **antique** song we heard last night;
Methought it did **relieve** my passion much;
More than **light airs** and **recollected** terms
Of these most **brisk** and giddy-paced times:--
Come, but one **verse**.

CURIO.
He is not here, so please your **lordship**, that should **sing** it.

DUKE.
Who was it?

CURIO.
Feste, the **jester**, my lord; a **fool** that the Lady Olivia's father took much **delight** in: he is about the house.

DUKE.
Seek him out, and **play** the **tune** the while.
[Exit CURIO. Music.]
Come **hither**, boy. If ever thou **shalt** love,
In the sweet pangs of it **remember** me:
For, such as I am, all true **lovers** are;
Unstaid and **skittish** in all **motions** else,

Spanish

airs: aires.
antique: antiguo, antigüedad, antigualla.
brisk: rápido.
delight: deleitar, delicia, encantar.
fool: engañar, necio, tonto.
hither: acá.
jester: bromista.
light: luz, claro, ligero, encender, alumbrar, débil, liviano, la luz, radiación visible, lámpara, iluminar.
lordship: señoría.

lovers: amantes.
morrow: día siguiente.
motions: movimientos.
play: jugar, jueguen, juega, juegan, juegue, jugad, jugáis, jugamos, juegas, juego, tocar.
recollected: recordado, acordado.
relieve: aliviar, alivie, alivias, aliviad, alivio, alivien, aliviamos, aliviáis, alivian, alivia, relevar.
remember: recordar, recuerde, recuerdo, recuerdan, recuerdas,

recuerden, recordamos, recordad, recordáis, recuerda, acordarse de.
shalt: irá, verbo auxiliar inglés para especificar futuro.
sing: cantar, cantan, cantas, canten, cantamos, cantáis, canta, cantad, canto, cante.
skittish: caprichoso, frívolo, nervioso, asustadizo.
thou: tú, usted, vosotros, ustedes, vos.
tune: melodía, acomodar, adaptar.
verse: verso, estrofa, copla, versículo.

Save in the **constant image** of the creature
That is belov'd.--How dost **thou** like this **tune**?

VIOLA.
It **gives** a very **echo** to the seat
Where Love is throned.

DUKE.
                    Thou dost **speak** masterly:
My life upon't, young though thou **art**, **thine** eye
Hath **stayed** upon some **favour** that it loves;
Hath it not, **boy**?

VIOLA.
              A little, by your favour.

DUKE.
What kind of woman is't?

VIOLA.
              Of your **complexion**.

DUKE.
She is not **worth thee**, then. What years, i' **faith**?

VIOLA.
About your years, my **lord**.

DUKE.
Too old, by **heaven**! Let still the woman take
An **elder** than **herself**; so **wears** she to him,
So sways she level in her husband's heart.
For, boy, however we do **praise** ourselves,
Our **fancies** are more **giddy** and unfirm,
More **longing**, **wavering**, **sooner lost** and won,
Than women's are.

VIOLA.
              I think it well, my lord.

Spanish

art: arte, el arte.
boy: chico, muchacho, niño, el muchacho, criado, chamaco.
complexion: cutis, tez.
constant: constante, continuo.
echo: eco, resonar, el eco.
elder: mayor, anciano, saúco.
faith: fe, la fe.
fancies: extravagante.
favour: favor, favorecer.
giddy: mareado.
gives: da.

heaven: cielo.
herself: sí, ella misma, se, sí misma.
image: imagen, grabado, retrato, reproducción.
longing: anhelo, anhelante.
lord: señor, caballero.
lost: perdido, adelgazado.
praise: alabar, alabanza, elogio, elogiar.
sooner: más pronto.
speak: hablar, hablamos, hablo, hablas, habláis, hablad, hablen, habla,

hablan, hable.
stayed: quedado, permanecido.
thee: ustedes, te, vosotros, usted, tú.
thine: tuyo, tuyos, tuyas, tuya, tus.
thou: tú, usted, vosotros, ustedes, vos.
tune: melodía, acomodar, adaptar.
wavering: vacilando, vacilación, duda, vacilante.
wears: lleva, usa.
worth: valor.

DUKE.
   Then let **thy** love be **younger** than thyself,
   Or thy **affection cannot** hold the bent:
   For women are as roses, whose fair flower,
   Being once display'd, doth fall that very hour.

VIOLA.
   And so they are: **alas**, that they are so;
   To **die**, even when they to **perfection grow**!

[Re-enter CURIO and CLOWN.]

DUKE.
   O, fellow, come, the song we had last night:--
   Mark it, Cesario; it is old and plain:
   The spinsters and the knitters in the sun,
   And the free maids, that **weave** their **thread** with bones,
   Do use to **chant** it: it is **silly** sooth,
   And **dallies** with the **innocence** of love
   Like the old age.

CLOWN.
   Are you ready, sir?

DUKE.
   Ay; pr'ythee, **sing**. [Music]

CLOWN.
   [Sings.]
      Come away, come away, death.
      And in sad **cypress** let me be laid;
      Fly away, **fly** away, breath;
      I am **slain** by a fair **cruel** maid.
      My **shroud** of white, **stuck** all with yew,
         O, **prepare** it!
      My part of death no one so true

Spanish

affection: afecto, cariño, afectuosidad, amor.
alas: ay, es una lástima.
cannot: presente de no poder.
chant: corear, canto.
cruel: cruel.
cypress: ciprés.
dallies: tarda.
die: morir, morid, mueran, muere, morís, mueren, mueres, muero, morimos, muera, molde.
fly: volar, voláis, vuelen, vuele, vuelas,

volamos, vuela, volad, vuelan, vuelo, mosca.
grow: crecer, crecen, crezco, crece, creced, crecemos, crezcan, crecéis, creces, crezca, cultivar.
innocence: inocencia, la inocencia.
perfection: perfección.
prepare: preparar, preparas, prepare, prepara, preparad, preparáis, preparan, preparo, preparen, preparamos, prepararse.
shroud: mortaja, obenque, protector,

protector de contacto.
silly: tonto, necio, absurdo, bobo.
sing: cantar, cantan, cantas, canten, cantamos, cantáis, canta, cantad, canto, cante.
slain: matado.
stuck: punzar, picar, atrancarse.
thread: hilo, rosca, hebra, el hilo.
thy: tu.
weave: tejer, tejido.
younger: menor.

Did share it.

Not a flower, not a flower sweet,
On my black coffin let there be strown:
Not a friend, not a friend greet
My poor corpse where my bones shall be thrown:
A thousand thousand sighs to save,
        Lay me, O, where
Sad true lover never find my grave,
        To weep there!

DUKE.
There's for thy pains.

CLOWN.
No pains, sir; I take pleasure in singing, sir.

DUKE.
I'll pay thy pleasure, then.

CLOWN.
Truly, sir, and pleasure will be paid one time or another.

DUKE.
Give me now leave to leave thee.

CLOWN.
Now the melancholy god protect thee; and the tailor make thy doublet of changeable taffeta, for thy mind is a very opal!--I would have men of such constancy put to sea, that their business might be everything, and their intent everywhere; for that's it that always makes a good voyage of nothing.--Farewell.
[Exit.]

DUKE.
Let all the rest give place.--
[Exeunt CURIO and Attendants.]

Spanish

bones: huesos, los huesos.
changeable: cambiable.
coffin: ataúd.
constancy: constancia.
corpse: cadáver.
doublet: jubón, doblete.
everything: todo.
everywhere: en todas partes, por todas partes.
flower: flor, la flor, florecer.
god: Dios.
intent: intento, intención, propósito.

lover: querido, amante, novio.
melancholy: melancolía, melancólico.
paid: pagado.
pains: dolores del parto, esfuerzos, desvelos.
pleasure: placer, agrado, gusto, complacencia, el gusto.
protect: proteger, protegéis, protejo, protejan, proteges, protegemos, proteged, protégé, protegen, proteja, guardar.
rest: descansar, descanso, resto,

detrito, desechos, reposar, reposo.
share: compartir, acción, parte, dividir, ración, cuota, lote.
singing: cantando, canto.
taffeta: tafetán, tafeta.
tailor: sastre, costurera.
thee: ustedes, te, vosotros, usted, tú.
thousand: mil.
thy: tu.
voyage: viaje.
weep: llorar, llore, lloren, llora, lloro, lloras, lloran, lloramos, lloráis, llorad.

Once more, Cesario,
Get **thee** to yond same **sovereign** cruelty:
Tell her my love, more **noble** than the world,
Prizes not **quantity** of **dirty** lands;
The parts that **fortune** hath bestow'd upon her,
Tell her, I hold as **giddily** as fortune;
But 'tis that **miracle** and **queen** of gems
That Nature **pranks** her in **attracts** my soul.

VIOLA.
But if she **cannot** love you, sir?

DUKE.
I cannot be so answer'd.

VIOLA.
'Sooth, but you must.
Say that some lady, as perhaps there is,
Hath for your love as great a **pang** of heart
As you have for Olivia: you cannot love her;
You tell her so. Must she not then be answer'd?

DUKE.
There is no woman's sides
Can **bide** the **beating** of so strong a passion
As love doth give my heart: no woman's heart
So big to hold so much; they lack retention.
Alas, their love may be called appetite,--
No **motion** of the **liver**, but the palate,--
That **suffer surfeit**, cloyment, and revolt;
But mine is all as **hungry** as the sea,
And can **digest** as much: make no compare
Between that love a woman can **bear** me
And that I **owe** Olivia.

Spanish

attracts: atrae, encanta.
bear: oso, llevar, el oso, bajista, producir, dar a luz, parir, portar, soportar.
beating: paliza, pulsación, latido.
bide: esperar, espera, esperad, esperáis, esperamos, esperan, esperas, espere, esperen, espero, aguardar.
cannot: presente de no poder.
digest: compendio, digerir.
dirty: sucio, ensuciar, verde, manchar.
fortune: suerte, fortuna.
giddily: mareadamente, frívolamente.
hungry: hambriento.
liver: hígado.
miracle: milagro.
motion: movimiento, moción, petición.
noble: hidalgo, noble.
owe: deber, adeudar.
pang: punzada.
pranks: bromas.
quantity: cantidad, la cantidad, magnitud, cuantidad.
queen: reina, la reina, dama.
sovereign: soberano.
suffer: sufrir, sufres, sufro, sufrís, sufrid, sufren, sufre, sufran, sufrimos, sufra, padecer.
surfeit: superabundancia, empacho, exceso, hartar, hartura, saciar, saciedad.
thee: ustedes, te, vosotros, usted, tú.

VIOLA.
                        Ay, but I know,--
DUKE.
    What dost **thou** know?
VIOLA.
    Too well what love women to men may owe.
    In **faith**, they are as true of **heart** as we.
    My father had a **daughter loved** a man,
    As it might be perhaps, were I a woman,
    I should your **lordship**.
DUKE.
                        And what's her **history**?
VIOLA.
    A **blank**, my lord. She never told her love,
    But let **concealment**, like a **worm** i' the bud,
    Feed on her **damask cheek**: she pined in thought;
    And with a **green** and **yellow** melancholy,
    She **sat** like **patience** on a monument,
    Smiling at **grief**. Was not this love, indeed?
    We men may say more, **swear** more; but indeed,
    Our **shows** are more than will; for still we prove
    Much in our **vows**, but little in our love.
DUKE.
    But **died thy sister** of her love, my **boy**?
VIOLA.
    I am all the **daughters** of my father's house,
    And all the **brothers** too;--and yet I know not.--
    Sir, shall I to this **lady**?
DUKE.
                        Ay, that's the theme.

Spanish

blank: blanco, espacio en blanco, en blanco, formulario, vacío, hoja.
boy: chico, muchacho, niño, el muchacho, criado, chamaco.
brothers: hermanos.
cheek: mejilla, la mejilla, carrillo.
concealment: ocultamiento, ocultación, encubrimiento.
damask: damasco.
daughter: hija, la hija, Nina.
daughters: hijas.
died: muerto.

faith: fe, la fe.
green: verde.
grief: pesar, dolor.
heart: corazón, cogollo.
history: historia, la historia.
lady: dama, señora.
lord: señor, caballero.
loved: amado, estimado, querido, considerado.
patience: paciencia.
sat: pret y pp de sit, sáb, servicio de administración tributaria, sentado,

sábado, soplado, asentado, empollado, se sentado, sentido.
shows: muestra.
sister: hermana, la hermana, cuñada.
swear: jurar, jura, jurad, juráis, juramos, juran, juras, juren, juro, jure, maldecir.
thou: tú, usted, vosotros, ustedes, vos.
thy: tu.
vows: promesas solemnes.
worm: gusano, lombriz, el gusano.
yellow: amarillo.

To her in **haste**: give her this **jewel**; say
My love can give no place, **bide** no denay.
[Exeunt.]

SCENE V. OLIVIA'S GARDEN.

[Enter SIR TOBY BELCH, SIR ANDREW AGUE-CHEEK, and FABIAN.]

SIR TOBY.
Come **thy ways**, Signior Fabian.

FABIAN.
Nay, I'll come; if I **lose** a **scruple** of this **sport** let me be **boiled** to death with
melancholy.

SIR TOBY.
Wouldst **thou** not be **glad** to have the **niggardly rascally** sheep-biter come by
some **notable shame**?

FABIAN.
I would **exult**, man; you know he brought me out o' **favour** with my lady
about a bear-baiting here.

SIR TOBY.
To **anger** him **we'll** have the bear again; and we will **fool** him black and
blue:--shall we not, Sir Andrew?

SIR ANDREW.
An we do not, it is **pity** of our lives.

[Enter MARIA.]

SIR TOBY.
Here comes the little villain:--How now, my **nettle** of India?

Spanish

anger: cólera, enojo, enfado, ira, enojar, furia.
bide: esperar, espera, esperad, esperáis, esperamos, esperan, esperas, espere, esperen, espero, aguardar.
boiled: hervido.
exult: regocijarse, exultar, exultas, exulto, exulte, exultan, exulta, exulten, exultáis, exultad, exultamos.
favour: favor, favorecer.
fool: engañar, necio, tonto.

glad: alegre, contento.
haste: prisa, precipitación.
jewel: joya, la joya.
lose: perder, pierda, pierdo, perdéis, perdemos, pierdan, pierde, pierden, pierdes, perded, adelgazar.
melancholy: melancolía, melancólico.
nettle: ortiga.
niggardly: mezquino, ávido, cicatero, ávidamente, tacaño, avariento.
notable: señalado, memorable, excelente, personaje, notabilidad,

insigne.
pity: dolerse por, piedad, compadecer a, lástima, compasión.
rascally: pícaro.
scruple: escrúpulo.
shame: vergüenza, verguenza, pudor, oprobio, avergonzar.
sport: deporte.
thou: tú, usted, vosotros, ustedes, vos.
thy: tu.
ways: maneras.
we'll: Haremos.

MARIA.
Get ye all three into the box-tree: Malvolio's coming down this **walk**; he has been **yonder** i' the **sun practising behaviour** to his own **shadow** this half **hour**: observe him, for the love of **mockery**; for I know this letter will make a **contemplative idiot** of him. Close, in the name of **jesting**! [The men hide themselves.] Lie thou there; [Throws down a letter] for here comes the **trout** that must be **caught** with tickling.

[Exit Maria.]

[Enter MALVOLIO.]

MALVOLIO.
'Tis but fortune; all is fortune. Maria once told me she did **affect** me: and I have heard herself come thus near, that, should she **fancy**, it should be one of my complexion. Besides, she **uses** me with a more **exalted** respect than any one else that **follows** her. What should I think on't?

SIR TOBY.
Here's an **overweening** rogue!

FABIAN.
O, peace! **Contemplation** makes a **rare** turkey-cock of him; how he **jets** under his advanced **plumes**!

SIR ANDREW.
'Slight, I could so beat the rogue:--

SIR TOBY.
Peace, I say.

MALVOLIO.
To be Count Malvolio;--

SIR TOBY.
Ah, rogue!

SIR ANDREW.
Pistol him, **pistol** him.

Spanish

affect: afectar, afecte, afectas, afecten, afectan, afectáis, afecta, afectad, afectamos, afecto, conmover.
behaviour: comportamiento, conducta.
caught: cogido, asido, acertado.
contemplation: contemplación.
contemplative: contemplativo.
exalted: exaltado.
fancy: figurarse, de fantasía, imaginación.
follows: sigue.

hour: hora, la hora.
idiot: idiota, bobo, estúpido.
jesting: chistes, dichos, en broma, chistoso, chanzas, bromas, bromeando, burlón, guasón.
jets: azabaches, chorros.
mockery: burla.
overweening: altranero, altivo, arrogante, presuntuoso.
pistol: pistola.
plumes: plumas.
practising: ejercicio, ejercicios,

entrenamiento, práctica, practicante, practicar, que ejerce.
rare: raro.
shadow: sombra, sombreado.
sun: sol, el sol.
trout: trucha.
uses: usa, utiliza.
walk: andar, andamos, ando, anden, ande, andas, andáis, andad, anda, andan, caminar.
yonder: allí, ahí, aquel.

SIR TOBY.
Peace, **peace**.

MALVOLIO.
There is **example** for't; the **lady** of the Strachy **married** the **yeoman** of the wardrobe.

SIR ANDREW.
Fie on him, Jezebel!

FABIAN.
O, peace! now he's **deeply** in; look how **imagination blows** him.

MALVOLIO.
Having been three months married to her, **sitting** in my state,--

SIR TOBY.
O for a stone-bow to **hit** him in the **eye**!

MALVOLIO.
Calling my **officers** about me, in my **branched velvet gown**; having come from a day-bed, where I have left Olivia **sleeping**.

SIR TOBY.
Fire and **brimstone**!

FABIAN.
O, peace, peace.

MALVOLIO.
And then to have the **humour** of state: and after a **demure travel** of regard,-- telling them I know my place as I would they should do theirs,--to **ask** for my **kinsman** Toby.

SIR TOBY.
Bolts and **shackles**!

FABIAN.
O, peace, peace, peace! Now, now.

Spanish

ask: preguntar, preguntáis, preguntad, pregunto, pregunten, preguntas, preguntan, preguntamos, pregunte, pregunta, pedir.
blows: golpes.
branched: ramificado.
brimstone: fuego del infierno, azufre.
deeply: profundamente.
demure: recatado, grave.
example: ejemplo, el ejemplo.
eye: ojo, el ojo, ojear, mirar.
gown: vestido, toga.

hit: golpear, acertar, golpe, pegar, llamar, éxito.
humour: humor.
imagination: imaginación.
kinsman: pariente.
lady: dama, señora.
married: casado, casada, se casado, conyugal.
officers: oficialidad, personal directivo, Mesa.
peace: paz, la paz.
shackles: grilletes.

sir: señor.
sitting: sesión, sentada.
sleeping: durmiendo, durmiente.
travel: viajar, viaje, viajo, viaja, viajas, viajan, viajamos, viajen, viajad, viajáis, conducir.
velvet: terciopelo, el terciopelo.
yeoman: hacendado.

MALVOLIO.
Seven of my people, with an **obedient** start, make out for him: I **frown** the
while, and perchance, wind up my **watch**, or play with some rich jewel. Toby
approaches; court'sies there to me:

SIR TOBY.
Shall this fellow live?

FABIAN.
Though our silence be **drawn** from us with **cars**, yet peace.

MALVOLIO.
I **extend** my hand to him thus, **quenching** my **familiar smile** with an **austere
regard** of control:

SIR TOBY.
And does not Toby take you a **blow** o' the lips then?

MALVOLIO.
Saying 'Cousin Toby, my fortunes having **cast** me on your niece, give me this
prerogative of speech':--

SIR TOBY.
What, what?

MALVOLIO.
'You must amend your drunkenness.'

SIR TOBY.
Out, **scab**!

FABIAN.
Nay, patience, or we break the **sinews** of our **plot**.

MALVOLIO.
'Besides, you **waste** the **treasure** of your time with a foolish knight';

SIR ANDREW.
That's me, I warrant you.

Spanish

approaches: aproches.
austere: austero.
blow: soplar, golpe.
cars: carros, los coches.
cast: lanzar, lanzamiento, arrojar, echar, colar, elenco, molde.
drawn: dibujado, encantado, trazado.
extend: extender, alargar, ampliar, extiende, amplías, extendéis, amplíen, amplío, extiendo, extended, extienden.
familiar: conocido.

frown: ceño, fruncir el entrecejo, fruncir el ceño.
obedient: obediente, dócil.
plot: parcela, trama, argumento, complot, gráfico, solar, trazar.
prerogative: prerrogativa.
quenching: extinción, temple, apagado, extinción sin conmutación.
regard: mirar, considerar, mira, miran, miráis, miro, miramos, mirad, miras, mire, miren.
scab: costra, esquirol, roña.

sinews: tendones, recursos.
smile: sonrisa, sonreír, la sonrisa, sonreírse.
treasure: tesoro, atesorar.
waste: desechos, desperdicio, residuo, residuos, detrito, gastar, acabar, desperdicios, derrochar, gasto, desecho.
watch: reloj, mirar, observar, reloj de pulsera, ver, contemplar, el reloj, prestar atención, vigilar, guardia, guardar.

MALVOLIO.
'One Sir Andrew':

SIR ANDREW.
I knew 'twas I; for many do **call** me fool.

MALVOLIO.
What **employment** have we here?
[Taking up the letter.]

FABIAN.
Now is the **woodcock near** the **gin**.

SIR TOBY.
O, **peace**! And the **spirit** of humours **intimate reading aloud** to him!

MALVOLIO.
By my life, this is my **lady's** hand: these be her very C's, her U's, and her T's;
and thus **makes** she her great P's. It is in **contempt** of question, her hand.

SIR ANDREW.
Her C's, her U's, and her T's. Why that?

MALVOLIO.
[Reads]
'To the **unknown beloved**, this, and my good wishes.' Her very phrases!--By
your **leave**, wax.--Soft!--and the impressure her Lucrece, with which she **uses**
to **seal**: 'tis my lady. To **whom** should this be?

FABIAN.
This **wins** him, **liver** and all.

MALVOLIO.
[Reads]
'Jove **knows** I love,
But who?
Lips, do not move,
No man must know.'

Spanish

aloud: en voz alta.
beloved: querido, amado, novio,
  dilecto.
call: llamada, llamar, llaman, llamen,
  llamad, llamas, llamo, llamamos,
  llamáis, llame, llama.
contempt: desprecio, menosprecio.
employment: empleo, trabajo,
  acomodo.
gin: ginebra, la ginebra.
intimate: íntimo, cómodo, intimo.
knows: sabe, conoce.

lady: dama, señora.
leave: salir, sal, sale, salís, salimos,
  salgo, salgan, salga, sales, salen,
  saled.
liver: hígado.
makes: hace, comete, confecciona.
near: cerca, próximo, cerca de,
  cercano, entrante, casi.
peace: paz, la paz.
reading: leyendo, lectura, la lectura.
seal: foca, sello, sellar, precinto,
  precintar.

sir: señor.
spirit: espíritu.
unknown: desconocido, incógnita.
uses: usa, utiliza.
whom: quien, quién, que.
wins: gana.
woodcock: becada.

'No man must know.'--What follows? the **numbers** alter'd!--'No man must know':--If this should be **thee**, Malvolio?

SIR TOBY.
Marry, **hang** thee, brock!

MALVOLIO.
'I **may command** where I adore:
But **silence**, like a Lucrece knife,
With **bloodless stroke** my heart doth gore;
M, O, A, I, doth **sway** my life.'

FABIAN.
A **fustian riddle**!

SIR TOBY.
Excellent **wench**, say I.

MALVOLIO.
'M, O, A, I, doth sway my life.'--Nay, but first let me see,--let me see,--let me see.

FABIAN.
What **dish** of **poison** has she **dressed** him!

SIR TOBY.
And with what **wing** the stannyel checks at it!

MALVOLIO.
'I may command where I adore.' Why, she may command me: I **serve** her, she is my **lady**. Why, this is **evident** to any **formal capacity**; there is no **obstruction** in this;--And the end,--What should that **alphabetical** position **portend**? If I could make that **resemble** something in me.--Softly!--M, O, A, I.--

SIR TOBY.
O, ay, make up that:--he is now at a **cold scent**.

Spanish

alphabetical: alfabético.
ay: sí.
bloodless: incruento.
capacity: capacidad.
cold: frío, resfriado, catarro, constipado.
command: mando, orden, mandato, comando, instrucción, capitanear, acaudillar.
dish: plato, el plato, guiso.
dressed: vestido, con guarnición de.
evident: evidente.

formal: formal.
fustian: fustán.
hang: colgar.
lady: dama, señora.
numbers: números.
obstruction: obstrucción, obstáculo.
poison: veneno, envenenar, intoxicar.
portend: presagiar.
resemble: parecerse, asemejarse, parecerse a.
riddle: enigma, acertijo, adivinanza.
scent: olor, perfume, aroma.

serve: servir, sirva, sirvo, servimos, servid, servís, sirvan, sirve, sirven, sirves.
silence: silencio, acallar, hacer callar, el silencio.
stroke: acariciar, caricia, apoplejía, carrera, golpe, derrame cerebral, recorrido.
sway: oscilación, vaivén.
thee: ustedes, te, vosotros, usted, tú.
wench: muchacha.
wing: ala, el ala, guardabarros, la ala.

FABIAN.
Sowter will cry upon't for all this, though it be as rank as a fox.

MALVOLIO.
M,--Malvolio; M,--why, that begins my name.

FABIAN.
Did not I say he would work it out? The **cur** is excellent at faults.

MALVOLIO.
M,--But then there is no consonancy in the **sequel**; that **suffers** under **probation**: A should follow, but O does.

FABIAN.
And O shall end, I hope.

SIR TOBY.
Ay, or I'll **cudgel** him, and make him cry 'O!'

MALVOLIO.
And then I comes behind.

FABIAN.
Ay, an you had any eye behind you, you might see more **detraction** at your **heels** than fortunes before you.

MALVOLIO.
M, O, A, I;--This **simulation** is not as the former:--and yet, to **crush** this a little, it would **bow** to me, for every one of these letters are in my name. Soft; here follows prose.-- 'If this fall into thy hand, **revolve**. In my stars I am above thee; but be not afraid of **greatness**. Some are born great, some achieve greatness, and some have greatness thrust upon them. Thy fates open their hands; let thy blood and spirit **embrace** them. And, to **inure thyself** to what thou art like to be, cast thy **humble slough** and appear fresh. Be opposite with a kinsman, **surly** with servants: let thy tongue **tang** arguments of state; put thyself into the **trick** of **singularity**: She thus **advises** thee that sighs for thee. Remember who **commended** thy yellow **stockings**, and wished to see thee ever cross-gartered. I say, remember. Go to; thou art made, if thou

Spanish

advises: aconseja.
bow: proa, arco, reverencia, inclinarse, lazo.
commended: alabado.
crush: compresión, aplastar.
cudgel: garrote corto.
cur: perro chusco o de mala casta, perro, hombre vil, de mala raza, chucho, canalla, vil.
detraction: detracción.
embrace: abrazar, abarcar.
greatness: grandeza.

heels: taco, tacón.
humble: humilde, humillar.
inure: habituar.
probation: libertad condicional.
revolve: girar, gira, gire, giro, revolver, giramos, giren, giran, giráis, girad, giras.
sequel: continuación.
simulation: simulación.
singularity: singularidad.
slough: pantano, Abismo, cenagal, Costra, fangal, Deshacerse Por,

Desprenderse De, Mudar, desprenderse, Mudar La Piel.
stockings: las medias.
suffers: sufre, padece.
surly: bronco, brusco, hosco.
tang: rabera, sabor, regusto, lengüeta, extremidad, espiga, dejo, chaveta, sabor picante, poner una espiga a.
thyself: ti, tú mismo, ti mismo, tú misma, te, ti misma.
trick: engañar, truco, resabio, mala costumbre.

desirest to be so; if not, let me see thee a steward still, the fellow of **servants**, and not **worthy** to **touch** fortune's fingers. Farewell. She that would **alter** services with thee,

THE FORTUNATE-UNHAPPY.

Daylight and champian **discovers** not more: this is open. I will be **proud**, I will read **politic** authors, I will **baffle** Sir Toby, I will **wash** off **gross** acquaintance, I will be point-device, the very man. I do not now fool myself to let imagination **jade** me; for every reason **excites** to this, that my lady loves me. She did **commend** my yellow stockings of late, she did praise my leg being cross-gartered; and in this she manifests herself to my love, and with a kind of **injunction**, **drives** me to these **habits** of her **liking**. I thank my stars I am happy. I will be **strange**, **stout**, in yellow stockings, and cross-gartered, even with the **swiftness** of putting on. Jove and my stars be praised!--Here is yet a **postscript**. 'Thou canst not choose but know who I am. If thou entertainest my love, let it appear in thy **smiling**; thy smiles become thee well: therefore in my presence still smile, dear my sweet, I pr'ythee.' Jove, I thank thee. I will smile; I will do everything that thou wilt have me.

[Exit.]

FABIAN.

I will not give my part of this sport for a **pension** of **thousands** to be paid from the Sophy.

SIR TOBY.

I could marry this wench for this device:

SIR ANDREW.

So could I too.

SIR TOBY.

And ask no other **dowry** with her but such another jest.

[Enter MARIA.]

SIR ANDREW.

Nor I neither.

Spanish

alter: cambiar, cambia, cambien, cambie, cambias, cambian, cambio, cambiamos, cambiáis, cambiad, alterar.
baffle: deflector, confundir, confusión, tilbe.
commend: alabar, alabo, alaben, alabe, alabas, alaban, alabamos, alabáis, alaba, alabad, recomendar.
discovers: descubre.
dowry: dote.
drives: conduce, maneja.
excites: instiga, excita.
gross: bruto, asqueroso, grueso, doce docenas.
habits: hábitos.
injunction: requerimiento, interdicto.
jade: fatigar, cansar, jade.
jove: Júpiter.
liking: afición, gusto.
pension: pensión.
politic: sagaz.
postscript: posdata, postdata.
proud: orgulloso.
servants: servicio.
smiling: sonriente.
stout: obstinado.
strange: extraño, raro, ajeno.
swiftness: ligereza, prontitud, rapidez.
thousands: miles.
touch: tocar, toque, tacto, palpar, contacto, rozar.
wash: lavar, lave, lavo, lava, lavad, laváis, lavamos, lavas, laven, lavan, lavarse.
worthy: digno.

FABIAN.
Here comes my **noble** gull-catcher.

SIR TOBY.
Wilt **thou** set **thy** foot o' my neck?

SIR ANDREW.
Or o' mine either?

SIR TOBY.
Shall I play my **freedom** at tray-trip, and become thy bond-slave?

SIR ANDREW.
I' faith, or I either?

SIR TOBY.
Why, thou **hast** put him in such a **dream**, that, when the image of it **leaves** him, he must run **mad**.

MARIA.
Nay, but say true; does it work upon him?

SIR TOBY.
Like **aqua**-vitae **with** a **midwife**.

MARIA.
If you will then see the fruits of the **sport**, **mark** his first approach before my lady: he will come to her in **yellow stockings**, and 'tis a **colour** she **abhors**, and cross-gartered, a **fashion** she **detests**; and he will smile upon her, which will now be so **unsuitable** to her **disposition**, being **addicted** to a **melancholy** as she is, that it **cannot** but turn him into a **notable contempt**; if you will see it, **follow** me.

SIR TOBY.
To the gates of Tartar, thou most excellent **devil** of wit!

SIR ANDREW.
I'll make one too.

[Exeunt.]

Spanish

abhors: detesta, aborrece, odia.
addicted: adicto.
aqua-vitae: aguardiente.
cannot: presente de no poder.
colour: color, colorear, coloración.
contempt: desprecio, menosprecio.
detests: detesta.
devil: diablo, el diablo.
disposition: disposición, talento, capacidad.
dream: soñar, sueño, ensueño.
fashion: moda.

follow: seguir, seguid, sigues, siguen, sigue, sigo, sigan, seguís, seguimos, siga, venir después.
freedom: libertad.
hast: haya.
leaves: sale, deja, hojas, las hojas.
mad: loco, enojado, chiflado, majara, majareta, demente, enfadado.
mark: señal, seña, marca, nota, marcar, sellar, signo, timbrar, señalar, marcos, marco.
melancholy: melancolía, melancólico.

midwife: comadrona, partera.
noble: hidalgo, noble.
notable: señalado, memorable, excelente, personaje, notabilidad, insigne.
sport: deporte.
stockings: las medias.
thou: tú, usted, vosotros, ustedes, vos.
thy: tu.
unsuitable: inadecuado.
wit: ingenio.
yellow: amarillo.

ACT III

SCENE I. OLIVIA'S GARDEN.

[Enter VIOLA, and CLOWN **with** a tabor.]

VIOLA.
Save **thee, friend,** and **thy music.** Dost **thou live** by thy tabor?

CLOWN.
No, **sir,** I live by the church.

VIOLA.
Art thou a **churchman?**

CLOWN.
No such **matter,** sir: I do live by the church; for I do live at my house, and my house doth **stand** by the church.

VIOLA.
So thou mayst say the **king** lies by a **beggar,** if a beggar **dwell near** him; or the church **stands** by thy tabor, if thy tabor stand by the church.

CLOWN.
You have said, sir.--To see this age!--A **sentence** is but a cheveril **glove** to a good wit. How **quickly** the **wrong** side may be **turned outward!**

Spanish

beggar: mendigo, pordiosero.
churchman: clérigo.
dwell: morar, morad, moren, moras, moráis, moran, moramos, mora, more, moro, habitar.
friend: amigo, amiga, el amigo.
glove: guante, el guante.
king: rey, el rey.
live: vivir, viven, vive, vivo, vivan, vivís, vivimos, vives, viva, vivid, habitar.
matter: materia, asunto, particular,

caso, importar.
music: música.
near: cerca, próximo, cerca de, cercano, entrante, casi.
outward: exterior.
quickly: rápidamente, de prisa, aprisa, pronto.
sentence: frase, condenar, sentencia, oración, la frase, pena, punición, condena.
sir: señor.
stand: estar de pie, puesto, levantarse,

granero, posición, cabina, soporte, base, estante, caseta, pararse.
stands: tenderetes, jaulas.
thee: ustedes, te, vosotros, usted, tú.
thou: tú, usted, vosotros, ustedes, vos.
thy: tu.
turned: girado, vuelto, trastornado.
wit: ingenio.
wrong: malo, mal, falso, incorrecto, entuerto, agravio, impropio, erróneo.

VIOLA.
Nay, that's certain; they that **dally nicely** with words may quickly make them **wanton**.

CLOWN.
I would, therefore, my **sister** had had no name, sir.

VIOLA.
Why, man?

CLOWN.
Why, sir, her name's a word; and to dally with that word might make my sister wanton. But indeed words are very rascals, since **bonds disgraced** them.

VIOLA.
Thy reason, man?

CLOWN.
Troth, sir, I can **yield** you none **without** words; and words are **grown** so **false** I am **loath** to **prove** reason with them.

VIOLA.
I **warrant**, thou art a **merry fellow**, and carest for nothing.

CLOWN.
Not so, sir, I do care for something: but in my **conscience**, sir, I do not care for you; if that be to care for nothing, sir, I would it would make you **invisible**.

VIOLA.
Art not thou the Lady Olivia's **fool**?

CLOWN.
No, indeed, sir; the Lady Olivia has no **folly**: she will keep no fool, sir, **till** she be **married**; and fools are as like husbands as pilchards are to **herrings**, the husband's the **bigger**; I am, indeed, not her fool, but her **corrupter** of words.

VIOLA.
I saw **thee** late at the Count Orsino's.

Spanish

bigger: más grande, mayor, más.
bonds: cautiverio, bonos, obligaciones.
conscience: conciencia.
corrupter: corruptor.
dally: perder el tiempo, tardar, tarda, tardo, tardas, tarde, tardan, tardamos, tardáis, tardad, tarden.
disgraced: deshonrado.
false: falso.
fellow: compañero, hombre, socio, tipo, becario.
folly: tontería.

fool: engañar, necio, tonto.
grown: crecido, aumentado, adulto.
herrings: arenque.
invisible: invisible.
loath: renuente.
married: casado, casada, se casado, conyugal.
merry: alegre.
nicely: agradablemente.
prove: probar, probad, prueban, pruebas, pruebo, probamos, probáis, prueben, prueba, pruebe, verificar.

sister: hermana, la hermana, cuñada.
thee: ustedes, te, vosotros, usted, tú.
thou: tú, usted, vosotros, ustedes, vos.
till: caja, hasta que, hasta, a que.
wanton: petulante, lascivo.
warrant: garantía, orden, orden por escrito, certificado, autorizar, autorización.
yield: ceder, cedemos, cedes, cedo, ceden, cedéis, ceded, cede, ceda, cedan, rendimiento.

CLOWN.

Foolery, sir, does walk about the **orb** like the sun; it **shines** everywhere. I would be **sorry**, sir, but the **fool** should be as **oft** with your master as with my **mistress**: I think I saw your **wisdom** there.

VIOLA.

Nay, an **thou pass** upon me, I'll no more with **thee**. Hold, there's **expenses** for thee.

CLOWN.

Now Jove, in his next **commodity** of hair, send thee a **beard**!

VIOLA.

By my **troth**, I'll tell thee, I am almost **sick** for one; though I would not have it grow on my **chin**. Is **thy** lady within?

CLOWN.

Would not a **pair** of these have **bred**, sir?

VIOLA.

Yes, being **kept** together and put to use.

CLOWN.

I would play Lord Pandarus of Phrygia, sir, to bring a Cressida to this Troilus.

VIOLA.

I understand you, sir; 'tis well **begged**.

CLOWN.

The matter, I hope, is not great, sir, **begging** but a **beggar**: Cressida was a beggar. My lady is within, sir. I will **construe** to them **whence** you come; who you are and what you would are out of my welkin: I might say element; but the   word   is   overworn.

[Exit.]

VIOLA.

This fellow's **wise** enough to play the fool;
And, to do that well, **craves** a kind of wit:

Spanish

beard: barba, la barba, arista.
beggar: mendigo, pordiosero.
begged: Mendigado.
begging: mendicidad, mendigando, mendigar.
bred: pret y pp de breed, Criado.
chin: barba, barbilla, la barbilla, mentón.
commodity: artículo, producto básico, producto, artículo de consumo.
construe: interpretar.
craves: ansía.

expenses: gastos, expensas.
fool: engañar, necio, tonto.
kept: guardado, vigilado, conservado, preservado.
mistress: señora.
oft: a menudo, mucho, con frecuencia, muchas veces.
orb: orbe.
pair: par, pareja, emparejar.
pass: pasar, adelantar, paso, pase, desfiladero, entregar, pasada, aprobar, alargar, paso de montaña,

llegar.
shines: brilla.
sick: enfermo.
sorry: afligido, arrepentido, pesaroso, siento, triste.
thee: ustedes, te, vosotros, usted, tú.
thou: tú, usted, vosotros, ustedes, vos.
thy: tu.
troth: fidelidad, fe.
whence: de dónde.
wisdom: sabiduría, sapiencia.
wise: sabio, sensato, guisa.

He must **observe** their **mood** on whom he jests,
The **quality** of persons, and the time;
And, like the **haggard**, **check** at every feather
That comes before his eye. This is a practice
As full of labour as a **wise** man's art:
For **folly**, that he **wisely** shows, is fit;
But wise men, folly-fallen, quite **taint** their wit.

[Enter SIR TOBY BELCH and SIR ANDREW AGUE-CHEEK.]

SIR TOBY.
Save you, gentleman.

VIOLA.
And you, sir.

SIR ANDREW.
*Dieu vous **garde**, monsieur.*

VIOLA.
Et vous aussi; votre serviteur.

SIR ANDREW.
I hope, sir, you are; and I am yours.

SIR TOBY.
Will you **encounter** the house? my **niece** is **desirous** you should enter, if your **trade** be to her.

VIOLA.
I am **bound** to your niece, sir: I mean, she is the **list** of my **voyage**.

SIR TOBY.
Taste your legs, sir; put them to motion.

VIOLA.
My legs do better understand me, sir, than I understand what you mean by **bidding** me **taste** my legs.

Spanish

bidding: licitación.
bound: encuadernado, saltar, salto, ligado, límite, obligado.
check: cheque, comprobar, revisar, control, controlar, cuenta, talón, verificación, contener, verificar, reprimir.
desirous: deseoso.
encounter: encuentro, encontrar, encuentran, encuentren, encuentre, encuentras, encuentra, encontramos, encontrad, encontráis, hallar.
folly: tontería.
garde: guarda.
haggard: ojeroso, macilento, demacrado.
list: lista, listar, la lista, listado, minuta.
mood: humor, el humor, estado de ánimo, capricho.
niece: sobrina, la sobrina.
observe: observar, observa, observen, observe, observas, observan, observad, observáis, observo, observamos, hacer.
quality: calidad, ralea, cualidad, la calidad.
taint: deterioración, putrefacción, mancha.
taste: gusto, saborear, sabor, probar, catar.
trade: comercio, oficio, negocio, intercambiar.
voyage: viaje.
wise: sabio, sensato, guisa.
wisely: sabiamente.

62 Twelfth Night

SIR TOBY.
I mean, to go, **sir**, to enter.

VIOLA.
I will **answer** you with **gait** and **entrance**: but we are prevented.
[Enter OLIVIA and MARIA.]
Most **excellent accomplished lady**, the **heavens rain** odours on you!

SIR ANDREW.
That **youth's** a **rare courtier**- 'Rain odours'! well.

VIOLA.
My matter hath no voice, lady, but to your own most **pregnant** and
vouchsafed car.

SIR ANDREW.
'Odours,' 'pregnant,' and 'vouchsafed':--I'll get 'em all three **ready**.

OLIVIA.
Let the **garden** door be **shut**, and leave me to my hearing.
[Exeunt SIR TOBY, SIR ANDREW, and MARIA.]
Give me your hand, sir.

VIOLA.
My **duty**, madam, and most **humble** service.

OLIVIA.
What is your name?

VIOLA.
Cesario is your **servant's** name, **fair princess**.

OLIVIA.
My servant, sir! 'Twas never **merry** world,
Since **lowly feigning** was call'd compliment:
You are servant to the Count Orsino, youth.

Spanish

accomplished: realizado, cumplido, consumado, dotado, talentoso, terminado.
answer: respuesta, responder, contestar, contestación, responder a, corresponder al, contestar a, la respuesta, réplica.
courtier: cortesano, palaciego.
duty: deber, servicio, obligación, impuesto.
entrance: entrada, la entrada.
excellent: excelente.

fair: justo, rubio, mercado, feria, verbena, bazar, equitativo, hermoso.
feigning: fingiendo, aparentando.
gait: paso.
garden: jardín, el jardín.
heavens: cielo, cielos.
humble: humilde, humillar.
lady: dama, señora.
lowly: humilde.
merry: alegre.
pregnant: embarazada, en estado, encinta, preñada.

princess: princesa.
rain: llover, lluvia, la lluvia.
rare: raro.
ready: listo, preparado, propenso, disponible.
servant: criado, criada, sirviente, servidor.
shut: cerrar, cerrado.
sir: señor.
vouchsafed: Concedido.
youth: juventud, joven, jóvenes, adolescencia.

VIOLA.
And he is **yours**, and his must needs be yours;
Your **servant's** servant is your servant, madam.

OLIVIA.
For him, I think not on him: for his thoughts,
Would they were **blanks** rather than fill'd with me!

VIOLA.
Madam, I come to **whet** your **gentle** thoughts
On his behalf:--

OLIVIA.
O, by your leave, I **pray** you:
I **bade** you never speak again of him:
But, would you **undertake** another suit,
I had rather hear you to **solicit** that
Than music from the **spheres**.

VIOLA.
Dear lady,--

OLIVIA.
Give me leave, **beseech** you: I did send,
After the last **enchantment** you did here,
A ring in **chase** of you; so did I abuse
Myself, my servant, and, I fear me, you:
Under your hard **construction** must I sit;
To force that on you, in a **shameful** cunning,
Which you knew none of yours. What might you think?
Have you not set mine **honour** at the stake,
And **baited** it with all the unmuzzl'd thoughts
That **tyrannous** heart can think? To one of your receiving
Enough is shown: a **cypress**, not a bosom,
Hides my heart: so let me hear you speak.

Spanish

bade: pret de bid, Mandó.
baited: Tentó.
beseech: supliquen, rogáis, rogamos, ruega, ruegan, ruegues, ruegue, rueguen, suplica, suplicamos, rogad.
blanks: segmentos lisos del cierre del cañón, recortes, cartones planos.
chase: cazar, perseguir, persecución, caza, cincelar.
construction: construcción.
cypress: ciprés.
enchantment: encantamiento.

gentle: dulce, suave, manso, apacible.
honour: honor, homenaje.
pray: rezar, rezáis, rezas, rezamos, rezad, reza, recen, rece, rezan, rezo, rogar.
servant: criado, criada, sirviente, servidor.
shameful: vergonzoso.
solicit: solicitar, solicita, solicitad, solicito, soliciten, solicitas, solicitan, solicitamos, solicitáis, solicite.
spheres: esferos.

tyrannous: tiránico, tirano.
undertake: emprender, emprenda, emprenden, emprended, emprendo, emprendes, emprendéis, emprendan, emprende, emprendemos, encargarse de.
whet: afilar, afile, afilen, afilas, afilan, afiláis, afilad, afila, afilo, afilamos.
yours: vuestro, suyo, el tuyo.

VIOLA.
I **pity** you.
OLIVIA.
That's a degree to love.
VIOLA.
No, not a grise; for 'tis a **vulgar** proof
That very **oft** we pity enemies.
OLIVIA.
Why, then, methinks 'tis time to smile again:
O world, how **apt** the poor are to be proud!
If one should be a **prey**, how much the better
To fall before the **lion** than the **wolf**! [Clock strikes.]
The **clock upbraids** me **with** the **waste** of time.--
Be not **afraid**, good **youth**, I will not have you:
And yet, when wit and youth is come to harvest,
Your wife is like to **reap** a **proper** man.
There lies your way, due-west.
VIOLA.
Then westward-ho:
Grace and good **disposition** 'tend your ladyship!
You'll nothing, madam, to my lord by me?
OLIVIA.
Stay:
I pr'ythee tell me what **thou** think'st of me.
VIOLA.
That you do think you are not what you are.
OLIVIA.
If I think so, I think the same of you.
VIOLA.
Then think you right; I am not what I am.

Spanish

afraid: miedoso, temeroso, asustado, medroso, miedo, encogido, angustioso, tímido, be - tener miedo.
apt: apropiado.
clock: reloj, el reloj, ceas.
disposition: disposición, talento, capacidad.
lion: león.
oft: a menudo, mucho, con frecuencia, muchas veces.
pity: dolerse por, piedad, compadecer a, lástima, compasión.

prey: presa.
proper: conveniente, preciso, correcto, apropiado, propio, debido.
reap: cosechar, cosechamos, cosechen, cosecho, cosecháis, cosechad, cosechas, cosechan, cosecha, coseche, segar.
thou: tú, usted, vosotros, ustedes, vos.
upbraids: reprende, reconviene, regaña.
vulgar: chabacano, cursi, grosero, cutre, corriente, vulgo, vulgar,

ramplón, ordinario, ordinaria, común.
waste: desechos, desperdicio, residuo, residuos, detrito, gastar, acabar, desperdicios, derrochar, gasto, desecho.
wit: ingenio.
wolf: lobo, el lobo.
youth: juventud, joven, jóvenes, adolescencia.

OLIVIA.
I would you were as I would have you be!

VIOLA.
Would it be better, madam, than I am,
I **wish** it might; for now I am your fool.

OLIVIA.
O what a **deal** of **scorn looks** beautiful
In the contempt and anger of his lip!
A murd'rous **guilt** shows not itself more soon
Than love that would **seem hid**: love's night is noon.
Cesario, by the roses of the spring,
By maidhood, honour, **truth**, and everything,
I love **thee** so that, maugre all **thy** pride,
Nor wit, nor **reason**, can my passion hide.
Do not **extort** thy reasons from this clause,
For, that I **woo**, thou therefore **hast** no cause:
But rather reason thus with reason fetter:
Love **sought** is good, but given unsought is better.

VIOLA.
By innocence I swear, and by my youth,
I have one heart, one **bosom**, and one truth,
And that no woman has; nor never none
Shall mistress be of it, **save** I alone.
And so **adieu**, good madam; never more
Will I my master's **tears** to you **deplore**.

OLIVIA.
Yet come again: for thou, perhaps, mayst move
That heart, which now **abhors**, to like his love.

[Exeunt.]

Spanish

abhors: detesta, aborrece, odia.
adieu: adiós.
bosom: pecho, seno.
deal: trato, transacción.
deplore: deplorar, deploro, deploren, deplore, deploráis, deploras, deplorad, deplora, deploran, deploramos.
extort: arrancar, arrancáis, arranquen, arranco, arrancas, arrancamos, arrancad, arranca, arrancan, arranque, extorsionar.

guilt: culpa.
hast: haya.
hid: escondió, pret de hide.
looks: mira.
reason: motivo, causa, razón, lugar, razonar.
save: guardar, guarda, guardan, guardáis, guardamos, guardas, guarde, guardo, guardad, guarden, salvar.
scorn: desdén, desdeñar.
seem: parecer, parezca, parecen,

parezcan, pareces, parezco, parecemos, parecéis, parece, pareced.
sought: buscado.
tears: desgarra, rasga.
thee: ustedes, te, vosotros, usted, tú.
thy: tu.
truth: verdad, veras, la verdad.
wish: desear, deseo, voluntad, querer, tener, gana.
woo: cortejar, corteje, cortejamos, cortejo, cortejen, cortejan, cortejáis, cortejad, corteja, cortejas.

SCENE II. A ROOM IN OLIVIA'S HOUSE.

[Enter SIR TOBY BELCH, SIR ANDREW AGUE-CHEEK, and FABIAN.]

SIR ANDREW.
No, faith, I'll not stay a **jot** longer.

SIR TOBY.
Thy reason, dear **venom**: give **thy** reason.

FABIAN.
You must needs yield your reason, Sir Andrew.

SIR ANDREW.
Marry, I saw your **niece** do more favours to the count's servingman than ever she **bestowed** upon me; I saw't i' the **orchard**.

SIR TOBY.
Did she see thee the while, old boy? tell me that.

SIR ANDREW.
As **plain** as I see you now.

FABIAN.
This was a great **argument** of love in her **toward** you.

SIR ANDREW.
'Slight! will you make an **ass** o' me?

FABIAN.
I will prove it **legitimate**, sir, upon the **oaths** of **judgment** and reason.

SIR TOBY.
And they have been **grand** jurymen since before Noah was a **sailor**.

FABIAN.
She did show favour to the youth in your **sight** only to **exasperate** you, to **awake** your **dormouse valour**, to put **fire** in your heart and **brimstone** in your liver. You should then have **accosted** her; and with some excellent **jests**,

Spanish

accosted: abordado.
argument: argumento, discusión, el argumento.
ass: burro, asno, culo.
awake: despierto, despertar, despertarse.
bestowed: conferido, otorgado, concedido.
brimstone: fuego del infierno, azufre.
dormouse: lirón.
exasperate: exasperar, exaspera, exasperen, exasperas, exasperan,

exasperamos, exasperáis, exasperad, exaspero, exaspere.
fire: fuego, incendio, despedir, disparar, el fuego, tirar, animar, incitar, lumbre, hacer fuego, encender.
grand: magnífico, grande, grandioso.
jests: bromas.
jot: pizca.
judgment: juicio, fallo, sentencia, criterio.
legitimate: legítimo.

niece: sobrina, la sobrina.
oaths: juramentos.
orchard: huerto, huerta.
plain: llanura, llano, claro, evidente, liso, plano.
sailor: marinero, navegante, el marinero, marino.
sight: vista, aspecto, mira, avistar.
thy: tu.
toward: hacia, a.
valour: valor.
venom: veneno.

fire-new from the **mint**, you should have banged the youth into **dumbness**. This was looked for at your hand, and this was baulked: the double **gilt** of this opportunity you let time wash off, and you are now **sailed** into the north of my lady's opinion; where you will hang like an **icicle** on Dutchman's beard, unless you do **redeem** it by some **laudable** attempt either of valour or policy.

SIR ANDREW.
And't be any way, it must be with valour: for policy I hate; I had as **lief** be a Brownist as a **politician**.

SIR TOBY.
Why, then, build me thy fortunes upon the basis of valour. Challenge me the count's youth to fight with him; **hurt** him in **eleven** places; my niece shall take note of it: and **assure** thyself there is no love-broker in the world can more **prevail** in man's **commendation** with woman than report of valour.

FABIAN.
There is no way but this, Sir Andrew.

SIR ANDREW.
Will either of you bear me a challenge to him?

SIR TOBY.
Go, write it in a **martial** hand; be curst and brief; it is no matter how witty, so it be **eloquent** and full of **invention**; **taunt** him with the **licence** of **ink**; if thou 'thou'st' him some **thrice**, it shall not be **amiss**; and as many lies as will lie in thy sheet of paper, although the sheet were big enough for the bed of Ware in England, set 'em down; go about it. Let there be **gall** enough in thy ink; though thou write with a goose-pen, no matter. About it.

SIR ANDREW.
Where shall I find you?

SIR TOBY.
We'll call thee at the cubiculo. Go.

[Exit SIR ANDREW.]

Spanish

amiss: errado.
assure: asegurar, asegura, aseguren, aseguras, aseguran, aseguramos, aseguráis, asegurad, aseguro, asegure, garantizar.
commendation: alabanza.
dumbness: mudez, tonterías comprensibles, estupidez.
eleven: once.
eloquent: elocuente.
gall: bilis, hiel, agalla.
gilt: dorado.

hurt: doler, herir, dañar, herida, lastimar.
icicle: carámbano.
ink: tinta, la tinta, entintar.
invention: invención, invento.
laudable: digno de loor.
licence: licencia, permiso.
lief: con placer.
martial: marcial.
mint: menta, hierbabuena, ceca.
politician: político, hombre político.
prevail: prevalecer, prevalecemos,

prevalece, prevaleced, prevalecéis, prevalezco, prevaleces, prevalezca, prevalezcan, prevalecen.
redeem: amortizar, redimir, rescatar, redima, redimimos, redimid, redimes, redimen, redime, rediman, redimo.
sailed: navegado.
taunt: insultar, insulto, insultas, insulten, insulta, insulte, insultamos, insultad, insultan, insultáis, mofarse.
thrice: tres veces.

FABIAN.
This is a dear manakin to you, Sir Toby.

SIR TOBY.
I have been dear to him, lad; some two thousand strong, or so.

FABIAN.
We shall have a rare letter from him: but you'll not deliver it.

SIR TOBY.
Never trust me then; and by all means **stir** on the youth to an answer. I think **oxen** and wainropes cannot **hale** them together. For Andrew, if he were opened and you find so much blood in his liver as will **clog** the foot of a **flea**, I'll eat the rest of the **anatomy**.

FABIAN.
And his opposite, the youth, bears in his **visage** no great **presage** of **cruelty**.

[Enter MARIA.]

SIR TOBY.
Look where the **youngest wren** of nine comes.

MARIA.
If you desire the **spleen**, and will laugh **yourselves** into **stitches**, follow me: yond gull Malvolio is turned **heathen**, a very renegado; for there is no Christian, that means to be saved by **believing rightly**, can ever believe such impossible passages of **grossness**. He's in yellow stockings.

SIR TOBY.
And cross-gartered?

MARIA.
Most **villainously**; like a **pedant** that keeps a school i' the church.--I have **dogged** him like his **murderer**. He does **obey** every point of the letter that I dropped to **betray** him. He does smile his face into more lines than is in the new map, with the **augmentation** of the Indies: you have not seen such a thing as 'tis; I can hardly **forbear hurling** things at him. I know my lady will strike him; if she do, he'll smile and take't for a great favour.

Spanish

anatomy: anatomía.
augmentation: aumento.
believing: creyendo.
betray: traicionar, traicionas, traiciono, traicionen, traiciona, traicionan, traicionamos, traicionad, traicionáis, traicione.
clog: obstruir, zueco, traba, empatar.
cruelty: crueldad, sevicia.
dogged: obstinado.
flea: pulga, la pulga.
forbear: antepasado.

grossness: grosería.
hale: sano.
heathen: pagano.
hurling: lanzar.
murderer: asesino.
obey: obedecer, obedecemos, obedezco, obedezcan, obedecen, obedecéis, obedeced, obedece, obedeces, obedezca.
oxen: buey.
pedant: pedante.
presage: agüero.

rightly: debidamente.
spleen: bazo.
stir: conmover, revolver, remover, agitar.
stitches: puntos de sutura, los puntos de sutura.
villainously: ruinmente, villanamente, malvadamente, malamente, vilmente.
visage: visaje, semblante, rostro, gesto.
wren: reyezuelo, chochín.
youngest: más joven.
yourselves: ustedes mismos.

SIR TOBY.
Come, bring us, bring us where he is.
[Exeunt.]

SCENE III. A STREET.

[Enter ANTONIO and SEBASTIAN.]
SEBASTIAN.
I would not by my will have **troubled** you;
But since you make your **pleasure** of your pains,
I will no further **chide** you.
ANTONIO.
I could not **stay** behind you: my desire,
More **sharp** than **filed steel**, did **spur** me **forth**;
And not all love to see you,--though so much,
As might have **drawn** one to a **longer** voyage,--
But **jealousy** what might **befall** your travel,
Being skilless in these **parts**; which to a stranger,
Unguided and **unfriended**, often prove
Rough and unhospitable. My **willing** love,
The rather by these **arguments** of fear,
Set forth in your **pursuit**.
SEBASTIAN.
                    My kind Antonio,
I can no other answer make but **thanks**,
And thanks, and ever thanks. Often good turns
Are **shuffled** off with such uncurrent pay;
But were my **worth**, as is my **conscience**, firm,

Spanish

arguments: argumentos.
befall: ocurrir, ocurrimos, ocurrís, ocurrid, ocurres, ocurren, ocurre, ocurran, ocurra, ocurro.
chide: regañar, reprender, reprended, reprende, reprendan, reprendemos, reprenden, reprendéis, regañas, regañen, regañan.
conscience: conciencia.
drawn: dibujado, encantado, trazado.
filed: archivado.
forth: adelante.

jealousy: celos.
longer: más, más tiempo.
parts: talento, regiones, piezas, partes.
pleasure: placer, agrado, gusto, complacencia, el gusto.
pursuit: persecución, acosamiento.
sharp: agudo, afilado, sostenido, justamente, acre, cortante, áspero.
shuffled: barajado.
spur: espolear, espuela, espolón, alimentación en derivación, línea en derivación, estimular.

stay: quedarse, quedar, queden, quede, quedas, quedan, quedamos, quedáis, quedad, queda, quedo.
steel: acero, ballena, el acero, acerar.
thanks: gracias, agradece.
troubled: molestar, de enfermedad, agitado, problema, desventurado, apurado, molestarse, dificultad, no sabroso, pasado difícilmente, pena.
unfriended: hostil.
willing: dispuesto, deseoso.
worth: valor.

You should find better **dealing**. What's to do?
Shall we go see the reliques of this **town**?

ANTONIO.
To-morrow, sir; best, first, go see your lodging.

SEBASTIAN.
I am not **weary**, and 'tis long to night;
I **pray** you, let us **satisfy** our eyes
With the memorials and the things of fame
That do **renown** this city.

ANTONIO.
                    Would you'd **pardon** me;
I do not without **danger** walk these streets:
Once in a sea-fight, 'gainst the **count**, his galleys,
I did some service; of such **note**, indeed,
That, were I ta'en here, it would **scarce** be **answered**.

SEBASTIAN.
Belike you **slew** great number of his people.

ANTONIO.
The **offence** is not of such a **bloody** nature;
Albeit the quality of the time and quarrel
Might well have given us bloody argument.
It might have since been answered in repaying
What we took from them; which, for traffic's sake,
Most of our city did: only myself **stood** out;
For which, if I be **lapsed** in this place,
I shall pay **dear**.

SEBASTIAN.
                    Do not then walk too open.

ANTONIO.
It doth not **fit** me. Hold, sir, here's my purse;

Spanish

answered: contesta, Contestado.
bloody: sangriento, sanguinario, cruento.
count: contar, recuento, cuenta, conde, calcular, entrar en cuenta, computar, unidad de cuenta, cargo.
danger: peligro, el peligro.
dealing: trato.
dear: caro, querido, estimado.
fit: adaptar, acomodar, ajustar, apoplejía, ajuste, caber, ataque, en forma, encajar.

lapsed: decrépito.
note: nota, apuntar, billete, anotar, apunte, anotación, notar.
offence: delito, escándalo, injuria.
pardon: perdón, perdonar, indulto, indultar.
pray: rezar, rezáis, rezas, rezamos, rezad, reza, recen, rece, rezan, rezo, rogar.
renown: hambre, renombre, conocimientos.
satisfy: complacer, complacen,

complazca, complazcan, complaces, complazco, complacéis, complace, complaced, complacemos, satisfacer.
scarce: escaso.
slew: cambio rápido de orientación, girar, giro sobre el eje, giro veloz, montón, pret de slay, torcer, torcerse a.
stood: pret y pp de stand.
town: ciudad, pueblo, población, el pueblo.
weary: cansado, fatigado.

In the south **suburbs**, at the Elephant,
Is best to **lodge**: I will **bespeak** our diet
Whiles you **beguile** the time and **feed** your knowledge
With **viewing** of the town; there shall you have me.

SEBASTIAN.
Why I your **purse**?

ANTONIO.
Haply your eye shall light upon some toy
You have desire to **purchase**; and your store,
I think, is not for **idle markets**, sir.

SEBASTIAN.
I'll be your purse-bearer, and leave you for
An hour.

ANTONIO.
　　　　To the Elephant.--

SEBASTIAN.
　　　　　　　　I do remember.

[Exeunt.]

SCENE IV. OLIVIA'S GARDEN.

[Enter OLIVIA and MARIA.]

OLIVIA.
I have sent after him. He says he'll come;
How shall I **feast** him? what **bestow** on him?
For **youth** is **bought** more **oft** than **begged** or borrowed.
I speak too loud.--
Where's Malvolio?--He is **sad** and civil,

Spanish

begged: Mendigado.
beguile: engañar, engañad, engaño, engañen, engañas, engañan, engañáis, engaña, engañamos, engañe.
bespeak: se encarga, ordenas, ordenáis, ordenamos, ordenad, ordenan, ordene, ordenen, ordena, os encargáis, apalabro.
bestow: conferir, otorgar.
bought: comprado.
feast: banquete, fiesta.

feed: alimentar, alimentad, alimenten, alimente, alimentas, alimentan, alimentáis, alimenta, alimentamos, alimento, dar de comer.
idle: ocioso, haraganear, perezoso, inactivo, en reposo.
lodge: alojar, hospedar, la casa del guarda.
markets: salidas.
oft: a menudo, mucho, con frecuencia, muchas veces.
purchase: compra, comprar,

adquisición, procurarse, la compra, adquirir.
purse: portamonedas, monedero, colecta, bolsa, bolso, la bolsa, cartera.
sad: triste, afligido.
suburbs: las afueras.
viewing: inspección, visita, ver la televisión, ver la tele, ver, programación, de los espectadores, censura, programas.
youth: juventud, joven, jóvenes, adolescencia.

Twelfth Night

And suits well for a **servant** with my fortunes;--
Where is Malvolio?

MARIA.
He's coming, **madam**: but in very **strange manner**. He is sure possessed.

OLIVIA.
Why, what's the matter? does he **rave**?

MARIA.
No, madam, he does nothing but **smile**: your **ladyship** were best to have
some **guard** about you if he come; For, sure, the man is **tainted** in his wits.

OLIVIA.
Go call him hither.--I'm as mad as he,
If **sad** and **merry madness equal** be.--
[Enter MALVOLIO.]
How now, Malvolio?

MALVOLIO.
Sweet lady, ho, ho.
[Smiles fantastically.]

OLIVIA.
Smil'st **thou**?
I sent for **thee** upon a sad **occasion**.

MALVOLIO.
Sad, lady? I could be sad: this does make some **obstruction** in the blood, this
cross-gartering. But what of that? If it please the eye of one, it is with me as
the very true **sonnet** is: 'Please one and please all.'

OLIVIA.
Why, how dost thou, man? what is the matter with thee?

MALVOLIO.
Not black in my mind, though **yellow** in my **legs**. It did come to his hands,
and commands shall be **executed**. I think we do know the **sweet** Roman
hand.

Spanish

equal: igual.
executed: ejecutado.
guard: guardia, guardar, vigilar,
  cobrador, guarda, revisor, defender,
  proteger, amparar.
ladyship: señora, señoría.
legs: las piernas.
mad: loco, enojado, chiflado, majara,
  majareta, demente, enfadado.
madness: locura, demencia,
  chifladura.
manner: manera.

merry: alegre.
obstruction: obstrucción, obstáculo.
occasion: motivo, ocasión, lugar,
  oportunidad.
rave: delirar, deliras, deliro, delire,
  deliran, deliramos, deliráis, delirad,
  delira, deliren.
sad: triste, afligido.
servant: criado, criada, sirviente,
  servidor.
smile: sonrisa, sonreír, la sonrisa,
  sonreírse.

sonnet: soneto.
strange: extraño, raro, ajeno.
sweet: dulce, caramelo, postre.
tainted: perdido, contaminado,
  corrompido, echado a perder,
  fraudulenta, infecto, manchado,
  pasado, viciado.
thee: ustedes, te, vosotros, usted, tú.
thou: tú, usted, vosotros, ustedes, vos.
yellow: amarillo.

OLIVIA.
Wilt **thou** go to bed, Malvolio?

MALVOLIO.
To bed? **ay, sweetheart**; and I'll come to **thee**.

OLIVIA.
God **comfort** thee! Why dost thou smile so, and **kiss thy** hand so **oft**?

MARIA.
How do you, Malvolio?

MALVOLIO.
At your **request**? Yes; **nightingales** answer daws.

MARIA.
Why appear you with this **ridiculous boldness** before my lady?

MALVOLIO.
'Be not **afraid** of **greatness**':--'twas well **writ**.

OLIVIA.
What **meanest** thou by that, Malvolio?

MALVOLIO.
'Some are born great,'--

OLIVIA.
Ha?

MALVOLIO.
'Some **achieve** greatness,'--

OLIVIA.
What say'st thou?

MALVOLIO.
'And some have greatness **thrust** upon them.'

OLIVIA.
Heaven **restore** thee!

Spanish

achieve: realizar, realizan, realizad, realice, realicen, realiza, realizamos, realizas, realizo, realizáis, conseguir.
afraid: miedoso, temeroso, asustado, medroso, miedo, encogido, angustioso, tímido, be - tener miedo.
ay: sí.
boldness: intrepidez.
comfort: comodidad, consolar, anchas, consuelo, confort.
greatness: grandeza.
kiss: besar, beso, besarse.

meanest: signifique.
nightingales: ruiseñores.
oft: a menudo, mucho, con frecuencia, muchas veces.
request: petición, pedir, solicitar, solicitud, demandar, solicitación, requerimiento, ruego, rogar, demanda.
restore: restaurar, restablecer, restaure, restaurad, restablezca, restableces, restablecen, restablecemos, restablecéis,

restableced, restablece.
ridiculous: ridículo.
sweetheart: novio, querido.
thee: ustedes, te, vosotros, usted, tú.
thou: tú, usted, vosotros, ustedes, vos.
thrust: empujar, empuje, empujón.
thy: tu.
writ: escritura, orden, escrito, orden por escrito.

MALVOLIO.
'Remember who **commended thy yellow stockings;**'--
OLIVIA.
Thy yellow stockings?
MALVOLIO.
'And **wished** to see **thee** cross-gartered.'
OLIVIA.
Cross-gartered?
MALVOLIO.
'Go to: **thou** an made, if thou desirest to be so:'--
OLIVIA.
Am I made?
MALVOLIO.
'If not, let me see thee a **servant** still.'
OLIVIA.
Why, this is very **midsummer** madness.
[Enter SERVANT.]
SERVANT.
Madam, the young **gentleman** of the Count Orsino's is **returned**; I could **hardly entreat** him back; he **attends** your ladyship's **pleasure.**
OLIVIA.
I'll come to him.
[Exit SERVANT.]
Good Maria, let this **fellow** be looked to. Where's my **cousin** Toby? Let some of my people have a special care of him; I would not have him **miscarry** for the half of my **dowry.**
[Exeunt OLIVIA and MARIA.]
MALVOLIO.
O, ho! do you come **near** me now? No **worse** man than Sir Toby to look to

Spanish

attends: asiste.
commended: alabado.
cousin: primo, prima, el primo.
dowry: dote.
entreat: demanden, rogáis, rueguen, ruegue, ruego, ruegas, ruegan, ruega, rogamos, demandad, demando.
fellow: compañero, hombre, socio, tipo, becario.
gentleman: caballero, señor, gentilhombre.
hardly: apenas.

midsummer: canícula.
miscarry: abortar, aborte, aborto, abortas, aborten, abortan, abortamos, abortáis, abortad, aborta.
near: cerca, próximo, cerca de, cercano, entrante, casi.
pleasure: placer, agrado, gusto, complacencia, el gusto.
returned: devuelto.
servant: criado, criada, sirviente, servidor.
stockings: las medias.

thee: ustedes, te, vosotros, usted, tú.
thou: tú, usted, vosotros, ustedes, vos.
thy: tu.
wished: deseado.
worse: peor.
yellow: amarillo.

me? This **concurs** directly with the letter: she **sends** him on purpose, that I may appear **stubborn** to him; for she **incites** me to that in the letter. 'Cast thy humble slough,' says she;--'be **opposite** with a kinsman, surly with servants,-- let thy tongue tang with arguments of state,--put thyself into the trick of singularity;--and **consequently**, sets down the manner how; as, a sad face, a **reverend carriage**, a **slow** tongue, in the **habit** of some sir of note, and so forth. I have **limed** her; but it is Jove's doing, and Jove make me **thankful!** And, when she went away now, 'Let this fellow be looked to;' Fellow! not Malvolio, nor after my degree, but fellow. Why, everything **adheres** together; that no **dram** of a scruple, no scruple of a scruple, no **obstacle**, no **incredulous** or **unsafe** circumstance,--What can be said? Nothing, that can be, can come between me and the full **prospect** of my hopes. Well, Jove, not I, is the **doer** of this, and he is to be thanked.

[Re-enter MARIA, with SIR TOBY BELCH and FABIAN.]

SIR TOBY.

Which way is he, in the name of **sanctity**? If all the **devils** of hell be drawn in little, and Legion himself **possessed** him, yet I'll speak to him.

FABIAN.

Here he is, here he is:--How is't with you, sir? how is't with you, man?

MALVOLIO.

Go off; I **discard** you; let me **enjoy** my private; go off.

MARIA.

Lo, how **hollow** the **fiend** speaks within him! did not I tell you?--Sir Toby, my lady **prays** you to have a care of him.

MALVOLIO.

Ah, ha! does she so?

SIR TOBY.

Go to, go to; peace, peace, we must deal **gently** with him; let me alone. How do you, Malvolio? how is't with you? What, man! defy the devil: consider, he's an enemy to **mankind**.

Spanish

adheres: adhiere.
carriage: coche, carro, cureña.
concurs: concurre.
consequently: por consiguiente.
devils: diablo.
discard: desecho, despedir, desechar, descartar.
doer: hacedor.
dram: aperitivo, dracma.
enjoy: disfrutar, disfrutas, disfrutan, disfrutamos, disfrutáis, disfrutad, disfruta, disfruto, disfruten, disfrute, gozar.
fiend: demonio.
gently: suavemente.
habit: costumbre, hábito, resabio, mala costumbre.
hollow: hueco, cavidad, hondonada, vacuo.
incites: incita.
incredulous: incrédulo.
limed: calcinado, Encalado.
mankind: humanidad.
obstacle: obstáculo, impedimento.
opposite: enfrente de, opuesto, contra, enfrente, contrario, frente a, frontero.
prays: reza, ruega, ora.
prospect: perspectiva.
reverend: reverendo, clérigo.
sanctity: santidad.
sends: envía, manda, despacha.
slow: lento.
stubborn: terco, testarudo, obstinado.
thankful: agradecido.
unsafe: inseguro, peligroso.

MALVOLIO.
Do you know what you say?

MARIA.
La you, an you **speak ill** of the **devil**, how he takes it at heart! **Pray** God he be not bewitched.

FABIAN.
Carry his water to the **wise** woman.

MARIA.
Marry, and it shall be done **to**-morrow morning, if I live. My **lady** would not **lose** him for more than I'll say.

MALVOLIO.
How now, **mistress**!

MARIA.
O lord!

SIR TOBY.
Pr'ythee hold **thy peace**; this is not the way. Do you not see you **move** him? let me **alone** with him.

FABIAN.
No way but **gentleness**; **gently**, gently: the **fiend** is **rough**, and will not be **roughly** used.

SIR TOBY.
Why, how now, my bawcock? how dost **thou**, **chuck**.

MALVOLIO.
Sir?

SIR TOBY.
Ay, Biddy, come with me. What, man! 'tis not for **gravity** to play at cherry-pit with Satan. **Hang** him, **foul collier**!

MARIA.
Get him to say his **prayers**; good Sir Toby, get him to pray.

Spanish

alone: solo, único, solamente, sólo.
chuck: caricia, acariciar, calzo, mandril.
collier: minero.
devil: diablo, el diablo.
fiend: demonio.
foul: falta, asqueroso, sucio.
gentleness: apacibilidad, suavidad.
gently: suavemente.
gravity: gravedad.
hang: colgar.
ill: enfermo, malo, doliente.

lady: dama, señora.
lose: perder, pierda, pierdo, perdéis, perdemos, pierdan, pierde, pierden, pierdes, perded, adelgazar.
mistress: señora.
move: mover, conmover, moverse, mudar, mudanza, movimiento, trasladar, traslado, mudarse, jugada.
peace: paz, la paz.
pray: rezar, rezáis, rezas, rezamos, rezad, reza, recen, rece, rezan, rezo, rogar.

prayers: ruegos, rezos, oraciones.
rough: áspero, crudo, desigual, bronco, brusco, grosero.
roughly: ásperamente, aproximadamente, bruscamente.
speak: hablar, hablamos, hablo, hablas, habláis, hablad, hablen, habla, hablan, hable.
thou: tú, usted, vosotros, ustedes, vos.
thy: tu.
to-morrow: mañana.
wise: sabio, sensato, guisa.

MALVOLIO.
My prayers, **minx**?

MARIA.
No, I warrant you, he will not hear of godliness.

MALVOLIO.
Go, hang yourselves all! you are idle **shallow** things: I am not of your element; you shall know more hereafter.
[Exit.]

SIR TOBY.
Is't possible?

FABIAN.
If this were **played** upon a **stage** now, I could **condemn** it as an **improbable fiction**.

SIR TOBY.
His very **genius** hath taken the **infection** of the device, man.

MARIA.
Nay, pursue him now; **lest** the device take air and **taint**.

FABIAN.
Why, we shall make him mad indeed.

MARIA.
The house will be the **quieter**.

SIR TOBY.
Come, **we'll** have him in a **dark** room and bound. My niece is already in the **belief** that he's mad; we may **carry** it thus, for our pleasure and his **penance**, till our very **pastime, tired** out of breath, **prompt** us to have **mercy** on him: at which time we will bring the device to the **bar**, and **crown** thee for a **finder** of **madmen**. But see, but see.

[Enter SIR ANDREW AGUE-CHEEK.]

Spanish

bar: barra, bar, salvo, cercar, taberna, obstrucción, impedir, impidan, cercad, cercáis, cercamos.
belief: creencia, credo, fe.
carry: llevar, llevamos, lleváis, llevad, lleva, lleven, llevo, llevan, llevas, lleve, cargar.
condemn: condenar, condenas, condenen, condenan, condenamos, condenáis, condenad, condeno, condene, condena, desaprobar.
crown: corona, coronar.

dark: oscuro, tenebroso.
fiction: ficción.
finder: descubridor.
genius: genio, ingenio.
improbable: inverosímil, improbable.
infection: infección.
lest: para que no, a no ser que, con el fin de, no sea que, si es necesario.
madmen: locos.
mercy: misericordia, compasión.
minx: bribona.
pastime: pasatiempo.

penance: penitencia.
played: jugado, tocado.
prompt: indicador, aviso.
quieter: más silencioso que.
shallow: poco profundo, somero, de poca profundidad, superficial.
stage: escenario, fase, etapa, escena, plataforma, estrado, organizar.
taint: deterioración, putrefacción, mancha.
tired: cansado.
we'll: Haremos.

FABIAN.
More matter for a May morning.

SIR ANDREW.
Here's the **challenge**, read it; I **warrant** there's **vinegar** and **pepper** in't.

FABIAN.
Is't so **saucy**?

SIR ANDREW.
Ay, is't, I warrant him; do but read.

SIR TOBY.
Give me. [Reads.] 'Youth, **whatsoever thou** art, thou art but a **scurvy** fellow.'

FABIAN.
Good and **valiant**.

SIR TOBY.
'Wonder not, nor **admire** not in **thy** mind, why I do call **thee** so, for I will show thee no reason for't.'

FABIAN.
A good note: that **keeps** you from the **blow** of the law.

SIR TOBY.
'Thou comest to the Lady Olivia, and in my sight she **uses** thee **kindly**: but thou liest in thy **throat**; that is not the matter I challenge thee for.'

FABIAN.
Very **brief**, and to **exceeding** good **senseless**.

SIR TOBY.
'I will **waylay** thee going home; where if it be thy chance to **kill** me,'--

FABIAN.
Good.

SIR TOBY.
'Thou kill'st me like a **rogue** and a villain.'

Spanish

admire: admirar, admiran, admiro, admiren, admiras, admiramos, admiráis, admirad, admira, admire.
blow: soplar, golpe.
brief: breve, corto, informe, conciso.
challenge: reto, desafiar, desafío, retar, recusación, impugnar.
exceeding: aventajando, excediendo, sobrepasando.
keeps: guarda, vigila, conserva, preserva.
kill: matar.

kindly: amablemente, bondadosamente, amable.
pepper: pimienta, la pimienta, pimiento.
rogue: pícaro.
saucy: descarado.
scurvy: escorbuto.
senseless: insensato.
thee: ustedes, te, vosotros, usted, tú.
thou: tú, usted, vosotros, ustedes, vos.
throat: garganta, la garganta.
thy: tu.

uses: usa, utiliza.
valiant: bravo, valiente.
vinegar: vinagre, el vinagre.
warrant: garantía, orden, orden por escrito, certificado, autorizar, autorización.
waylay: acechar, aceche, acechan, acecho, acechen, acechas, acecháis, acechamos, acecha, acechad.
whatsoever: lo que, en absoluto, todo lo que, cualquier cosa, cualquier.

FABIAN.
Still you keep o' the **windy** side of the law. Good.
SIR TOBY.
'Fare thee well; and God have mercy upon one of our souls! He may have mercy upon mine; but my hope is better, and so look to thyself. Thy friend, as thou usest him, and thy sworn enemy, Andrew Ague-Cheek.' If this letter move him not, his legs cannot: I'll give't him.
MARIA.
You may have very fit occasion for't; he is now in some **commerce** with my lady, and will by and by **depart**.
SIR TOBY.
Go, Sir Andrew; **scout** me for him at the **corner** of the orchard, like a bum-bailiff; so soon as ever thou seest him, draw; and as thou drawest, swear **horrible**; for it comes to pass oft that a **terrible oath**, with a **swaggering accent sharply twanged** off, gives **manhood** more **approbation** than ever proof itself would have **earned** him. Away.
SIR ANDREW.
Nay, let me alone for swearing.
[Exit.]
SIR TOBY.
Now will not I deliver his letter; for the behaviour of the young gentleman gives him out to be of good capacity and **breeding**; his employment between his lord and my niece **confirms** no less; therefore this letter, being so excellently **ignorant**, will breed no **terror** in the youth: he will find it comes from a clodpole. But, sir, I will deliver his challenge by word of mouth, set upon Ague-cheek notable report of valour, and drive the gentleman,--as I know his youth will **aptly** receive it,--into a most hideous opinion of his **rage, skill, fury**, and **impetuosity**. This will so **fright** them both that they will kill one another by the look, like cockatrices.
[Enter OLIVIA and VIOLA.]

Spanish

accent: acento, acentuar, acentúan, acentúas, acentúo, acentúen, acentuáis, acentuad, acentúa, acentúe, acentuamos.
approbation: aprobación.
aptly: propensamente, acertadamente, capazmente, hábilmente, habilidoso, oportunamente.
breed: raza, casta, criar.
breeding: cría, crianza, reproducción.
commerce: comercio.
confirms: confirma.

corner: esquina, ángulo, rincón.
depart: salir, salís, salgo, salga, sales, salen, saled, sale, salgan, salimos, sal.
earned: ganado.
fright: espanto, susto, miedo, angustia, terror.
fury: furia, furor.
horrible: temeroso, abominable, lúgubre, horroroso, horrible.
ignorant: ignorante.
impetuosity: irreflexión, impetuosidad.

manhood: hombría.
oath: juramento.
rage: rabia, furia, furor, ira.
scout: explorador, explorar.
sharply: bruscamente.
skill: destreza, habilidad, arte, agilidad.
swaggering: pavoneándose, fanfarrón.
terrible: terrible.
terror: terror.
twanged: Vibrado.
windy: ventoso.

FABIAN.
Here he comes with your **niece**; give them way till he take leave, and **presently** after him.

SIR TOBY.
I will **meditate** the while upon some **horrid message** for a challenge.

[Exeunt SIR TOBY, FABIAN, and MARIA.]

OLIVIA.
I have said too much **unto** a heart of stone,
And laid mine honour too unchary on it:
There's something in me that **reproves** my **fault**;
But such a **headstrong potent** fault it is
That it but **mocks reproof**.

VIOLA.
With the same 'haviour that your **passion** bears
Goes on my master's griefs.

OLIVIA.
Here, wear this **jewel** for me; 'tis my picture;
Refuse it not; it hath no tongue to **vex** you:
And, I **beseech** you, come again **to**-morrow.
What shall you ask of me that I'll deny,
That, honour saved, may upon **asking** give?

VIOLA.
Nothing but this, your true love for my master.

OLIVIA.
How with mine honour may I give him that
Which I have given to you?

VIOLA.
                                I will **acquit** you.

OLIVIA.
Well, come again to-morrow. **Fare thee** well;

Spanish

acquit: absolver, absuelvan, absuelve, absuelvo, absuelves, absolvemos, absuelven, absolvéis, absolved, absuelva, pagar.
asking: preguntando, pidiendo, solicitando.
beseech: supliquen, rogáis, rogamos, ruega, ruegan, ruegas, ruegue, rueguen, suplica, suplicamos, rogad.
fare: tarifa, pasaje.
fault: culpa, defecto, avería, falla, falta, fallo, error, imperfección.

headstrong: terco, cabezudo, caprichoso, impetuoso, obstinado, testarudo, testarudo tozudo, voluntarioso, ingobernable.
horrid: hórrido.
jewel: joya, la joya.
meditate: meditar, medite, meditamos, medito, mediten, meditan, meditáis, meditad, medita, meditas.
message: mensaje, recado, noticias, publicación, noticia, el mensaje.

mocks: ridiculiza, trisca, befa, desbarata, escarnece, mofa, remeda.
niece: sobrina, la sobrina.
passion: pasión.
potent: potente, poderoso.
presently: por ahora.
reproof: reparo, censura, reprobación.
reproves: reprueba.
thee: ustedes, te, vosotros, usted, tú.
to-morrow: mañana.
unto: hacia.
vex: vejar.

A fiend like thee might bear my soul to hell.
[Exit.]
[Re-enter SIR TOBY BELCH and SIR FABIAN.]
SIR TOBY.
Gentleman, God save thee.
VIOLA.
And you, sir.
SIR TOBY.
That defence thou hast, **betake** thee to't. Of what nature the wrongs are thou hast done him, I know not; but thy intercepter, full of despite, bloody as the hunter, attends thee at the orchard end: **dismount** thy **tuck**, be yare in thy preparation, for thy **assailant** is quick, **skilful**, and deadly.
VIOLA.
You mistake, sir; I am sure no man hath any quarrel to me; my remembrance is very free and clear from any image of offence done to any man.
SIR TOBY.
You'll find it otherwise, I assure you: therefore, if you hold your life at any price, betake you to your guard; for your opposite hath in him what youth, strength, skill, and **wrath**, can **furnish** man **withal**.
VIOLA.
I pray you, sir, what is he?
SIR TOBY.
He is knight, **dubbed** with unhacked **rapier** and on carpet consideration; but he is a devil in private **brawl**; souls and bodies hath he divorced three; and his incensement at this moment is so **implacable** that satisfaction can be none but by pangs of death and **sepulchre**: hob, nob is his word; give't or take't.
VIOLA.
I will return again into the house and desire some conduct of the lady. I am no fighter. I have heard of some kind of men that put quarrels **purposely** on others to taste their valour: belike this is a man of that **quirk**.

Spanish

assailant: agresor, atacador, atacante.
betake: recurres, vayan, vaya, vamos, van, voy, vais, va, recurro, recurrís, recurrimos.
brawl: reyerta, pelearse, alboroto.
dismount: apearse, desmontar, desmontad, desmonta, desmonto, desmonten, desmonte, desmontáis, desmontamos, desmontan, desmontas.
dubbed: se apodado, reproducido, dobló, doblado.

furnish: amueblar, amueblas, amueblen, amueblo, amueble, amueblamos, amuebláis, amuebla, amueblan, amueblad, suministrar.
hob: hornillo, fresa-madre, fresamatriz, hornilla, quemador, punzón de acuñación, placa, cubierta.
implacable: cosa implacable.
nob: personaje, pez gordo, majo, golpear a la cabeza, currutaco, cholla, cabeza.
purposely: intencionalmente,

deliberadamente, a propósito.
quirk: ocurrencia, rareza, mediacaña, chifladura, rasgo, moldurera, juntera, cimacio, capricho, escapatoria, peculiaridad.
rapier: estoque.
sepulchre: mausoleo, sepulcro, sepultura, tumba.
skilful: hábil, experto.
tuck: alforza.
withal: además.
wrath: ira.

SIR TOBY.
Sir, no; his **indignation** **derives** itself out of a very **competent** **injury**; therefore, get you on and give him his desire. Back you shall not to the house, unless you undertake that with me which with as much **safety** you might answer him: therefore on, or **strip** your **sword** **stark** **naked**; for **meddle** you must, that's certain, or **forswear** to wear **iron** about you.

VIOLA.
This is as **uncivil** as strange. I **beseech** you, do me this **courteous** office as to know of the **knight** what my offence to him is; it is something of my **negligence**, nothing of my purpose.

SIR TOBY.
I Will do so. Signior Fabian, stay you by this gentleman till my return. [Exit SIR TOBY.]

VIOLA.
Pray you, sir, do you know of this matter?

FABIAN.
I know the knight is **incensed** against you, even to a **mortal** arbitrement; but nothing of the **circumstance** more.

VIOLA.
I beseech you, what manner of man is he?

FABIAN.
Nothing of that **wonderful** promise, to read him by his form, as you are like to find him in the proof of his **valour**. He is indeed, sir, the most **skilful**, bloody, and **fatal** opposite that you could **possibly** have found in any part of Illyria. Will you walk towards him? I will make your peace with him if I can.

VIOLA.
I shall be much bound to you for't. I am one that would rather go with sir **priest** than sir knight: I care not who knows so much of my **mettle**.

[Exeunt.]
[Re-enter SIR TOBY With SIR ANDREW.]

Spanish

beseech: supliquen, rogáis, rogamos, ruega, ruegan, ruegas, ruegue, rueguen, suplica, suplicamos, rogad.
circumstance: condición, circunstancia.
competent: competente.
courteous: cortés.
derives: deriva.
fatal: mortal.
forswear: abjurar, abjuráis, abjuro, abjuren, abjure, abjuras, abjuramos, abjurad, abjura, abjuran.

incensed: encolerizado, indignado, inciensado.
indignation: indignación.
injury: lesión, herida, daño.
iron: hierro, planchar, plancha, de hierro, el hierro, fierro.
knight: caballero, caballo.
meddle: entrometerse.
mettle: temple.
mortal: mortal.
naked: desnudo.
negligence: negligencia, descuido.

possibly: posiblemente, quizás, tal vez.
priest: sacerdote, cura, preste.
safety: seguridad.
skilful: hábil, experto.
stark: severo.
strip: tira, raya, faja, desnudarse, franja, desmontar, banda.
sword: espada.
uncivil: descortés, incivil.
valour: valor.
wonderful: maravilloso.

SIR TOBY.
Why, man, he's a very devil; I have not seen such a **virago**. I had a pass with him, **rapier**, **scabbard**, and all, and he gives me the stuck-in with such a mortal motion that it is **inevitable**; and on the answer, he **pays** you as **surely** as your **feet** hit the **ground** they **step** on. They say he has been **fencer** to the Sophy.

SIR ANDREW.
Pox on't, I'll not **meddle** with him.

SIR TOBY.
Ay, but he will not now be **pacified**: Fabian can scarce hold him **yonder**.

SIR ANDREW.
Plague on't; an I thought he had been **valiant**, and so cunning in fence, I'd have seen him **damned ere** I'd have **challenged** him. Let him let the matter **slip** and I'll give him my horse, grey Capilet.

SIR TOBY.
I'll make the motion. Stand here, make a good show on't; this shall end without the **perdition** of souls. [Aside.] Marry, I'll ride your horse as well as I ride you.
[Re-enter FABIAN and VIOLA.]
I have his horse [To FABIAN.] to take up the **quarrel**; I have persuaded him the youth's a devil.

FABIAN.
He is as **horribly conceited** of him; and **pants** and looks **pale**, as if a bear were at his heels.

SIR TOBY.
There's no remedy, sir: he will **fight** with you for's oath **sake**: marry, he hath better **bethought** him of his quarrel, and he finds that now scarce to be worth **talking** of: therefore, draw for the supportance of his **vow**; he protests he will not hurt you.

Spanish

bethought: pret y pp de bethink.
challenged: Desafiado, recibe.
conceited: presumido, hueco.
damned: condenado, maldito.
ere: antes de.
feet: los pies, pies.
fence: reja, valla, cerca, vallado, obstrucción, la cerca, cercado.
fencer: esgrimidor, floretista.
fight: luchar, pelear, lucha, combate, pelea, batallar, riña, combatir.
ground: suelo, terreno, tierra, molido,

masa, conexión a tierra, el suelo, fondo, fundamento.
horribly: horriblemente.
inevitable: inevitable.
meddle: entrometerse.
pacified: apaciguado, pacificado.
pale: pálido, palidecer, descolorido.
pants: pantalón, pantalones.
pays: paga.
perdition: perdición.
quarrel: disputar, reñir, riña, pelear.
rapier: estoque.

sake: motivo, fin, bien, causa.
scabbard: vaina.
slip: deslizamiento, resbalar, desliz, deslizar, combinación.
step: paso, escalón, peldaño.
surely: seguramente, ciertamente.
talking: hablando, parlante, charlando, hablar.
valiant: bravo, valiente.
virago: arpía.
vow: voto.
yonder: allí, ahí, aquel.

VIOLA.
[Aside]
Pray God **defend** me! A little thing would make me tell them how much I **lack** of a man.

FABIAN.
Give ground if you see him **furious**.

SIR TOBY.
Come, Sir Andrew, there's no **remedy**; the gentleman will, for his honour's **sake**, have one **bout** with you: he **cannot** by the duello **avoid** it; but he has **promised** me, as he is a gentleman and a **soldier**, he will not **hurt** you. Come on: to't.

SIR ANDREW.
Pray God he keep his oath!
[Draws.]
[Enter ANTONIO.]

VIOLA.
I do **assure** you 'tis against my will.
[Draws.]

ANTONIO.
Put up your sword:--if this young gentleman
Have done **offence**, I take the **fault** on me;
If you **offend** him, I for him **defy** you.
[Drawing.]

SIR TOBY.
You, sir! why, what are you?

ANTONIO.
One, sir, that for his love **dares** yet do more
Than you have heard him **brag** to you he will.

Spanish

assure: asegurar, asegura, aseguren, aseguras, aseguran, aseguramos, aseguráis, asegurad, aseguro, asegure, garantizar.
avoid: evitar, evito, evitan, evitamos, evitáis, evitad, eviten, evita, evitas, evite, eludir.
bout: rato, ataque, combate.
brag: jactarse, fanfarronear.
cannot: presente de no poder.
dares: aventura, desafía, osa, se arriesga, se atreve.

defend: defender, defiendes, defiendo, defendéis, defendemos, defiendan, defienden, defended, defiende, defienda.
defy: desafiar, desafiáis, desafío, desafíen, desafías, desafiamos, desafiad, desafía, desafían, desafíe.
fault: culpa, defecto, avería, falla, falta, fallo, error, imperfección.
furious: torcido, furioso, furibundo.
hurt: doler, herir, dañar, herida, lastimar.

lack: falta, carencia, escasez, faltar, carecer de, carecer.
offence: delito, escándalo, injuria.
offend: ofender, ofendo, ofendan, ofende, ofended, ofendéis, ofendemos, ofenden, ofendes, ofenda, injuriar.
promised: prometido.
remedy: curar, remedio, recurso, medio, remediar.
sake: motivo, fin, bien, causa.
soldier: soldado, el soldado.

SIR TOBY.
Nay, if you be an **undertaker**, I am for you.
[Draws.]
[Enter two OFFICERS.]

FABIAN.
O good Sir Toby, **hold**; here come the officers.

SIR TOBY.
[To ANTONIO]
I'll be with you **anon**.

VIOLA.
[To SIR ANDREW.]
Pray, **sir**, put your **sword** up, if you **please**.

SIR ANDREW.
Marry, will I, sir; and for that I **promised** you, I'll be as good as my word. He will **bear** you **easily** and **reins** well.

FIRST OFFICER.
This is the man; do **thy** office.

SECOND OFFICER.
Antonio, I **arrest thee** at the **suit** of Count Orsino.

ANTONIO.
You do **mistake** me, sir.

FIRST OFFICER.
No, sir, no **jot**; I know your **favour** well,
Though now you have no sea-cap on your head.--
Take him away; he **knows** I know him well.

ANTONIO.
I Must obey.--This **comes** with **seeking** you;
But there's no **remedy**; I shall **answer** it.
What will you do? Now my **necessity**

Spanish

anon: pronto.
answer: respuesta, responder, contestar, contestación, responder a, corresponder al, contestar a, la respuesta, réplica.
arrest: detención, detener, arrestar, arresto, prender.
bear: oso, llevar, el oso, bajista, producir, dar a luz, parir, portar, soportar.
comes: Viene.
easily: fácilmente.

favour: favor, favorecer.
hold: tener, sujetar, continuar, retención, sostener, contener, mantener, retenido, presa, bodega.
jot: pizca.
knows: sabe, conoce.
mistake: error, equivocación, yerro, la falta.
necessity: necesidad.
please: por favor, agradar, gustar, complacer, haz el favor, contentar, haz favor.

promised: prometido.
reins: riñones, rienda, riendas.
remedy: curar, remedio, recurso, medio, remediar.
seeking: buscando.
sir: señor.
suit: traje, convenir, el traje, pleito.
sword: espada.
thee: ustedes, te, vosotros, usted, tú.
thy: tu.
undertaker: enterrador.

Makes me to ask you for my **purse**. It **grieves** me
Much more for what I **cannot** do for you
Than what **befalls** myself. You stand amazed;
But be of comfort.

SECOND OFFICER.
Come, sir, away.

ANTONIO.
I must **entreat** of you some of that money.

VIOLA.
What money, sir?
For the fair **kindness** you have **showed** me here,
And part being **prompted** by your present trouble,
Out of my **lean** and low ability
I'll **lend** you something; my having is not much;
I'll make **division** of my present with you:
Hold, there is half my **coffer**.

ANTONIO.
Will you **deny** me now?
Is't possible that my deserts to you
Can lack **persuasion**? Do not **tempt** my misery,
Lest that it make me so **unsound** a man
As to **upbraid** you with those kindnesses
That I have done for you.

VIOLA.
I know of none,
Nor know I you by voice or any feature:
I **hate ingratitude** more in a man
Than **lying**, **vainness**, **babbling**, drunkenness,
Or any **taint** of **vice** whose strong corruption
Inhabits our **frail** blood.

Spanish

babbling: balbuceando, balbuceo.
befalls: ocurre.
cannot: presente de no poder.
coffer: panel empotrado.
deny: negar, negad, niego, niegas, niegan, negáis, negamos, nieguen, niega, niegue, desmentir.
division: división, escisión.
entreat: demanden, rogáis, rueguen, ruegue, ruego, ruegas, ruegan, ruega, rogamos, demandad, demando.
frail: frágil.

grieves: aflige, apena.
hate: odiar, odio, aborrecer, detestar.
ingratitude: ingratitud.
kindness: amabilidad, la bondad.
lean: apoyarse, fino, magro, enjuto, apoyar, delgado.
lend: prestar, presto, preste, presten, prestas, prestan, prestamos, prestáis, prestad, presta.
lying: mentiroso.
persuasion: persuasión.
prompted: interactiva, incitado.

purse: portamonedas, monedero, colecta, bolsa, bolso, la bolsa, cartera.
showed: mostrado, pret de show.
taint: deterioración, putrefacción, mancha.
tempt: tentar, tentad, tiento, tienten, tientas, tientan, tentamos, tentáis, tienta, tiente.
unsound: enfermo.
upbraid: regañar.
vainness: vanidad.
vice: vicio, virtud, tornillo de banco.

ANTONIO.
O **heavens** themselves!
SECOND OFFICER.
Come, sir, I **pray** you go.
ANTONIO.
Let me speak a little. This **youth** that you see here
I **snatched** one half out of the **jaws** of death,
Relieved him with such **sanctity** of love,--
And to his image, which methought did promise
Most **venerable** worth, did I **devotion**.
FIRST OFFICER.
What's that to us? The time **goes** by; away.
ANTONIO.
But O how **vile** an **idol proves** this god!
Thou **hast**, Sebastian, done good **feature** shame.
In nature there's no **blemish** but the mind;
None can be call'd deform'd but the unkind:
Virtue is **beauty**; but the beauteous-evil
Are **empty trunks**, o'erflourished by the **devil**.
FIRST OFFICER.
The man **grows mad**; away with him. Come, come, sir.
ANTONIO.
Lead me on.
[Exeunt Officers with ANTONIO.]
VIOLA.
Methinks his words do from such **passion** fly
That he **believes** himself; so do not I.
Prove true, **imagination**; O prove true,
That I, **dear** brother, be now ta'en for you!

Spanish

beauty: belleza, la belleza.
believes: cree.
blemish: defecto, mancha.
dear: caro, querido, estimado.
devil: diablo, el diablo.
devotion: devoción.
empty: vacío, vaciar, evacuar, desocupado, desocupar.
feature: característica, facción, función, rasgo.
goes: va, marcha.
grows: crece, aumenta.

hast: haya.
heavens: cielo, cielos.
idol: ídolo.
imagination: imaginación.
jaws: mordazas.
mad: loco, enojado, chiflado, majara, majareta, demente, enfadado.
passion: pasión.
pray: rezar, rezáis, rezas, rezamos, rezad, reza, recen, rece, rezan, rezo, rogar.
prove: probar, probad, prueban,

pruebas, pruebo, probamos, probáis, prueben, prueba, pruebe, verificar.
proves: prueba, verifica.
sanctity: santidad.
snatched: arrebatado.
trunks: traje de baño, bañador, mampara encerradora de la escotilla, pantaloneta, pantalón de baño.
venerable: venerado.
vile: vil.
youth: juventud, joven, jóvenes, adolescencia.

SIR TOBY.
Come **hither**, knight; come hither, Fabian; **we'll whisper o'er** a **couplet** or two of most **sage** saws.

VIOLA.
He **named** Sebastian; I my brother know
Yet **living** in my **glass**; even such and so
In favour was my brother; and he went
Still in this fashion, colour, ornament,
For him I **imitate**. O, if it prove,
Tempests are kind, and salt **waves** fresh in love!
[Exit.]

SIR TOBY.
A very **dishonest paltry** boy, and more a **coward** than a **hare**: his **dishonesty appears** in **leaving** his friend here in necessity, and **denying** him; and for his cowardship, ask Fabian.

FABIAN.
A coward, a most **devout** coward, **religious** in it.

SIR ANDREW.
'Slid, I'll after him again and beat him.

SIR TOBY.
Do, **cuff** him **soundly**, but never draw **thy** sword.

SIR ANDREW.
And I do not,--
[Exit.]

FABIAN.
Come, let's see the event.

SIR TOBY.
I dare **lay** any money 'twill be nothing yet.
[Exeunt.]

Spanish

appears: aparece, comparece.
couplet: pareado.
coward: cobarde, el cobarde.
cuff: puño, puño de la camisa.
denying: negando, desmintiendo.
devout: devoto.
dishonest: improbo, deshonesto.
dishonesty: deshonestidad.
glass: vidrio, vaso, cristal, copa, el vidrio.
hare: liebre.
hither: acá.

imitate: imitar, imite, imito, imitamos, imitas, imitáis, imitan, imitad, imita, imiten.
lay: poner, colocar, coloque, colocamos, pongan, ponga, pones, ponen, ponemos, ponéis, poned.
leaving: saliendo, dejando.
living: viviendo, habitando, vivo, viviente.
named: denominado.
o'er: sobre.
paltry: vil, mezquino, ínfimo,

despreciable, ruin, miserable.
religious: religioso.
sage: salvia, sabio.
soundly: sanamente, solventemente, sólidamente, razonablemente, profundamente, firmemente, vigorosamente.
thy: tu.
waves: olas.
we'll: Haremos.
whisper: cuchichear, cuchicheo, susurrar, susurro, murmurar.

ACT IV

SCENE I. THE STREET BEFORE OLIVIA'S HOUSE.

[Enter SEBASTIAN and CLOWN.]

CLOWN.
Will you make me believe that I am not **sent** for you?

SEBASTIAN.
Go to, go to, **thou art** a **foolish** fellow;
Let me be clear of **thee**.

CLOWN.
Well **held** out, i' **faith**! No, I do not know you; **nor** I am not sent to you by my **lady**, to **bid** you come **speak** with her; nor your name is not Master Cesario; nor this is not my **nose** neither.-- Nothing that is so is so.

SEBASTIAN.
I pr'ythee **vent thy folly somewhere** else. Thou know'st not me.

CLOWN.
Vent my folly! he has **heard** that **word** of some great man, and now **applies** it to a fool. Vent my folly! I am **afraid** this great **lubber**, the world, will **prove** a

Spanish

afraid: miedoso, temeroso, asustado, medroso, miedo, encogido, angustioso, tímido, be - tener miedo.
applies: emplea, aplica.
art: arte, el arte.
bid: ofrecer, licitación, postura, oferta, solicitar, licitar, pedir, demandar, rogar, puja.
faith: fe, la fe.
folly: tontería.
fool: engañar, necio, tonto.
foolish: zote, tonto, necio, bobo.

heard: oído.
held: tuvo lugar, sostuvo.
lady: dama, señora.
lubber: palurdo.
nor: ni, tampoco.
nose: nariz, la nariz, proa.
prove: probar, probad, prueban, pruebas, pruebo, probamos, probáis, prueben, prueba, pruebe, verificar.
sent: enviado, mandado, despachado.
somewhere: en alguna parte.
speak: hablar, hablamos, hablo,

hablas, habláis, hablad, hablen, habla, hablan, hable.
thee: ustedes, te, vosotros, usted, tú.
thou: tú, usted, vosotros, ustedes, vos.
thy: tu.
vent: abertura, respiradero, desahogar.
word: palabra, la palabra, vocablo, término, formular.

cockney.--I **pr'ythee** now, **ungird thy strangeness,** and tell me what I shall **vent** to my **lady.** Shall I vent to her that **thou art coming?**

SEBASTIAN.
I pr'ythee, **foolish** Greek, **depart** from me;
There's money for thee; if you **tarry** longer
I shall give **worse** payment.

CLOWN.
By my **troth,** thou **hast** an open hand:--These **wise** men that give fools money get themselves a good report after **fourteen** years' **purchase.**

[Enter SIR ANDREW, SIR TOBY, and FABIAN.]

SIR ANDREW.
Now, sir, have I **met** you again? there's for you.
[Striking SEBASTIAN.]

SEBASTIAN.
Why, there's for thee, and there, and there.
Are all the people mad?
[Beating SIR ANDREW.]

SIR TOBY.
Hold, sir, or I'll **throw** your **dagger o'er** the house.

CLOWN.
This will I tell my lady **straight.** I would not be in some of your **coats** for twopence.
[Exit.]

SIR TOBY.
Come on, sir; hold.
[Holding SEBASTIAN.]

SIR ANDREW.
Nay, let him **alone;** I'll go another way to work with him; I'll have an action of **battery** against him, if there be any law in Illyria: though I **struck** him first, yet it's no matter for that.

Spanish

alone: solo, único, solamente, sólo.
art: arte, el arte.
battery: batería, pila, acumulador.
coats: membranas.
coming: viniendo, proveniente, próximo, originario, natural.
dagger: daga, puñal.
depart: salir, salis, salgo, salga, sales, salen, saled, sale, salgan, salimos, sal.
foolish: zote, tonto, necio, bobo.
fourteen: catorce.
hast: haya.

lady: dama, señora.
met: encontrado, hallado.
o'er: sobre.
purchase: compra, comprar, adquisición, procurarse, la compra, adquirir.
straight: derecho, recto, directamente, recta.
strangeness: extrañeza.
struck: pret y pp de strike, golpeado.
tarry: quedarse atrás, alquitranado.
thee: ustedes, te, vosotros, usted, tú.

thou: tú, usted, vosotros, ustedes, vos.
throw: lanzar, echar, tirar, tirada, arrojar, lanzamiento.
thy: tu.
troth: fidelidad, fe.
ungird: Desciña, desceñir, desceño, desceñís, desceñimos, desceñid, desceñes, desceñen, desceñe, desceña, desceñan.
vent: abertura, respiradero, desahogar.
wise: sabio, sensato, guisa.
worse: peor.

SEBASTIAN.
Let go **thy** hand.
SIR TOBY.
Come, sir, I will not let you go. Come, my young **soldier**, put up your **iron**: you are well fleshed; come on.
SEBASTIAN.
I will be free from **thee**. What wouldst **thou** now? If thou dar'st **tempt** me further, **draw** thy sword.
[Draws.]
SIR TOBY.
What, what? **Nay**, then I must have an **ounce** or two of this malapert blood from you.
[Draws.]
[Enter OLIVIA.]
OLIVIA.
Hold, Toby; on thy life, I **charge** thee hold.
SIR TOBY.
Madam?
OLIVIA.
Will it be ever thus? **Ungracious** wretch,
Fit for the **mountains** and the **barbarous** caves,
Where **manners ne'er** were preach'd! Out of my sight!
Be not **offended**, dear Cesario!--
Rudesby, be gone!--I pr'ythee, **gentle** friend,
[Exeunt SIR TOBY, SIR ANDREW, and FABIAN.]
Let thy **fair wisdom**, not thy **passion**, sway
In this **uncivil** and **unjust** extent
Against thy peace. Go with me to my house,
And hear thou there how many **fruitless** pranks
This **ruffian** hath botch'd up, that thou **thereby**

Spanish

barbarous: bárbaro.
charge: carga, cargo, acusación, gastos, cargar, cobro, cobrar, imputación.
draw: dibujar, dibujáis, dibujad, dibujen, dibuje, dibujas, dibujamos, dibuja, dibujan, dibujo, tirar.
fair: justo, rubio, mercado, feria, verbena, bazar, equitativo, hermoso.
fruitless: infructuoso.
gentle: dulce, suave, manso, apacible.
iron: hierro, planchar, plancha, de hierro, el hierro, fierro.

manners: modales, educación.
mountains: sierra, monta a.
nay: más aún, más bien, voto negativo, voto en contra, no, negativa, mejor dicho.
ne'er: nunca.
offended: ofendido, injuriado, ultrajado, insultado, delinquido.
ounce: onza.
passion: pasión.
ruffian: rufián.
soldier: soldado, el soldado.

tempt: tentar, tentad, tiento, tienten, tientas, tientan, tentamos, tentáis, tienta, tiente.
thee: ustedes, te, vosotros, usted, tú.
thereby: en consecuencia de esto, por lo tanto.
thou: tú, usted, vosotros, ustedes, vos.
thy: tu.
uncivil: descortés, incivil.
ungracious: descortés, poco gracioso.
unjust: injusto.
wisdom: sabiduría, sapiencia.

Mayst smile at this: **thou shalt** not **choose** but go;
Do not **deny**. Beshrew his **soul** for me,
He **started** one poor heart of mine in thee.

SEBASTIAN.
What **relish** is in this? how **runs** the stream?
Or I am mad/ or else this is a dream:--
Let **fancy** still my sense in Lethe steep;
If it be thus to dream, still let me **sleep**!

OLIVIA.
Nay, come, I pr'ythee. Would thou'dst be **ruled** by me!

SEBASTIAN.
Madam, I will.

OLIVIA.
O, say so, and so be!

[Exeunt.]

SCENE II. A ROOM IN OLIVIA'S HOUSE.

[Enter MARIA and CLOWN.]

MARIA.
Nay, I pr'ythee, put on this **gown** and this **beard**; make him believe thou art
Sir Topas the **curate**; do it quickly: I'll call Sir Toby the **whilst**.

[Exit MARIA.]

CLOWN.
Well, I'll put it on, and I will **dissemble** myself in't; and I would I were the
first that ever **dissembled** in such a gown. I am not tall enough to become the
function well: nor **lean** enough to be thought a good **student**: but to be said,

Spanish

beard: barba, la barba, arista.
choose: escoger, escojan, escoges, escogen, escogemos, escogéis, escoged, escojo, escoge, escoja, elegir.
curate: coadjutor, cura.
deny: negar, negad, niego, niegas, niegan, negáis, negamos, nieguen, niega, niegue, desmentir.
dissemble: disimular, disimula, disimulo, disimulen, disimulas, disimulan, disimulamos, disimuláis, disimulad, disimule, ocultar.

dissembled: disimulado.
fancy: figurarse, de fantasía, imaginación.
function: función, funcionar, cargo, oficio.
gown: vestido, toga.
lean: apoyarse, fino, magro, enjuto, apoyar, delgado.
relish: paladear, condimento, saborear.
ruled: reglado.
runs: corre.

shalt: irá, verbo auxiliar inglés para especificar futuro.
sleep: dormir, duerme, duermes, dormimos, duermen, duermo, dormís, dormid, duerma, duerman, sueño.
soul: alma, espíritu, ánimo.
started: comenzado, encaminado.
student: estudiante, alumno, el estudiante.
thou: tú, usted, vosotros, ustedes, vos.
whilst: mientras.

an **honest** man and a good **housekeeper,** goes as **fairly** as to say, a **careful** man and a great **scholar.** The **competitors** enter.

[Enter SIR TOBY BELCH and MARIA.]

SIR TOBY.

Jove **bless thee,** Master Parson.

CLOWN.

Bonos dies, Sir Toby: for as the old **hermit** of Prague, that never saw **pen** and **ink,** very **wittily** said to a **niece** of King Gorboduc, 'That that is, is'; so I, being **master parson,** am master parson: for what is that but that? and is but is?

SIR TOBY.

To him, Sir Topas.

CLOWN.

What, hoa, I say,--Peace in this **prison!**

SIR TOBY.

The **knave** counterfeits well; a good knave.

MALVOLIO.

[In an **inner** chamber.]

Who **calls** there?

CLOWN.

Sir Topas the **curate,** who comes to visit Malvolio the **lunatic.**

MALVOLIO.

Sir Topas, Sir Topas, good Sir Topas, go to my lady.

CLOWN.

Out, **hyperbolical fiend!** how vexest **thou** this man? talkest thou nothing but of **ladies?**

SIR TOBY.

Well said, master parson.

Spanish

bless: bendecir, bendecimos, bendigo, bendigan, bendices, bendicen, bendecís, bendecid, bendice, bendiga.
calls: llama, llamadas.
careful: cuidadoso, prudente, circunspecto, precavido.
competitors: competencia.
curate: coadjutor, cura.
dies: muere.
fairly: bastante, con justicia.
fiend: demonio.
hermit: ermitaño.

honest: honrado, sincero, honesto.
housekeeper: ama de casa, ama de llaves.
hyperbolical: hiperbólico.
ink: tinta, la tinta, entintar.
inner: interior, interno, interna.
knave: bribón.
ladies: damas, señoras.
lunatic: lunático.
master: maestro, amo, dueño, patrón, principal, magister.
niece: sobrina, la sobrina.

parson: sacerdote, cura, párroco.
pen: pluma, la pluma, corral, un bolígrafo.
prison: prisión, cárcel, presidio, encierro.
scholar: erudito, estudiante, escolar.
thee: ustedes, te, vosotros, usted, tú.
thou: tú, usted, vosotros, ustedes, vos.
wittily: chistoso, ingeniosamente, graciosamente.

MALVOLIO.
Sir Topas, never was man thus **wronged**: good Sir Topas, do not think I am mad; they have laid me here in **hideous darkness**.

CLOWN.
Fie, thou dishonest Sathan! I call **thee** by the most **modest terms**; for I am one of those **gentle** ones that will use the **devil** himself with **courtesy**. Say'st thou that house is dark?

MALVOLIO.
As hell, Sir Topas.

CLOWN.
Why, it hath **bay windows transparent** as barricadoes, and the clear storeys **toward** the south-north are as **lustrous** as **ebony**; and yet complainest thou of **obstruction**?

MALVOLIO.
I am not mad, Sir Topas; I say to you this house is dark.

CLOWN.
Madman, thou errest. I say there is no darkness but **ignorance**; in which thou art more **puzzled** than the Egyptians in their **fog**.

MALVOLIO.
I say this house is as dark as ignorance, though ignorance were as dark as hell; and I say there was never man thus **abused**. I am no more mad than you are; make the **trial** of it in any constant question.

CLOWN.
What is the **opinion** of Pythagoras **concerning** wild-fowl?

MALVOLIO.
That the **soul** of our grandam might **haply inhabit** a **bird**.

CLOWN.
What thinkest thou of his opinion?

Spanish

abused: maltratado.
bay: bahía, caballo bayo, compartimiento, bayo, ladrar.
bird: pájaro, ave.
concerning: en cuanto a, acerca de, por lo tocante a, respecto de.
courtesy: cortesía.
darkness: tinieblas, oscuridad, la oscuridad.
devil: diablo, el diablo.
dishonest: improbo, deshonesto.
ebony: ébano.

fog: niebla, bruma, neblina, la neblina.
gentle: dulce, suave, manso, apacible.
haply: posiblemente.
hideous: horroroso, abominable, horrible.
ignorance: ignorancia.
inhabit: habitar, habite, habitan, habito, habitas, habitamos, habitáis, habitad, habita, habiten.
lustrous: lustroso.
modest: modesto.
obstruction: obstrucción, obstáculo.

opinion: opinión, dictamen, juicio, parecer.
puzzled: perplejo, desconcertado.
soul: alma, espíritu, ánimo.
terms: condiciones, condición.
thee: ustedes, te, vosotros, usted, tú.
thou: tú, usted, vosotros, ustedes, vos.
toward: hacia, a.
transparent: transparente.
trial: ensayo, juicio, prueba.
windows: ventanas, ojal.
wronged: explotado.

MALVOLIO.
I think **nobly** of the soul, and no way **approve** his opinion.

CLOWN.
Fare thee well. **Remain** thou still in darkness: thou **shalt** hold the opinion of Pythagoras **ere** I will allow of thy wits; and fear to kill a **woodcock**, **lest** thou **dispossess** the soul of thy grandam. Fare thee well.

MALVOLIO.
Sir Topas, Sir Topas!

SIR TOBY.
My most exquisite Sir Topas!

CLOWN.
Nay, I am for all **waters**.

MARIA.
Thou mightst have done this without thy beard and gown: he **sees** thee not.

SIR TOBY.
To him in **thine** own voice, and bring me word how thou findest him; I would we were well **rid** of this **knavery**. If he may be **conveniently** delivered, I would he were; for I am now so far in offence with my niece that I **cannot** pursue with any safety this sport to the **upshot**. Come by and by to my chamber.

[Exeunt SIR TOBY and MARIA.]

CLOWN.
[Singing.]
'Hey, Robin, **jolly** Robin,
Tell me how thy lady does.'

MALVOLIO.
Fool,--

CLOWN.
'My lady is **unkind**, perdy.'

Spanish

approve: aprobar, aprueban, apruebo, apruebas, aprueba, aprobamos, aprobáis, aprobad, aprueben, apruebe.
cannot: presente de no poder.
conveniently: convenientemente.
dispossess: desposeer, desposea, desposeo, desposees, desposeen, desposeemos, desposeéis, desposeed, desposee, desposean, desapoderar.
ere: antes de.
jolly: alegre, jovial.

knavery: bribonada.
lest: para que no, a no ser que, con el fin de, no sea que, si es necesario.
nobly: con nobleza, noblemente, hidalgamente, nobiliariamente, noble, prócermente, generosamente, personaje.
remain: quedarse, restar, permanecer, restas, resto, reste, restan, restamos, restáis, restad, resta.
rid: librar, libro, librad, librado, libráis, libramos, libran, libras, libre, libren,

libra.
sees: Ve, serra.
shalt: irá, verbo auxiliar inglés para especificar futuro.
thine: tuyo, tuyos, tuyas, tuya, tus.
unkind: brusco, bronco.
upshot: resultado.
waters: aguas.
woodcock: becada.

MALVOLIO.
   Fool,--
CLOWN.
   'Alas, why is she so?'
MALVOLIO.
   Fool, I say;--
CLOWN.
   'She **loves** another'--Who **calls**, **ha**?
MALVOLIO.
   Good **fool**, as ever **thou wilt deserve** well at my hand, help me to a **candle**, and **pen**, **ink**, and paper; as I am a **gentleman**, I will live to be **thankful** to **thee** for't.
CLOWN.
   Master Malvolio!
MALVOLIO.
   Ay, good fool.
CLOWN.
   Alas, sir, how fell you **besides** your five wits?
MALVOLIO.
   Fool, there was never man so **notoriously abused**; I am as well in my wits, fool, as thou art.
CLOWN.
   But as well? then you are **mad** indeed, if you be no better in your wits than a fool.
MALVOLIO.
   They have here **propertied** me; keep me in **darkness**, **send ministers** to me, asses, and do all they can to face me out of my wits.
CLOWN.
   Advise you what you say: the minister is here.--Malvolio, **thy** wits the

Spanish

abused: maltratado.
besides: además, demás, además de, amén de.
calls: llama, llamadas.
candle: vela, la vela, bujía, candela, cirio.
darkness: tinieblas, oscuridad, la oscuridad.
deserve: merecer, merecemos, merezcan, merezco, merecen, mereced, merece, mereces, merecéis, merezca.

fool: engañar, necio, tonto.
gentleman: caballero, señor, gentilhombre.
ha: ah, decir ah, ja.
ink: tinta, la tinta, entintar.
loves: amor.
mad: loco, enojado, chiflado, majara, majareta, demente, enfadado.
ministers: asiste, atiende, auxilia, oficia.
notoriously: notoriamente.
pen: pluma, la pluma, corral, un

bolígrafo.
propertied: adinerado, propietario, hacendado.
send: enviar, envío, envía, envíe, enviad, enviáis, enviamos, envían, envías, envíen, mandar.
thankful: agradecido.
thee: ustedes, te, vosotros, usted, tú.
thou: tú, usted, vosotros, ustedes, vos.
thy: tu.
wilt: marchitarse, marchitar.

heavens restore! endeavour thyself to sleep, and leave thy **vain bibble-**babble.

MALVOLIO.
Sir Topas,--

CLOWN.
Maintain no words with him, good **fellow**. Who, I, sir? not I, sir. God b' wi' you, good Sir Topas.--Marry, amen.--I will sir, I will.

MALVOLIO.
Fool, **fool**, fool, I say,--

CLOWN.
Alas, sir, be patient. What say you, sir? I am shent for **speaking** to you.

MALVOLIO.
Good fool, help me to some light and some **paper**;
I tell **thee** I am as well in my wits as any man in Illyria.

CLOWN.
Well-a-day,--that you were, sir!

MALVOLIO.
By this hand, I am: Good fool, some **ink**, paper, and light, and **convey** what I will set down to my lady; it shall **advantage** thee more than ever the **bearing** of letter did.

CLOWN.
I will help you to't. But tell me true, are you not mad indeed? or do you but **counterfeit**?

MALVOLIO.
Believe me, I am not; I tell thee true.

CLOWN.
Nay, I'll **ne'er** believe a **madman** till I see his brains.
I will **fetch** you light, and paper, and ink.

Spanish

advantage: ventaja, provecho, la ventaja.
b: si, segundo.
bearing: cojinete, abolas, rodamiento.
convey: alargar, entregar, llevar, entrega, entregan, entreguen, entregue, entregas, entregamos, entregáis, entregad.
counterfeit: falsificación, falsificar, contrahecho.
endeavour: tratar de, esforzarse por, esfuerzo.

fellow: compañero, hombre, socio, tipo, becario.
fetch: traer, traemos, traed, trae, traéis, traes, traigo, traigan, traen, traiga, coger.
fool: engañar, necio, tonto.
heavens: cielo, cielos.
ink: tinta, la tinta, entintar.
madman: loco.
ne'er: nunca.
paper: papel, documento, el papel, papel pintado, ponencia, tapizar,

periódico.
restore: restaurar, restablecer, restaure, restaurad, restablezca, restableces, restablecen, restablecemos, restablecéis, restableced, restablece.
speaking: hablando, parlante.
thee: ustedes, te, vosotros, usted, tú.
thy: tu.
thyself: ti, tú mismo, ti mismo, tú misma, te, ti misma.
vain: vano, hueco, vanidoso.

MALVOLIO.
Fool, I'll **requite** it in the **highest degree**: I pr'ythee be **gone**.
CLOWN.
[Singing.]
'I am gone, sir,
And **anon**, sir,
I'll be with you again,
In a trice,
Like to the old vice
Your need to sustain;
Who with **dagger** of lath,
In his **rage** and his wrath,
Cries **ah, ha**! to the devil:
Like a **mad** lad,
Pare **thy nails**, dad.
Adieu, goodman drivel.
[Exit.]

SCENE III. OLIVIA'S GARDEN.

[Enter SEBASTIAN.]
SEBASTIAN.
This is the **air**; that is the **glorious** sun;
This **pearl** she gave me, I do feel't and see't:
And though 'tis **wonder** that **enwraps** me thus,
Yet 'tis not **madness**. Where's Antonio, then?
I could not find him at the Elephant;
Yet there he was; and there I found this credit,
That he did **range** the **town** to **seek** me out.

Spanish

ah: ay.
air: aire, airear, el aire, aéreo, orear.
anon: pronto.
dagger: daga, puñal.
degree: grado, título, licencia.
enwraps: envuelve.
glorious: glorioso, famoso.
gone: ido, marchado.
ha: ah, decir ah, ja.
highest: sumo, el más alto, suma, máximo, sumamente, alto, máxima.
mad: loco, enojado, chiflado, majara,

majareta, demente, enfadado.
madness: locura, demencia, chifladura.
nails: clavos.
pearl: perla, la perla.
rage: rabia, furia, furor, ira.
range: alcance, gama, rango, intervalo, ámbito, margen, recorrido.
requite: reembolse, compensar, recompensar, pagar.
seek: buscar, busque, busca, buscan, buscamos, busquen, buscas, buscáis,

buscad, busco.
thy: tu.
town: ciudad, pueblo, población, el pueblo.
wonder: preguntarse, maravilla, asombrarse, prodigio, preguntar.

His **counsel** now might do me golden service;
For though my soul disputes well with my sense,
That this may be some **error**, but no madness,
Yet doth this **accident** and **flood** of fortune
So far **exceed** all **instance**, all discourse,
That I am ready to **distrust** mine eyes
And **wrangle** with my reason, that **persuades** me
To any other trust but that I am mad,
Or else the lady's mad; yet if 'twere so,
She could not **sway** her house, command her followers,
Take and give back affairs and their despatch
With such a smooth, **discreet**, and **stable** bearing,
As I **perceive** she does: there's something in't
That is deceivable. But here comes the lady.

[Enter OLIVIA and a PRIEST.]

OLIVIA.
Blame not this **haste** of mine. If you mean well,
Now go with me and with this **holy** man
Into the **chantry** by: there, before him
And **underneath** that **consecrated** roof,
Plight me the full assurance of your faith,
That my most **jealous** and too **doubtful** soul
May live at peace. He shall **conceal** it
Whiles you are willing it shall come to note;
What time we will our **celebration** keep
According to my birth.--What do you say?

SEBASTIAN.
I'll follow this good man, and go with you;
And, having **sworn** truth, ever will be true.

Spanish

accident: accidente, desgracia, un accidente, el accidente.
celebration: fiesta, celebración, festividad.
chantry: capellanía, capilla.
conceal: ocultar, ocultamos, oculten, ocultan, ocultáis, ocultad, oculta, ocultas, oculto, oculte, recatar.
consecrated: consagrado.
counsel: consejo, aconsejar, abogado, anunciar.
discreet: discreto.

distrust: desconfianza.
doubtful: dudoso.
error: equivocación, error, yerro.
exceed: aventajar, aventajan, aventajen, aventajo, aventajas, aventajáis, aventajad, aventaja, aventaje, aventajamos, exceder.
flood: diluvio, inundación, enterrar, pleamar, inundar.
haste: prisa, precipitación.
holy: santo, sagrado.
instance: instancia, ejemplo, ejemplar.

jealous: celoso.
perceive: percibir, perciben, percibes, percibe, perciban, percibid, percibimos, percibís, percibo, perciba.
persuades: convence, persuade.
stable: cuadra, establo, estable, fijo, caballeriza.
sway: oscilación, vaivén.
sworn: jurado.
underneath: abajo, debajo, debajo de, en el fondo.
wrangle: disputa, disputar, reñir.

OLIVIA.
   Then   lead the way, good father;--And **heavens** so shine
   That they may **fairly note** this act of **mine**!
   [Exeunt.]

ACT V

SCENE I. THE STREET BEFORE OLIVIA'S HOUSE.

[Enter CLOWN and FABIAN.]

FABIAN.
Now, as **thou** lovest me, let me see his **letter**.

CLOWN.
Good Master Fabian, **grant** me another **request**.

FABIAN.
Anything.

CLOWN.
Do not **desire** to see this letter.

FABIAN.
This is to give a **dog**; and in **recompense** desire my dog again.

[Enter DUKE, VIOLA, and Attendants.]

DUKE.
Belong you to the Lady Olivia, **friends**?

Spanish

desire: desear, deseo, tener, querer, gana, codiciar.
dog: perro, el perro, la perra, can.
friends: amigos, los amigos.
grant: subvención, concesión, beca, conceder, subsidio, otorgar, otorgamiento, donación, ceder.
letter: carta, letra, la carta.
recompense: recompensa.
request: petición, pedir, solicitar, solicitud, demandar, solicitación, requerimiento, ruego, rogar,

demanda.
thou: tú, usted, vosotros, ustedes, vos.

CLOWN.
Ay, **sir**; we are some of her trappings.

DUKE.
I know **thee** well. How dost **thou**, my good **fellow**?

CLOWN.
Truly, sir, the better for my foes and the **worse** for my **friends**.

DUKE.
Just the **contrary**; the better for **thy** friends.

CLOWN.
No, sir, the worse.

DUKE.
How can that be?

CLOWN.
Marry, sir, they **praise** me and make an **ass** of me; now my foes tell me **plainly** I am an ass: so that by my foes, sir, I **profit** in the **knowledge** of **myself**, and by my friends I am **abused**: so that, conclusions to be as **kisses**, if your four **negatives** make your two **affirmatives**, why then, the worse for my friends and the better for my foes.

DUKE.
Why, this is **excellent**.

CLOWN.
By my **troth**, sir, no; though it **please** you to be one of my friends.

DUKE.
Thou **shalt** not be the worse for me; there's **gold**.

CLOWN.
But that it would be **double**-dealing, sir, I would you could make it another.

DUKE.
O, you give me **ill counsel**.

Spanish

abused: maltratado.
affirmatives: afirmativo.
ass: burro, asno, culo.
contrary: contrario.
counsel: consejo, aconsejar, abogado, anunciar.
double-dealing: falsía.
excellent: excelente.
fellow: compañero, hombre, socio, tipo, becario.
friends: amigos, los amigos.
gold: oro, el oro, de oro.

ill: enfermo, malo, doliente.
kisses: besos.
knowledge: conocimiento, saber.
myself: yo mismo.
negatives: negativos.
plainly: simplemente.
please: por favor, agradar, gustar, complacer, haz el favor, contentar, haz favor.
praise: alabar, alabanza, elogio, elogiar.
profit: beneficio, provecho, ganancia, aprovecharse, ganar, lucro, rendimiento.

shalt: irá, verbo auxiliar inglés para especificar futuro.
sir: señor.
thee: ustedes, te, vosotros, usted, tú.
thou: tú, usted, vosotros, ustedes, vos.
thy: tu.
troth: fidelidad, fe.
worse: peor.

CLOWN.
Put your grace in your **pocket**, sir, for this once, and let your flesh and blood **obey** it.

DUKE.
Well, I will be so much a **sinner** to be a **double**-dealer: there's another.

CLOWN.
Primo, secundo, tertio, is a good play; and the old saying is, the third **pays** for all; the **triplex**, sir, is a good **tripping measure**; or the **bells** of Saint Bennet, sir, may put you in mind; one, two, three.

DUKE.
You can fool no more money out of me at this throw: if you will let your lady know I am here to speak with her, and bring her **along** with you, it may awake my **bounty** further.

CLOWN.
Marry, sir, **lullaby** to your bounty till I come again. I go, sir; but I would not have you to think that my desire of having is the sin of **covetousness**: but, as you say, sir, let your bounty take a **nap**; I will awake it anon.
[Exit.]

[Enter ANTONIO and OFFICERS.]

VIOLA.
Here comes the man, sir, that did **rescue** me.

DUKE.
That face of his I do remember well:
Yet when I saw it last it was besmeared
As black as Vulcan in the **smoke** of war:
A bawbling **vessel** was he **captain** of,
For shallow **draught** and **bulk** unprizable;
With which such scathful **grapple** did he make
With the most noble **bottom** of our **fleet**

Spanish

along: a lo largo de, por.
bells: las campanas.
bottom: fondo, suelo, inferior, lado inferior, el fondo, culo, posaderas, trasero.
bounty: liberalidad, generosidad.
bulk: volumen, granel, bulto, a granel, masa.
captain: capitán.
covetousness: deseo.
double-dealer: traidor.
draught: calado, trago.

fleet: flota, parque.
grapple: agarrar, asir, coger.
lullaby: arrullo, canción de cuna.
measure: medida, medir.
nap: siesta, la siesta, echar la siesta.
obey: obedecer, obedecemos, obedezco, obedezcan, obedecen, obedecéis, obedeced, obedece, obedeces, obedezca.
pays: paga.
pocket: bolsillo, el bolsillo, bolsa, casilla.

rescue: salvar, rescate, rescatar, socorro, salvamento.
sin: pecado, pecar.
sinner: pecador.
smoke: fumar, fumo, fume, fumas, fuman, fumamos, fumáis, fumad, fuma, fumen, humo.
triplex: triple.
tripping: desconexión.
vessel: vaso, embarcación, barco, estuche, recipiente, vasija, olla, buque, jarro, caja.

That very envy and the tongue of los
Cried **fame** and honour on him.--What's the matter?

FIRST OFFICER.
Orsino, this is that Antonio
That took the Phoenix and her **fraught** from Candy:
And this is he that did the Tiger board
When your young **nephew** Titus lost his leg:
Here in the **streets**, desperate of shame and state,
In **private** brabble did we **apprehend** him.

VIOLA.
He did me kindness, sir; drew on my side;
But, in conclusion, put strange speech upon me.
I know not what 'twas, but **distraction**.

DUKE.
Notable **pirate**! thou salt-water **thief**!
What foolish boldness brought thee to their mercies,
Whom thou, in terms so bloody and so dear,
Hast made **thine** enemies?

ANTONIO.
                              Orsino, noble sir,
Be pleased that I shake off these **names** you give me:
Antonio never yet was thief or pirate,
Though, I **confess**, on **base** and ground enough,
Orsino's enemy. A **witchcraft** drew me hither:
That most ingrateful boy there, by your side
From the **rude** sea's **enraged** and **foamy** mouth
Did I redeem; a **wreck** past hope he was:
His life I gave him, and did **thereto** add
My love, without **retention** or restraint,
All his in **dedication**: for his sake,
Did I **expose** myself, **pure** for his love,

Spanish

apprehend: aprehender, aprehendemos, aprehendéis, aprehendo, aprehenden, aprehende, aprehendes, aprehendan, aprehended, aprehenda.
base: basar, pie, fundar, base, basamento, casquillo, fundamentar.
confess: confesar, confiesan, confiesen, confieso, confiesas, confesamos, confesad, confesáis, confiesa, confiese, declarar.
dedication: dedicación, dedicatoria.
distraction: distracción.
enraged: enfurecido.
expose: exponer, exponen, expongo, expongan, expones, exponemos, exponéis, exponed, expon, expone, exponga.
fame: fama, hambre, conocimientos, la fama, gloria.
foamy: espumoso, espumante.
fraught: cargado.
names: nombres, Michael.
nephew: sobrino, el sobrino.
pirate: pirata.
private: privado, soldado raso.
pure: puro, limpio.
retention: retención, conservación.
rude: grosero, rudo, insolente, descortés.
streets: calles, las calles.
thereto: a eso.
thief: ladrón.
thine: tuyo, tuyos, tuyas, tuya, tus.
witchcraft: brujería.
wreck: naufragio, desbaratar.

Into the **danger** of this **adverse** town;
Drew to **defend** him when he was beset:
Where being **apprehended**, his **false** cunning,--
Not meaning to **partake** with me in danger,--
Taught him to face me out of his acquaintance,
And **grew** a twenty-years-removed thing
While one would **wink**; **denied** me **mine** own purse,
Which I had **recommended** to his use
Not half an hour before.

VIOLA.

How can this be?

DUKE.

When came he to this town?

ANTONIO.

To-day, my lord; and for three months before,--
No **interim**, not a minute's vacancy,--
Both day and night did we keep company.

[Enter OLIVIA and ATTENDANTS.]

DUKE.

Here comes the **countess**; now **heaven walks** on earth.--
But for **thee, fellow**, fellow, **thy** words are madness:
Three months this **youth** hath **tended** upon me;
But more of that anon.--Take him **aside**.

OLIVIA.

What would my lord, but that he may not have,
Wherein Olivia may seem serviceable!--
Cesario, you do not keep **promise** with me.

VIOLA.

Madam?

Spanish

adverse: adverso, contrario.
apprehended: aprehendido.
aside: aparte, al lado.
countess: condesa.
danger: peligro, el peligro.
defend: defender, defiendes, defiendo, defendéis, defendemos, defiendan, defienden, defended, defiende, defienda.
denied: negado, desmentido.
false: falso.
fellow: compañero, hombre, socio,

tipo, becario.
grew: creció, pret de grow, crecida.
heaven: cielo.
interim: interino.
mine: mina, mío, minar.
partake: compartir, compartan, comparto, compartís, compartimos, compartid, compartes, comparte, comparta, comparten.
promise: prometer, prometéis, prometemos, prometen, prometo, promete, prometan, prometa,

prometes, prometed, promesa.
recommended: recomendado, ensalzado, encarecido.
tended: cuidado, Tendido.
thee: ustedes, te, vosotros, usted, tú.
thy: tu.
walks: anda, camina.
wink: guiño, pestañeo, parpadeo, guiñar.
youth: juventud, joven, jóvenes, adolescencia.

DUKE.
   Gracious Olivia,--
OLIVIA.
   What do you say, Cesario?--Good my lord,--
VIOLA.
   My lord would **speak**, my **duty** hushes me.
OLIVIA.
   If it be **aught** to the old **tune**, my lord,
   It is as **fat** and **fulsome** to **mine** ear
   As **howling** after music.
DUKE.
                      Still so **cruel**?
OLIVIA.
   Still so **constant**, lord.
DUKE.
   What! to **perverseness**? you **uncivil** lady,
   To whose **ingrate** and unauspicious altars
   My **soul** the faithfull'st **offerings** hath **breathed** out
   That **e'er devotion** tender'd! What shall I do?
OLIVIA.
   Even what it please my lord, that shall become him.
DUKE.
   Why should I not, had I the **heart** to do it.
   Like to the Egyptian **thief**, at point of death,
   Kill what I love; a **savage** jealousy
   That **sometime savours** nobly.--But hear me this:
   Since you to non-regardance **cast** my faith,
   And that I **partly** know the instrument
   That **screws** me from my true place in your favour,
   Live you the marble-breasted **tyrant** still;

Spanish

aught: algo.
breathed: respirado.
cast: lanzar, lanzamiento, arrojar, echar, colar, elenco, molde.
constant: constante, continuo.
cruel: cruel.
devotion: devoción.
duty: deber, servicio, obligación, impuesto.
e'er: nunca en la vida.
fat: gordo, grasa, grueso, manteca.
fulsome: de mal gusto.

heart: corazón, cogollo.
howling: aullido, lamentarse, clamoroso, aullador, alarido, aullar, lamento, gritar, rugir, grito, dar alaridos.
ingrate: desagradecido, ingrato, desleal.
mine: mina, mío, minar.
offerings: productos.
partly: en parte, parcialmente.
perverseness: obstinación, perversidad.

savage: fiero, salvaje.
savours: sabores.
screws: tornillos.
sometime: algún día.
soul: alma, espíritu, ánimo.
speak: hablar, hablamos, hablo, hablas, habláis, hablad, hablen, habla, hablan, hable.
thief: ladrón.
tune: melodía, acomodar, adaptar.
tyrant: tirano.
uncivil: descortés, incivil.

But this your **minion**, whom I know you love,
And whom, by heaven I **swear**, I **tender** dearly,
Him will I **tear** out of that cruel eye
Where he **sits crowned** in his master's sprite.--
Come, boy, with me; my **thoughts** are **ripe** in mischief:
I'll **sacrifice** the lamb that I do love,
To **spite** a raven's heart within a dove.
[Going.]
VIOLA.
And I, most **jocund**, **apt**, and willingly,
To do you rest, a thousand deaths would die.
OLIVIA.
Where goes Cesario?
VIOLA.
After him I love
More than I love these eyes, more than my life,
More, by all **mores**, than **e'er** I shall love wife;
If I do **feign**, you witnesses above
Punish my life for **tainting** of my love!
OLIVIA.
Ah me, **detested**! how am I beguil'd!
VIOLA.
Who does **beguile** you? who does do you wrong?
OLIVIA.
Hast thou forgot **thyself**? Is it so long?-- Call forth the holy father.
[Exit an ATTENDANT.]
DUKE.
[To VIOLA.]
Come, away!

Spanish

apt: apropiado.
beguile: engañar, engañad, engaño, engañen, engañas, engañan, engañáis, engaña, engañamos, engañe.
crowned: verdadero, coronado.
detested: detestado.
e'er: nunca en la vida.
feign: fingir, fingen, finjo, finjan, finja, fingís, fingimos, finges, finge, fingid, aparentar.
jocund: jocundo.

minion: favorito.
mores: moralidad, costumbres, tradiciones.
ripe: maduro.
sacrifice: sacrificio, sacrificar, ofrecer, presentar.
sits: asienta, siente, sopla, empolla, se sienta.
spite: rencor.
swear: jurar, jura, jurad, juráis, juramos, juran, juras, juren, juro, jure, maldecir.

tainting: Manchar.
tear: lágrima, desgarrar, rajar, romper, rasgar, desgarro.
tender: tierno, oferta, dulce, subasta, proposición, ofrecer, destajo, licitación, presentar, reproducir, retratar.
thou: tú, usted, vosotros, ustedes, vos.
thyself: ti, tú mismo, ti mismo, tú misma, te, ti misma.

OLIVIA.
  Whither, my lord? Cesario, **husband**, stay.
DUKE.
  Husband?
OLIVIA.
             Ay, husband, can he that **deny**?
DUKE.
  Her husband, sirrah?
VIOLA.
             No, my lord, not I.
OLIVIA.
  Alas, it is the **baseness** of **thy** fear
  That makes **thee strangle** thy propriety:
  Fear not, Cesario, take thy fortunes up;
  Be that **thou** know'st thou art, and then thou art
  As great as that thou fear'st--O, **welcome**, father!
  [Re-enter ATTENDANT and PRIEST.]
  Father, I charge thee, by thy reverence,
  Here to unfold,--though **lately** we intended
  To keep in **darkness** what occasion now
  Reveals before 'tis ripe,--what thou dost know
  Hath **newly passed** between this **youth** and me.
PRIEST.
  A **contract** of **eternal bond** of love,
  Confirmed by **mutual joinder** of your hands,
  Attested by the **holy** close of lips,
  Strengthen'd by interchangement of your rings;
  And all the **ceremony** of this compact
  Sealed in my function, by my testimony:

Spanish

baseness: bajeza.
bond: lazo, bono, obligación, fianza, cinta, adherencia, enlace.
ceremony: ceremonia.
contract: contrato, contrata, destajo, contraer.
darkness: tinieblas, oscuridad, la oscuridad.
deny: negar, negad, niego, niegas, niegan, negáis, negamos, nieguen, niega, niegue, desmentir.
eternal: eterno.

holy: santo, sagrado.
husband: marido, esposo, el esposo.
joinder: reunión, acumulación, acumulación de acciones, comunidad, asociación.
lately: últimamente.
mutual: mutuo, mutua.
newly: nuevamente, recién, recientemente.
passed: pasado.
strangle: estrangular, estranguláis, estrangulen, estrangulamos,

estrangulan, estrangulo, estrangula, estrangulas, estrangulad, estrangule.
thee: ustedes, te, vosotros, usted, tú.
thou: tú, usted, vosotros, ustedes, vos.
thy: tu.
welcome: dar la bienvenida, bienvenida, bienvenido, acoger, grato, agradable, acogida, acogen, acojan, acojo, acoges.
youth: juventud, joven, jóvenes, adolescencia.

Since when, my watch hath told me, **toward** my grave,
I have **travelled** but two hours.

DUKE.
O **thou dissembling cub**! What **wilt** thou be,
When time hath **sowed** a **grizzle** on **thy** case?
Or will not else thy **craft** so quickly grow
That **thine** own **trip** shall be thine overthrow?
Farewell, and take her; but **direct** thy feet
Where thou and I **henceforth** may never **meet**.

VIOLA.
My lord, I do protest,--

OLIVIA.
O, do not swear;
Hold little **faith**, though thou has too much fear.

[Enter SIR ANDREW AGUE-CHEEK, with his head **broke**.]

SIR ANDREW.
For the love of God, a **surgeon**; send one **presently** to Sir Toby.

OLIVIA.
What's the matter?

SIR ANDREW.
He has broke my head across, and has given Sir Toby a bloody **coxcomb** too:
for the love of God, your help: I had rather than forty **pound** I were at home.

OLIVIA.
Who has done this, Sir Andrew?

SIR ANDREW.
The Count's **gentleman**, one Cesario: we took him for a **coward**, but he's the
very **devil** incardinate.

DUKE.
My gentleman, Cesario?

Spanish

broke: bollado, rotura, rompió, romper, pret de break, interrupción, fracturar, sin blanca, comienzo, pelado, descanso.
coward: cobarde, el cobarde.
coxcomb: cresta de crías de gallina, cresta de gallo, fatuo, mequetrefe.
craft: astucia, destreza, embarcación, oficio.
cub: cachorro.
devil: diablo, el diablo.
direct: directo, mandar, guiar,
derecho, dirigir.
dissembling: disimulando.
faith: fe, la fe.
gentleman: caballero, señor, gentilhombre.
grizzle: color gris, gimoteado, gimotear.
henceforth: de aquí en adelante.
meet: encontrar, encontrad, encuentro, encuentren, encuentre, encuentras, encuentran, encontramos, encontráis, encuentra, quedar.
pound: libra, la libra.
presently: por ahora.
sowed: sembrado.
surgeon: cirujano, el cirujano.
thine: tuyo, tuyos, tuyas, tuya, tus.
thou: tú, usted, vosotros, ustedes, vos.
thy: tu.
toward: hacia, a.
travelled: viaje, moverse, viajado, viajar, viajar por, camino.
trip: viaje, disparo, excursión, el viaje.
wilt: marchitarse, marchitar.

110 Twelfth Night

SIR ANDREW.
Od's lifelings, here he is:--You **broke** my head for nothing; and that that I did, I was set on to do't by Sir Toby.

VIOLA.
Why do you **speak** to me? I never **hurt** you: You drew your **sword** upon me without cause; But I bespake you **fair** and hurt you not.

SIR ANDREW.
If a **bloody coxcomb** be a hurt, you have hurt me; I think you set nothing by a bloody coxcomb.
[Enter SIR TOBY BELCH, **drunk**, led by the CLOWN.]
Here comes Sir Toby **halting**; you shall hear more: but if he had not been in **drink** he would have **tickled** you othergates than he did.

DUKE.
How now, **gentleman**? how is't with you?

SIR TOBY.
That's all one; he has hurt me, and there's the end on't.--Sot, didst see Dick Surgeon, **sot**?

CLOWN.
O, he's drunk, Sir Toby, an hour agone; his eyes were set at eight i' the morning.

SIR TOBY.
Then he's a **rogue**. After a passy-measure, or a pavin, I **hate** a **drunken** rogue.

OLIVIA.
Away with him. Who hath made this **havoc** with them?

SIR ANDREW.
I'll help you, Sir Toby, because **we'll** be **dressed** together.

SIR TOBY.
Will you help an ass-head, and a coxcomb, and a **knave**? a thin-faced knave, a **gull**?

Spanish

bloody: sangriento, sanguinario, cruento.
broke: bollado, rotura, rompió, romper, pret de break, interrupción, fracturar, sin blanca, comienzo, pelado, descanso.
coxcomb: cresta de crías de gallina, cresta de gallo, fatuo, mequetrefe.
dressed: vestido, con guarnición de.
drink: beber, bebida, tomar, el refresco, trago, copa.
drunk: borracho, bebido, ebrio.

drunken: borracho, ebrio.
fair: justo, rubio, mercado, feria, verbena, bazar, equitativo, hermoso.
gentleman: caballero, señor, gentilhombre.
gull: gaviota.
halting: parar, detenerse, hacer alto, renqueante, parada, interrupción, interrumpir, claudicante, vacilante, alto, detener.
hate: odiar, odio, aborrecer, detestar.
havoc: estrago, destrucción.

hurt: doler, herir, dañar, herida, lastimar.
knave: bribón.
rogue: pícaro.
sot: beodo, borrachín, borracho.
speak: hablar, hablamos, hablo, hablas, habláis, hablad, hablen, habla, hablan, hable.
sword: espada.
tickled: Cosquilleó.
we'll: Haremos.

OLIVIA.
Get him to **bed**, and let his **hurt** be looked to.
[Exeunt CLOWN, SIR TOBY, and SIR ANDREW.]
[Enter SEBASTIAN.]
SEBASTIAN.
I am **sorry**, madam, I have hurt your kinsman;
But, had it been the **brother** of my blood,
I must have done no less, **with** wit and safety.
You **throw** a **strange regard** upon me, and by that
I do **perceive** it hath **offended** you;
Pardon me, **sweet** one, even for the vows
We made each other but so **late ago**.
DUKE.
One face, one voice, one **habit**, and two persons;
A **natural perspective**, that is, and is not.
SEBASTIAN.
Antonio, O my **dear** Antonio!
How have the **hours** rack'd and tortur'd me
Since I have **lost thee**.
ANTONIO.
Sebastian are you?
SEBASTIAN.
                    Fear'st **thou** that, Antonio?
ANTONIO.
How have you made **division** of yourself?--
An **apple**, **cleft** in two, is not more twin
Than these two creatures. Which is Sebastian?
OLIVIA.
Most **wonderful**!

Spanish

ago: hace.
apple: manzana, la manzana.
bed: cama, lecho, cauce, la cama, bancada, cuadro, madre.
brother: hermano, el hermano, cofrade.
cleft: hendido, grieta.
dear: caro, querido, estimado.
division: división, escisión.
habit: costumbre, hábito, resabio, mala costumbre.
hours: horas, las horas.

hurt: doler, herir, dañar, herida, lastimar.
late: tarde, tardío, tardo.
lost: perdido, adelgazado.
natural: natural.
offended: ofendido, injuriado, ultrajado, insultado, delinquido.
perceive: percibir, perciben, percibes, percibe, perciban, percibid,
percibimos, percibís, percibo, perciba.
perspective: perspectiva.
regard: mirar, considerar, mira, miran,

miráis, miro, miramos, mirad, miras, mire, miren.
sorry: afligido, arrepentido, pesaroso, siento, triste.
strange: extraño, raro, ajeno.
sweet: dulce, caramelo, postre.
thee: ustedes, te, vosotros, usted, tú.
thou: tú, usted, vosotros, ustedes, vos.
throw: lanzar, echar, tirar, tirada, arrojar, lanzamiento.
wit: ingenio.
wonderful: maravilloso.

SEBASTIAN.
Do I stand there? I never had a brother:
Nor can there be that **deity** in my nature
Of here and everywhere. I had a sister
Whom the **blind waves** and surges have devoured:--
[To VIOLA.]
Of **charity**, what **kin** are you to me?
What **countryman**, what name, what **parentage**?

VIOLA.
Of Messaline: Sebastian was my father;
Such a Sebastian was my brother too:
So went he **suited** to his **watery** tomb:
If **spirits** can **assume** both form and suit,
You come to **fright** us.

SEBASTIAN.
                    A spirit I am indeed:
But am in that **dimension grossly** clad,
Which from the **womb** I did participate.
Were you a woman, as the rest goes even,
I should my tears let fall upon your cheek,
And say--Thrice welcome, **drowned** Viola!

VIOLA.
My father had a **mole** upon his **brow**.

SEBASTIAN.
And so had mine.

VIOLA.
And died that day when Viola from her birth
Had **numbered thirteen** years.

SEBASTIAN.
O, that **record** is **lively** in my soul!

Spanish

assume: asumir, asumen, asumo, asumís, asumimos, asumes, asume, asuman, asumid, asuma, suponer.
blind: ciego, persiana, deslumbrar, deslumbrad, deslumbre, deslumbras, deslumbran, deslumbro, deslumbramos, deslumbráis, deslumbren.
brow: ceja, frente.
charity: caridad, limosna, misericordia, beneficencia.
countryman: compatriota.
deity: deidad.
dimension: dimensión, tamaño.
drowned: se ahogado, ahogado.
fright: espanto, susto, miedo, angustia, terror.
grossly: groseramente.
kin: parientes.
lively: animado, vivo, alegre.
mole: topo, lunar, mol.
numbered: foliado, numerado, contado.
parentage: linaje.
record: registro, registrar, récord, disco, expediente, grabar, inscribir, acta, certificar, ficha.
spirits: alcohol.
suited: demanda, conveniente, traje, satisfacer, preparado, pleito, idóneo, ajustarse a, adecuado, acomodado, conjunto.
thirteen: trece.
watery: acuoso, aguado.
waves: olas.
womb: útero, matriz.

He finished, indeed, his **mortal** act
That day that made my sister **thirteen** years.
VIOLA.
If nothing **lets** to make us happy both
But this my **masculine** usurp'd attire,
Do not **embrace** me **till** each circumstance
Of place, time, **fortune**, do **cohere**, and jump
That I am Viola: which to confirm,
I'll bring you to a **captain** in this town,
Where **lie** my **maiden weeds**; by whose **gentle** help
I was preserv'd to serve this **noble** count;
All the **occurrence** of my fortune since
Hath been between this lady and this lord.
SEBASTIAN.
[To OLIVIA]
So comes it, lady, you have been mistook:
But nature to her **bias** drew in that.
You would have been **contracted** to a maid;
Nor are you **therein**, by my life, deceived;
You are betroth'd both to a maid and man.
DUKE.
Be not **amazed**; right noble is his blood.--
If this be so, as yet the glass seems true,
I shall have share in this most happy wreck:
[To VIOLA]
Boy, **thou hast** said to me a thousand times,
Thou never shouldst love woman like to me.
VIOLA.
And all those **sayings** will I over-swear;
And all those swearings keep as true in **soul**

Spanish

amazed: asombrado, maravillado, pasmado, atónito.
bias: sesgo, prejuicio, parcialidad, error sistemático, tendencia, polarización.
captain: capitán.
cohere: pegan, unen, unes, unís, une, unan, una, peguen, pegue, pego, pegas.
contracted: contraído, contratado.
embrace: abrazar, abarcar.
fortune: suerte, fortuna.

gentle: dulce, suave, manso, apacible.
hast: haya.
lets: deja, alquila.
lie: mentir, mentira, yacer, estar tendido, embuste, echarse.
maid: criada, sirvienta, doncella, la criada.
maiden: doncella, soltera.
masculine: masculino, varonil.
mortal: mortal.
noble: hidalgo, noble.
occurrence: ocurrencia, suceso,

acaecimiento, aparición, acontecimiento.
sayings: dichos.
soul: alma, espíritu, ánimo.
therein: en eso, adjunto.
thirteen: trece.
thou: tú, usted, vosotros, ustedes, vos.
till: caja, hasta que, hasta, a que.
weeds: malas hierbas, hierbajos.

As doth that **orbed continent** the fire
That **severs** day from night.

DUKE.
Give me **thy** hand;
And let me see **thee** in thy woman's **weeds**.

VIOLA.
The **captain** that did bring me first on shore
Hath my maid's **garments**: he, upon some action,
Is now in durance, at Malvolio's suit;
A **gentleman** and **follower** of my lady's.

OLIVIA.
He shall **enlarge** him:--Fetch Malvolio hither:--
And yet, **alas**, now I remember me,
They say, poor gentleman, he's much distract.
[Re-enter CLOWN, with a **letter**.]
A most **extracting frenzy** of **mine** own
From my **remembrance** clearly **banished** his.--
How does he, sirrah?

CLOWN.
Truly, **madam**, he holds Belzebub at the stave's end as well as a man in his case may do: he has here **writ** a letter to you; I should have given it you to-day morning, but as a madman's epistles are no gospels, so it **skills** not much when they are **delivered**.

OLIVIA.
Open it, and read it.

CLOWN.
Look then to be well **edified** when the **fool delivers** the madman:--'By the Lord, madam,--'

OLIVIA.
How now! **art thou** mad?

Spanish

alas: ay, es una lástima.
art: arte, el arte.
banished: Desterrado.
captain: capitán.
continent: continente, el continente.
delivered: entregado.
delivers: entrega.
edified: edificado.
enlarge: ampliar, amplíe, amplía, amplíen, amplías, amplían, ampliamos, ampliáis, ampliad, amplío, agrandar.

extracting: extraer.
follower: seguidor.
fool: engañar, necio, tonto.
frenzy: frenesí.
garments: ornamentos.
gentleman: caballero, señor, gentilhombre.
letter: carta, letra, la carta.
mad: loco, enojado, chiflado, majara, majareta, demente, enfadado.
mine: mina, mío, minar.
orbed: redondo, esférico.

remembrance: recuerdo.
severs: separa.
skills: competencia.
thee: ustedes, te, vosotros, usted, tú.
thou: tú, usted, vosotros, ustedes, vos.
thy: tu.
to-day: hoy.
weeds: malas hierbas, hierbajos.
writ: escritura, orden, escrito, orden por escrito.

CLOWN.

No, madam, I do but read **madness**: an your **ladyship** will have it as it **ought** to be, you must **allow** vox.

OLIVIA.

Pr'ythee, read i' **thy** right wits.

CLOWN.

So I do, **madonna**; but to read his right wits is to read thus; therefore **perpend**, my **princess**, and give **ear**.

OLIVIA.

[To FABIAN]
Read it you, sirrah.

FABIAN.

[Reads]
'By the Lord, madam, you wrong me, and the world shall know it: though you have put me into **darkness** and given your **drunken cousin rule** over me, yet have I the **benefit** of my **senses** as well as your ladyship. I have your own letter that **induced** me to the **semblance** I put on; with the which I **doubt** not but to do myself much right or you much **shame**. Think of me as you please. I leave my **duty** a little **unthought** of, and speak out of my injury.
                         THE MADLY-USED MALVOLIO'

OLIVIA.

Did he write this?

CLOWN.

Ay, madam.

DUKE.

This **savours** not much of **distraction**.

OLIVIA.

See him **delivered**, Fabian: bring him hither.
[Exit FABIAN.]
My lord, so please you, these things further thought on,

Spanish

allow: permitir, permitan, permitid, permiten, permites, permitimos, permite, permito, permitís, permita, dejar.
benefit: beneficio, ventaja, provecho, prestación, subsidio, beneficiar, lucro.
cousin: primo, prima, el primo.
darkness: tinieblas, oscuridad, la oscuridad.
delivered: entregado.
distraction: distracción.
doubt: dudar, duda.

drunken: borracho, ebrio.
duty: deber, servicio, obligación, impuesto.
ear: oreja, espiga, la oreja, oído.
induced: inducido.
ladyship: señora, señoría.
madness: locura, demencia, chifladura.
madonna: Madona.
ought: haber que, deba, deber, haber de.
perpend: perpiaño, pesar, considerar,

meditar.
princess: princesa.
rule: regla, gobernar, la regla, norma, fallar, refrenar, dominio, subyugar, reprimir, regir, contener.
savours: sabores.
semblance: semejanza.
senses: juicio, los sentidos, sentido.
shame: vergüenza, verguenza, pudor, oprobio, avergonzar.
thy: tu.
unthought: desaconsejado.

To think me as well a **sister** as a wife,
One day shall **crown** the **alliance** on't, so please you,
Here at my house, and at my **proper** cost.

DUKE.
Madam, I am most **apt** to **embrace** your offer.--
[To VIOLA]
Your **master quits** you; and, for your service done him,
So much against the **mettle** of your **sex**,
So far **beneath** your **soft** and **tender breeding**,
And since you called me master for so long,
Here is my hand; you shall from this time be
You master's **mistress**.

OLIVIA.
A sister?--you are she.

[Re-enter FABIAN with MALVOLIO.]

DUKE.
Is this the **madman**?

OLIVIA.
Ay, my **lord**, this same;
How now, Malvolio?

MALVOLIO.
Madam, you have done me **wrong**,
Notorious wrong.

OLIVIA.
Have I, Malvolio? no.

MALVOLIO.
Lady, you have. **Pray** you **peruse** that letter:
You must not now **deny** it is your hand,
Write from it, if you can, in hand or phrase;
Or say 'tis not your **seal**, not your invention:

Spanish

alliance: alianza.
apt: apropiado.
beneath: debajo de, debajo, abajo.
breeding: cría, crianza, reproducción.
crown: corona, coronar.
deny: negar, negad, niego, niegas, niegan, negáis, negamos, nieguen, niega, niegue, desmentir.
embrace: abrazar, abarcar.
lord: señor, caballero.
madman: loco.
master: maestro, amo, dueño, patrón,

principal, magister.
mettle: temple.
mistress: señora.
peruse: lean, examina, leo, lees, leen, leemos, leéis, leed, lee, examino, examinen.
pray: rezar, rezáis, rezas, rezamos, rezad, reza, recen, rece, rezan, rezo, rogar.
proper: conveniente, preciso, correcto, apropiado, propio, debido.
quits: abandona, en paz.

seal: foca, sello, sellar, precinto, precintar.
sex: sexo, el sexo, tener sexo.
sister: hermana, la hermana, cuñada.
soft: blando, suave, tierno, dulce.
tender: tierno, oferta, dulce, subasta, proposición, ofrecer, destajo, licitación, presentar, reproducir, retratar.
wrong: malo, mal, falso, incorrecto, entuerto, agravio, impropio, erróneo.

You can say none of this. Well, grant it then,
And tell me, in the **modesty** of honour,
Why you have given me such clear **lights** of favour;
Bade me come **smiling** and cross-garter'd to you;
To put on yellow **stockings**, and to frown
Upon Sir Toby and the **lighter** people:
And, **acting** this in an **obedient** hope,
Why have you suffer'd me to be imprison'd,
Kept in a dark house, **visited** by the priest,
And made the most **notorious** geck and gull
That **e'er invention** played on? tell me why.

OLIVIA.
Alas, Malvolio, this is not my writing,
Though, I **confess**, much like the character:
But out of question, 'tis Maria's hand.
And now I do **bethink** me, it was she
First told me **thou** wast mad; then cam'st in smiling,
And in such **forms** which here were presuppos'd
Upon **thee** in the letter. Pr'ythee, be content:
This **practice** hath most **shrewdly** pass'd upon thee:
But, when we know the grounds and authors of it,
Thou **shalt** be both the **plaintiff** and the judge
Of **thine** own cause.

FABIAN.
                    Good madam, hear me speak;
And let no **quarrel**, nor no **brawl** to come,
Taint the **condition** of this present hour,
Which I have wonder'd at. In hope it shall not,
Most **freely** I confess, myself and Toby
Set this device against Malvolio here,
Upon some **stubborn** and **uncourteous** parts

Spanish

acting: acción, interino.
bethink: recapacitar, acordarse de, recordar.
brawl: reyerta, pelearse, alboroto.
condition: condición, acondicionar, estado.
confess: confesar, confiesan, confiesen, confieso, confiesas, confesamos, confesad, confesáis, confiesa, confiese, declarar.
e'er: nunca en la vida.
forms: formas, Formularios.

freely: libremente.
invention: invención, invento.
lighter: encendedor, mechero, gabarra.
lights: luces.
modesty: modestia, pudor.
notorious: notorio, fragante, infamo.
obedient: obediente, dócil.
plaintiff: demandante, querellante.
practice: ejercicio, practicar, emplear, práctica, ejercer.
quarrel: disputar, reñir, riña, pelear.
shalt: irá, verbo auxiliar inglés para

especificar futuro.
shrewdly: astutamente, perspicazmente, con perspicacia, sagazmente, mañosamente.
smiling: sonriente.
stockings: las medias.
stubborn: terco, testarudo, obstinado.
thee: ustedes, te, vosotros, usted, tú.
thine: tuyo, tuyos, tuyas, tuya, tus.
thou: tú, usted, vosotros, ustedes, vos.
uncourteous: descortés.
visited: visitado.

We had conceiv'd against him. **Maria** writ
The letter, at Sir Toby's great importance;
In **recompense whereof** he hath married her.
How with a **sportful malice** it was follow'd
May rather **pluck** on **laughter** than revenge,
If that the **injuries** be **justly** weigh'd
That have on both **sides** past.

OLIVIA.
Alas, poor **fool**! how have they **baffled thee**!

CLOWN.
Why, 'some are born great, some achieve **greatness**, and some have greatness **thrown** upon them.' I was one, sir, in this interlude;:--one Sir Topas, sir; but that's all one:--'By the Lord, fool, I am not mad;'--But do you remember? 'Madam, why laugh you at such a **barren rascal**? An you smile not, he's gagged'? And thus the **whirligig** of time **brings** in his revenges.

MALVOLIO.
I'll be revenged on the whole **pack** of you.
[Exit.]

OLIVIA.
He hath been most **notoriously** abus'd.

DUKE.
Pursue him, and **entreat** him to a peace:--
He hath not told us of the **captain** yet;
When that is known, and **golden** time convents,
A **solemn combination** shall be made
Of our dear souls.--Meantime, **sweet** sister,
We will not part from hence.--Cesario, come:
For so you shall be while you are a man;
But, when in other **habits** you are seen,
Orsino's **mistress**, and his fancy's queen.

Spanish

baffled: confundido.
barren: árido, estéril, yermo.
brings: trae.
captain: capitán.
combination: combinación.
entreat: demanden, rogáis, rueguen, ruegue, ruego, ruegas, ruegan, ruega, rogamos, demandad, demando.
fool: engañar, necio, tonto.
golden: dorado, áureo, de oro.
greatness: grandeza.
habits: hábitos.

injuries: las lesiones.
justly: justamente.
laugh: reír, reírse, risa, carcajada.
laughter: risa, la risa, carcajada.
malice: malicia.
maria: María.
mistress: señora.
notoriously: notoriamente.
pack: paquete, empacar, embalar, empaquetar, manada, envolver.
pluck: arrancar, tirón, cortar, desplumar.

rascal: bribón.
recompense: recompensa.
sides: costados, Lados.
solemn: solemne.
sportful: alegre.
sweet: dulce, caramelo, postre.
thee: ustedes, te, vosotros, usted, tú.
thrown: tirado, pp de throw.
whereof: de que, de lo cual, cuyo, del cual.
whirligig: molinete, movimiento confuso, tiovivo.

[Exeunt.]
CLOWN.
[Sings.]
When   that I was and a little **tiny** boy,
With **hey**, ho, the **wind** and the **rain**,
A **foolish** thing was but a toy,
For the rain it raineth every day.

But when I came to man's estate,
With hey, ho, the wind and the rain,
'Gainst **knave** and **thief** men **shut** their gate,
For the rain it raineth every day.

But when I came, **alas**! to wive,
With hey, ho, the wind and the rain,
By **swaggering** could I never thrive,
For the rain it raineth every day.

But when I came **unto** my bed,
With hey, ho, the wind and the rain,
With toss-pots still had **drunken** head,
For the rain it raineth every day.

A great while **ago** the world begun,
With hey, ho, the wind and the rain,
But that's all one, our **play** is done,
And **we'll strive** to **please** you every day.
[Exit.]

Spanish

ago: hace.
alas: ay, es una lástima.
drunken: borracho, ebrio.
foolish: zote, tonto, necio, bobo.
hey: eh, hola.
knave: bribón.
play: jugar, jueguen, juega, juegan, juegue, jugad, jugáis, jugamos, juegas, juego, tocar.
please: por favor, agradar, gustar, complacer, haz el favor, contentar, haz favor.
rain: llover, lluvia, la lluvia.
shut: cerrar, cerrado.
strive: esforzarse.
swaggering: pavoneándose, fanfarrón.
thief: ladrón.
tiny: diminuto.
unto: hacia.
we'll: Haremos.
wind: viento, serpentear, el viento, enrollar, devanar.

GLOSSARY

abatement: descuento, rebaja, reducción, disminución, supresión, baja, Abolición
abhors: detesta, aborrece, odia
abjured: abjurado, renunciado, contramandado
absence: ausencia, falta
absent: ausente
abused: maltratado
accent: acento, acentuar, acentúan, acentúas, acentúo, acentúen, acentuáis, acentuad, acentúa, acentúe, acentuamos
access: acceso, instinto, entrada, ataque, acceder, agresión, acometida
accident: accidente, desgracia, un accidente, el accidente
accomplished: realizado, cumplido, consumado, dotado, talentoso, terminado
accost: abordar, dirigirse a, abordamos, abordo, aborden, aborde, abordan, abordáis, abordad, aborda, abordas
accosted: abordado
accounted: contabilizados, contabilizo
achieve: realizar, realizan, realizad, realice, realicen, realiza, realizamos, realizas, realizo, realizáis, conseguir
acquaintance: conocido, conocimiento, notoriedad
acquit: absolver, absuelvan, absuelve, absuelvo, absuelves, absolvemos, absuelven, absolvéis, absolved, absuelva, pagar
acting: acción, interino
actions: acciones
a-day: día de llegada
add: sumar, sumad, sumáis, sumamos, suman, sumas, sume, sumen, suma, sumo, agregar
addicted: adicto
address: dirección, dirigir, discurso, señas, dirigirse a, alocución, dirigirse, domicilio, dirigir la palabra a

adds: suma, agrega, añade
adheres: adhiere
adieu: adiós
admirable: admirable, estupendo
admire: admirar, admiran, admiro, admiren, admiras, admiramos, admiráis, admirad, admira, admire
admit: confesar, confesad, confesáis, confieso, confiesen, confiese, confiesas, confiesan, confiesa, confesamos, admitir
adore: adorar, adoran, adoren, adore, adoro, adoras, adoramos, adoráis, adora, adorad
adored: adorado
adores: adora
advanced: avanzado, adelantado
advantage: ventaja, provecho, la ventaja
adverse: adverso, contrario
advises: aconseja
affairs: asuntos
affect: afectar, afecte, afectas, afecten, afectan, afectáis, afecta, afectad, afectamos, afecto, conmover
affection: afecto, cariño, afectuosidad, amor
affirmatives: afirmativo
afraid: miedoso, temeroso, asustado, medroso, miedo, encogido, angustioso, tímido, be - tener miedo
ago: hace
ah: ay
air: aire, airear, el aire, aéreo, orear
airs: aires
alas: ay, es una lástima
ale: cerveza
allay: calmar, aliviar
alliance: alianza
allied: aliado
allow: permitir, permitan, permitid, permiten, permites, permitimos, permite, permito, permitís, permita, dejar
allowed: permitido, dejado
alone: solo, único, solamente, sólo
along: a lo largo de, por

aloud: en voz alta
alphabetical: alfabético
alter: cambiar, cambia, cambien, cambie, cambias, cambian, cambio, cambiamos, cambiáis, cambiad, alterar
altered: cambiado, alterado, mudado
altogether: todo, en conjunto
amazed: asombrado, maravillado, pasmado, atónito
amend: enmendar, enmienden, enmiendas, enmiendan, enmendamos, enmendáis, enmendad, enmiendo, enmiende, enmienda, corregir
amends: enmienda, corrige, compensación
amiss: errado
ample: amplio, abundante
anatomy: anatomía
andrew: Andrés
anger: cólera, enojo, enfado, ira, enojar, furia
anne: Ana
anon: pronto
answer: respuesta, responder, contestar, contestación, responder a, corresponder al, contestar a, la respuesta, réplica
answered: contesta, Contestado
antique: antiguo, antigüedad, antigualla
apartment: apartamento, piso, cuarto
appear: aparecer, aparece, aparezco, aparezcan, apareces, aparecen, aparecemos, aparecéis, apareced, aparezca, parecer
appeared: Aparecido, comparecido
appears: aparece, comparece
appetite: apetito, el apetito
apple: manzana, la manzana
applies: emplea, aplica
apprehend: aprehender, aprehendemos, aprehendéis, aprehendo, aprehenden, aprehende, aprehendes, aprehendan, aprehended, aprehenda

apprehended: aprehendido
approach: aproximación, enfoque,
aproximarse, acercarse, acercar,
acercamiento, método,
planteamiento
approaches: aproches
approbation: aprobación
approve: aprobar, aprueban,
apruebo, apruebas, aprueba,
aprobamos, aprobáis, aprobad,
aprueben, apruebe
apt: apropiado
aptly: propensamente,
acertadamente, capazmente,
hábilmente, habilidoso,
oportunamente
aqua-vitae: aguardiente
argument: argumento, discusión, el
argumento
arguments: argumentos
arion: Programa de Visitas de
Estudio para Especialistas en Temas
Educativos
arrest: detención, detener, arrestar,
arresto, prender
arrived: llegado
art: arte, el arte
arts: letras, artes
aside: aparte, al lado
ask: preguntar, preguntáis,
preguntad, pregunto, pregunten,
preguntas, preguntan, preguntamos,
pregunte, pregunta, pedir
asking: preguntando, pidiendo,
solicitando
asleep: dormido
aspect: aspecto, vista
ass: burro, asno, culo
assail: asaltar, asalto, asalta, asaltáis,
asaltad, asaltamos, asaltan, asaltas,
asalten, asalte
assailant: agresor, atacador, atacante
assume: asumir, asumen, asumo,
asumís, asumimos, asumes, asume,
asuman, asumid, asuma, suponer
assurance: garantía, convicción,
aseguramiento
assure: asegurar, asegura, aseguren,
aseguras, aseguran, aseguramos,
aseguráis, asegurad, aseguro,
asegure, garantizar
attempt: intentar, intenta, intentad,
intentáis, intentamos, intentas,
intente, intenten, intentan, intento,
tentativa
attend: asistir, asistan, asisto, asistís,
asistimos, asistid, asistes, asisten,
asiste, asista, visitar
attendance: asistencia, servicio
attendant: asistente, sirviente,
acompañante
attendants: asistentes

attended: asistido
attending: asistiendo
attends: asiste
attire: atavío, indumentaria, atraer
attracts: atrae, encanta
audience: audiencia, público
aught: algo
augmentation: aumento
austere: austero
avoid: evitar, evito, evitan, evitamos,
evitáis, evitad, eviten, evita, evitas,
evite, eludir
awake: despierto, despertar,
despertarse
awhile: durante un rato, por un rato,
un momento, un rato
ay: sí
b: si, segundo
babbling: balbuceando, balbuceo
babylon: babel, Babilonia
bachelor: bachiller, soltero, solterón
bad: malo, mal, podrido
bade: pret de bid, Mandó
baffle: deflector, confundir,
confusión, tilbe
baffled: confundido
baited: Tentó
banished: Desterrado
bank: banco, orilla, ribera, el banco,
talud, batería, escaño
bar: barra, bar, salvo, cercar, taberna,
obstrucción, impedir, impidan,
cercad, cercáis, cercamos
barbarous: bárbaro
barren: árido, estéril, yermo
base: basar, pie, fundar, base,
basamento, casquillo, fundamentar
baseness: bajeza
basis: base
battery: batería, pila, acumulador
bay: bahía, caballo bayo,
compartimiento, bayo, ladrar
beagle: sabueso
bear: oso, llevar, el oso, bajista,
producir, dar a luz, parir, portar,
soportar
beard: barba, la barba, arista
bearing: cojinete, abolas, rodamiento
beat: golpear, batido, batir, pegar,
apalear, pulsación, latido,
batimiento
beating: paliza, pulsación, latido
beauteous: bello, bonito, hermoso
beautiful: bonito, hermoso, bello,
precioso
beauty: belleza, la belleza
becomes: acontece
bed: cama, lecho, cauce, la cama,
bancada, cuadro, madre
beds: las camas
beef: carne de vaca
befall: ocurrir, ocurrimos, ocurrís,

ocurrid, ocurres, ocurren, ocurre,
ocurran, ocurra, ocurro
befalls: ocurre
beggar: mendigo, pordiosero
begged: Mendigado
begging: mendicidad, mendigando,
mendigar
begin: empezar, empiecen, empezad,
empezáis, empiece, empieza,
empiezan, empiezas, empiezo,
empezamos, comenzar
begins: empieza, principia
beguile: engañar, engañad, engaño,
engañen, engañas, engañan,
engañáis, engaña, engañamos,
engañe
behaviour: comportamiento,
conducta
behold: tenga
belch: eructo, eructar
belie: desmentir, desmientes,
desmentid, desmiento, desmienten,
desmiente, desmientan, desmienta,
desmentís, desmentimos
belief: creencia, credo, fe
believes: cree
believing: creyendo
bells: las campanas
beloved: querido, amado, novio,
dilecto
bench: banco, estrado, banquillo,
escaño
beneath: debajo de, debajo, abajo
benefit: beneficio, ventaja, provecho,
prestación, subsidio, beneficiar,
lucro
bennet: cariofilada, hierba de san
benito
beseech: supliquen, rogáis, rogamos,
ruega, ruegan, ruegas, ruegue,
rueguen, suplica, suplicamos, rogad
besides: además, demás, además de,
amén de
bespeak: se encarga, ordenas,
ordenáis, ordenamos, ordenad,
ordenan, ordene, ordenen, ordena,
os encargáis, apalabro
bestow: conferir, otorgar
bestowed: conferido, otorgado,
concedido
betake: recurres, vayan, vaya, vamos,
van, voy, vais, va, recurro, recurrís,
recurrimos
bethink: recapacitar, acordarse de,
recordar
bethought: pret y pp de bethink
betimes: al alba, a tiempo
betray: traicionar, traiciona,
traiciono, traicionen, traiciona,
traicionan, traicionamos, traicionad,
traicionáis, traicione
betters: mejor

bewitched: embrujado

bias: sesgo, prejuicio, parcialidad, error sistemático, tendencia, polarización

bid: ofrecer, licitación, postura, oferta, solicitar, licitar, pedir, demandar, rogar, puja

bidding: licitación

bide: esperar, espera, esperad, esperáis, esperamos, esperan, esperas, espere, esperen, espero, aguardar

bigger: más grande, mayor, más

bind: liar, ligar, encuadernar, enlazar, obligar, comprometer, lazo

bird: pájaro, ave

blank: blanco, espacio en blanco, en blanco, formulario, vacío, hoja

blanks: segmentos lisos del cierre del cañón, recortes, cartones planos

blazon: blasón

blemish: defecto, mancha

blent: pret y pp de blend

bless: bendecir, bendecimos, bendigo, bendigan, bendices, bendicen, bendecís, bendecid, bendice, bendiga

blind: ciego, persiana, deslumbrar, deslumbrad, deslumbre, deslumbras, deslumbran, deslumbro, deslumbramos, deslumbráis, deslumbren

blood: sangre, la sangre

bloodless: incruento

bloody: sangriento, sanguinario, cruento

blow: soplar, golpe

blows: golpes

board: tabla, tablero, bordo, cartón, placa, panel, abordar, junta, tablón, cuadro, consejo

boat: barco, bote, barca, el barco

boiled: hervido

bold: grueso, negrita, audaz

boldly: audazmente

boldness: intrepidez

bond: lazo, bono, obligación, fianza, cinta, adherencia, enlace

bonds: cautiverio, bonos, obligaciones

bones: huesos, los huesos

boots: botas

bore: aburrir, barrena, taladrar, calibre, perforar, barrenar, barreno, perforación

born: nacido, nato

bosom: pecho, seno

bottom: fondo, suelo, inferior, lado inferior, el fondo, culo, posaderas, trasero

bought: comprado

bound: encuadernado, saltar, salto, ligado, límite, obligado

bounty: liberalidad, generosidad

bout: rato, ataque, combate

bow: proa, arco, reverencia, inclinarse, lazo

bowers: Enramadas

boy: chico, muchacho, niño, el muchacho, criado, chamaco

brag: jactarse, fanfarronear

brain: cerebro, seso

brains: sesos, inteligencia

branched: ramificado

brawl: reyerta, pelearse, alboroto

breach: brecha, infracción, contravención, incumplimiento, violación, violar

break: romper, descanso, interrupción, rotura, quebrar, corte, pausa, adiestrar, fractura, interrumpir

breast: pecho, seno, pechuga, mama

breath: aliento, respiración, hálito

breathed: respirado

breathes: respira

bred: pret y pp de breed, Criado

breed: raza, casta, criar

breeding: cría, crianza, reproducción

brief: breve, corto, informe, conciso

brimstone: fuego del infierno, azufre

brine: salmuera, escabeche

bring: traer, traigan, trae, traed, traéis, traemos, traen, traigo, traes, traiga, llevar

brings: trae

brisk: rápido

bristle: cerda, erizarse

broke: bollado, rotura, rompió, romper, pret de break, interrupción, fracturar, sin blanca, comienzo, pelado, descanso

brother: hermano, el hermano, cofrade

brothers: hermanos

brought: Traído

brow: ceja, frente

build: construir, edificar, tipo

bulk: volumen, granel, bulto, a granel, masa

bullets: balas, destacadores

burn: arder, quemar, quemadura, quemarse, encender, la quemadura, abrasar

cabin: cabaña, camarote, cabina, litera

cakes: pasteles, tortas, tarta

calamity: calamidad

call: llamada, llamar, llaman, llamen, llamad, llamas, llamo, llamamos, llamáis, llame, llama

calls: llama, llamadas

canary: canario

candle: vela, la vela, bujía, candela, cirio

cannon: cañón

cannot: presente de no poder

canopied: doselado, endoselado

capacity: capacidad

caper: cabriola, alcaparra

captain: capitán

careful: cuidadoso, prudente, circunspecto, precavido

carpet: alfombra, la alfombra, alfombrar

carriage: coche, carro, cureña

carry: llevar, llevamos, lleváis, llevad, lleva, lleven, llevo, llevan, llevas, lleve, cargar

cars: carros, los coches

cast: lanzar, lanzamiento, arrojar, echar, colar, elenco, molde

catch: coger, cogéis, cojan, coged, cogemos, cogen, coges, coja, coge, cojo, asir

catches: coge, ase, acierta

catechize: catequizar, catequizáis, catequizo, catequizas, catequizamos, catequizad, catequiza, catequicen, catequice, catequizan

caterwauling: maullidos, aullidos, maullido, maullar, chillidos

caught: cogido, asido, acertado

cause: causa, causar, ocasionar, dar lugar a, instigar, producir, maquinar, provocar

celebration: fiesta, celebración, festividad

ceremony: ceremonia

chain: cadena, la cadena, encadenar

challenge: reto, desafiar, desafío, retar, recusación, impugnar

challenged: Desafiado, recibe

chamber: cámara, habitación, cuarto

chance: azar, suerte, acontecimiento, acaso, oportunidad

changeable: cambiable

chant: corear, canto

chantry: capellañía, capilla

chapter: capítulo, capitulo, sección

charge: carga, cargo, acusación, gastos, cargar, cobro, cobrar, imputación

charges: cargos

charity: caridad, limosna, misericordia, beneficencia

chase: cazar, perseguir, persecución, caza, cincelar

check: cheque, comprobar, revisar, control, controlar, cuenta, talón, verificación, contener, verificar, reprimir

cheek: mejilla, la mejilla, carrillo

chide: regañar, reprender, reprended, reprende, reprendan, reprendemos, reprenden, reprendéis, regañas,

regañen, regañan
chin: barba, barbilla, la barbilla,
mentón
choose: escoger, escojan, escoges,
escogen, escogemos, escogéis,
escoged, escojo, escoge, escoja, elegir
christian: cristiano
chuck: caricia, acariciar, calzo,
mandril
churchman: clérigo
churlish: rústico
circumstance: condición,
circunstancia
civil: civil
clamorous: clamoroso
clearly: claramente
cleft: hendido, grieta
clock: reloj, el reloj, ceas
clog: obstruir, zueco, traba, empatar
cloistress: monja
close: cerrar, cierras, cierra, cierren,
cerráis, cerrad, cerramos, cierro,
cierre, cierran, cerca
clothes: ropa, viste, la ropa, ropaje
clown: payaso, el payaso
coats: membranas
codling: bacalao, bacalao pequeño
coffer: panel empotrado
coffin: ataúd
cohere: pegan, unen, unes, unís, une,
unan, una, peguen, pegue, pego,
pegas
cold: frío, resfriado, catarro,
constipado
collier: minero
colour: color, colorear, coloración
colours: bandera
combination: combinación
comedian: cómico, comediante
comes: Viene
comfort: comodidad, consolar,
anchas, consuelo, confort
comfortable: cómodo, agradable
coming: viniendo, proveniente,
próximo, originario, natural
command: mando, orden, mandato,
comando, instrucción, capitanear,
acaudillar
commend: alabar, alabo, alaben,
alabe, alabas, alaban, alabamos,
alabáis, alaba, alabad, recomendar
commendation: alabanza
commended: alabado
commerce: comercio
commission: comisión, encargar,
encargo, comisionar
commodity: artículo, producto
básico, producto, artículo de
consumo
common: común
compare: comparar, comparas,
comparen, comparo, compare,

comparan, comparamos, comparáis,
compara, comparad, cotejar
competent: competente
competitors: competencia
complexion: cutis, tez
con: estafas, estudien, estudie,
estudias, estudian, estudiamos,
estudiáis, estudiad, estudia, estafo,
estudio
conceal: ocultar, ocultamos, oculten,
ocultan, ocultáis, ocultad, oculta,
ocultas, oculto, oculte, recatar
concealment: ocultamiento,
ocultación, encubrimiento
conceited: presumido, hueco
concerning: en cuanto a, acerca de,
por lo tocante a, respecto de
concerns: concierne
conclusion: conclusión
concurs: concurre
condemn: condenar, condenas,
condenen, condenan, condenamos,
condenáis, condenad, condeno,
condene, condena, desaprobar
condition: condición, acondicionar,
estado
conduct: conducir, guiar, dirigir,
conducta, comportamiento
confess: confesar, confiesan,
confiesen, confieso, confiesas,
confesamos, confesad, confesáis,
confiesa, confiese, declarar
confine: limitar, confín
confirms: confirma
cons: estafa, estudia, engaña,
CONTRA
consanguineous: consanguíneo
conscience: conciencia
consecrated: consagrado
consequently: por consiguiente
consider: considerar, considerad,
considero, consideren, consideras,
consideran, consideramos,
consideráis, considera, considere,
contemplar
consideration: consideración,
contraprestación, contemplación
consist: consistir, consista, consiste,
consisten, consistan
consists: consiste
constancy: constancia
constant: constante, continuo
constantly: constantemente, siempre,
continuamente
constellation: constelación
constitution: constitución,
complexión
constrained: encogido
construction: construcción
construe: interpretar
contagion: contagio
contagious: contagioso

contemplation: contemplación
contemplative: contemplativo
contempt: desprecio, menosprecio
continent: continente, el continente
continuance: persistencia
continue: continuar, continúe,
continuad, continuáis, continuamos,
continúan, continúas, continúen,
continúo, continúa, durar
contract: contrato, contrata, destajo,
contraer
contracted: contraído, contratado
contrary: contrario
conveniently: convenientemente
convey: alargar, entregar, llevar,
entrega, entregan, entreguen,
entregue, entregas, entregamos,
entregáis, entregad
copy: copiar, copia, traslado,
trasladar, la copia
corner: esquina, ángulo, rincón
coroner: médico forense
corpse: cadáver
corrupter: corruptor
cost: costar, costo, coste, gastos
counsel: consejo, aconsejar, abogado,
anunciar
count: contar, recuento, cuenta,
conde, calcular, entrar en cuenta,
computar, unidad de cuenta, cargo
counterfeit: falsificación, falsificar,
contrahecho
countess: condesa
countryman: compatriota
couplet: pareado
courteous: cortés
courtesy: cortesía
courtier: cortesano, palaciego
cousin: primo, prima, el primo
covetousness: deseo
coward: cobarde, el cobarde
coxcomb: cresta de crías de gallina,
cresta de gallo, fatuo, mequetrefe
craft: astucia, destreza, embarcación,
oficio
cram: atestar, empollar, apretura,
abarrotado, repaso de última hora,
rellenar con, hartarse de comer,
emborrar, cebar, atiborrar,
atiborramiento
crammed: Atracado, hasta los topes
crave: ansiar, pedir, ansía, ansío,
ansíen, ansíe, ansías, ansían, ansiad,
ansiáis, ansiamos
craves: ansía
credit: crédito, haber, acreditar
creep: arrastrarse, arrastrar,
deslizamiento, arrastre, fluencia,
arrastras, arrastren, arrastran,
arrastramos, arrastráis, arrastrad
crow: el cuervo, corneja, cuervo
crown: corona, coronar

crowned: verdadero, coronado
cruel: cruel
cruelty: crueldad, sevicia
crush: compresión, aplastar
cry: llorar, grito, gritar, lamento
cub: cachorro
cuckold: cornudo
cudgel: garrote corto
cuff: puño, puño de la camisa
cunning: astucia, astuto, hábil
cup: taza, la taza, copa
cur: perro chusco o de mala casta, perro, hombre vil, de mala raza, chucho, canalla, vil
curate: coadjutor, cura
curio: curiosidad
curl: rizo, bucle, rizar, rizarse, rotacional, encrespar
curtain: cortina, la cortina
cut: cortar, corte, cortado, cortadura
cypress: ciprés
dagger: daga, puñal
dallies: tarda
dally: perder el tiempo, tardar, tarda, tardo, tardas, tarde, tardan, tardamos, tardáis, tardad, tarden
damask: damasco
damned: condenado, maldito
dance: bailar, baile, danza, danzar, el baile
dancing: bailando, baile
danger: peligro, el peligro
dare: atreverse, reto, cariño
dares: aventura, desafía, osa, se arriesga, se atreve
dark: oscuro, tenebroso
darkly: cetrinamente, misteriosamente, oscuramente, tristemente
darkness: tinieblas, oscuridad, la oscuridad
daughter: hija, la hija, Nina
daughters: hijas
dead: muerto
deadly: mortal
deal: trato, transacción
dealing: trato
dear: caro, querido, estimado
debt: deuda
decreed: decretado
dedication: dedicación, dedicatoria
deed: escritura, acto, hecho, hazaña
deem: creer, crea, creemos, crees, creo, creen, creéis, creed, crean, cree, contemplar
deeply: profundamente
defence: defensa, retaguardia
defend: defender, defiendes, defiendo, defendéis, defendemos, defiendan, defienden, defended, defiende, defienda
defy: desafiar, desafiáis, desafío,

desafíen, desafías, desafiamos, desafiad, desafía, desafían, desafíe
degree: grado, título, licencia
deity: deidad
delay: retraso, retardo, demora, retrasar, demorar, retardar
delight: deleitar, delicia, encantar
deliver: entregar, entregas, entrego, entregan, entregamos, entregáis, entregad, entreguen, entrega, entregue
delivered: entregado
delivers: entrega
demure: recatado, grave
denial: negación, denegación
denied: negado, desmentido
deny: negar, negad, niego, niegas, niegan, negáis, negamos, nieguen, niega, niegue, desmentir
denying: negando, desmintiendo
depart: salir, salís, salgo, salga, sales, salen, saled, sale, salgan, salimos, sal
deplore: deplorar, deploro, deploren, deplore, deploráis, deploras, deplorad, deplora, deploran, deploramos
derives: deriva
deserve: merecer, merecemos, merezcan, merezco, merecen, mereced, merece, mereces, merecéis, merezca
desire: desear, deseo, tener, querer, gana, codiciar
desirous: deseoso
desperate: desesperado
despite: a pesar de
determinate: determinado
detested: detestado
detests: detesta
detraction: detracción
device: aparato, dispositivo, artefacto, mecanismo
devil: diablo, el diablo
devils: diablo
devotion: devoción
devout: devoto
dialogue: diálogo
die: morir, morid, mueran, muere, morís, mueren, mueres, muero, morimos, muera, molde
died: muerto
dies: muere
digest: compendio, digerir
dimension: dimensión, tamaño
direct: directo, mandar, guiar, derecho, dirigir
directly: directamente, seguido
dirty: sucio, ensuciar, verde, manchar
discard: desecho, despedir, desechar, descartar
discourse: discurso
discovers: descubre

discreet: discreto
disgraced: deshonrado
disguise: disfraz, disfrazar
dish: plato, el plato, guiso
dishonest: ímprobo, deshonesto
dishonesty: deshonestidad
dislike: aversión, repugnancia, detestar, detesto, detesten, deteste, detestas, detestan, detesta, detestamos, detestáis
dismiss: despedir, despedimos, despido, despiden, despide, despides, despedís, despedid, despidan, despida, expedir
dismount: apearse, desmontar, desmontad, desmonta, desmonto, desmonten, desmonte, desmontáis, desmontamos, desmontan, desmontas
disposed: dispuesto
disposition: disposición, talento, capacidad
dispossess: desposeer, desposea, desposeo, desposees, desposeen, desposeemos, desposeéis, desposeed, desposease, desposean, desapoderar
dissemble: disimular, disimula, disimulo, disimulen, disimulas, disimulan, disimulamos, disimuláis, disimulad, disimule, ocultar
dissembled: disimulado
dissembling: disimulando
distaff: tareas femeninas, rueca
distemper: moquillo, pintura al temple
distempered: destemplado
distinction: distinción
distraction: distracción
distrust: desconfianza
divers: varios, diversos
divinity: divinidad
division: división, escisión
divorced: divorciado
divulged: divulgado
doctrine: doctrina
doer: hacedor
dog: perro, el perro, la perra, can
dogged: obstinado
dogs: los perros, las perras
doors: las puertas
dormouse: lirón
dote: chochear, chochean, chochee, chocheen, chocheas, chocheáis, chochea, chochead, chocheo, chocheamos
double: doble, doblar, doblado
double-dealer: traidor
double-dealing: falsía
doublet: jubón, doblete
doubt: dudar, duda
doubtful: dudoso

dowry: dote
dram: aperitivo, dracma
draught: calado, trago
draw: dibujar, dibujáis, dibujad, dibujen, dibuje, dibujas, dibujamos, dibuja, dibujan, dibujo, tirar
drawn: dibujado, encantado, trazado
dream: soñar, sueño, ensueño
dressed: vestido, con guarnición de
drink: beber, bebida, tomar, el refresco, trago, copa
drinking: potable, el beber, bebida, beber
drive: conducir, conducen, conduzcan, conduzco, conducís, conducimos, conduzca, conduces, conduce, conducid, propulsión
drives: conduce, maneja
driving: conduciendo, manejando, conducción, conducir
drop: gota, caer, disminuir, amainar, decrecer, menguar, caída, descenso, dejar caer
dropped: soltar
drown: ahogarse, ahogar
drowned: se ahogado, ahogado
drowns: se ahoga
drunk: borracho, bebido, ebrio
drunken: borracho, ebrio
drunkenness: embriaguez, ebriedad, borrachera
dry: seco, secar, enjugar
dubbed: se apodado, reproducido, dobló, doblado
duke: duque
dulcet: dulce
dumbness: mudez, tonterías comprensibles, estupidez
dust: polvo, quitar el polvo, quitar el polvo a
duty: deber, servicio, obligación, impuesto
dwell: morar, morad, moren, moras, moráis, moran, moramos, mora, more, moro, habitar
dwelt: pret de dwell, pp de dwell
dying: muriendo, agonizante
ear: oreja, espiga, la oreja, oído
earlier: mas temprano
earned: ganado
ears: orejas, las orejas, oídos
easily: fácilmente
easy: fácil
eat: comer, comemos, comes, coméis, comed, coman, como, comen, coma, Come
eater: tener siempre buen apetito, comedero, comedor, manzana, agua
eating: comiendo
ebony: ébano
echo: eco, resonar, el eco
edified: edificado

e'er: nunca en la vida
egyptian: egipcio, egipcíaco
eight: ocho
elder: mayor, anciano, saúco
eldest: mayor
element: elemento, ingrediente
elements: elementos, abecé, alfabeto
eleven: once
eloquent: elocuente
em: ingeniero de mineras
embassy: embajada
embrace: abrazar, abarcar
employment: empleo, trabajo, acomodo
empty: vacío, vaciar, evacuar, desocupado, desocupar
enchantment: encantamiento
encounter: encuentro, encontrar, encuentran, encuentren, encuentre, encuentras, encuentra, encontramos, encontrad, encontráis, hallar
endeavour: tratar de, esforzarse por, esfuerzo
ended: finalizó, terminado
endue: dotar
endure: durar, duráis, duro, duren, dure, duras, duran, duramos, dura, durad, tolerar
enemy: enemigo
enjoy: disfrutar, disfrutas, disfrutan, disfrutamos, disfrutáis, disfrutad, disfruta, disfruto, disfruten, disfrute, gozar
enlarge: ampliar, amplíe, amplía, amplíen, amplías, amplían, ampliamos, ampliáis, ampliad, amplío, agrandar
enraged: enfurecido
enter: entrar, entro, entra, entrad, entráis, entramos, entran, entras, entren, entre, inscribir
enters: entra, inscribe, monta
entertainment: recreación, entretenimiento, diversión, función
entrance: entrada, la entrada
entreat: demanden, rogáis, rueguen, ruegue, ruego, ruegas, ruegan, ruega, rogamos, demandad, demando
envy: envidiar, envidiad, envidiáis, envidiamos, envidian, envidias, envidie, envidien, envidio, envidia
enwraps: envuelve
equal: igual
equinoctial: equinoccial
ere: antes de
error: equivocación, error, yerro
escape: escaparse, escapar, huida, fuga, escape, evadir, escapada, huir
estate: finca, granja, propiedad, herencia, hacienda, patrimonio
estimable: apreciable, estimable

eternal: eterno
eunuch: eunuco
event: acontecimiento, evento, suceso, acaecimiento, ocurrencia
everything: todo
everywhere: en todas partes, por todas partes
evident: evidente
exalted: exaltado
example: ejemplo, el ejemplo
exasperate: exasperar, exaspera, exasperen, exasperas, exasperan, exasperamos, exasperáis, exasperad, exaspero, exaspere
exceed: aventajar, aventajan, aventajen, aventajo, aventajas, aventajáis, aventajad, aventaja, aventaje, aventajamos, exceder
exceeding: aventajando, excediendo, sobrepasando
excellence: excelencia
excellent: excelente
excellently: magníficamente, relevantemente, excelentemente, muy bien, sobresalientemente
except: excepto, menos, exceptuar, además de, amén de
excepted: excepto, exceptuando
exceptions: excepciones
excess: exceso, excedente
excites: instiga, excita
excuse: excusa, excusar, disculpa, disculpar
executed: ejecutado
exeunt: salen
expenses: gastos, expensas
expose: exponer, exponen, expongo, expongan, expones, exponemos, exponéis, exponed, expon, expone, exponga
express: expresar, expresa, expresas, expresen, expresan, expresamos, expresáis, expresad, expreso, exprese
exquisite: exquisito
extend: extender, alargar, ampliar, extiende, amplías, extendéis, amplíen, amplío, extiendo, extended, extienden
extort: arrancar, arrancáis, arranquen, arranco, arrancas, arrancamos, arrancad, arranca, arrancan, arranque, extorsionar
extracting: extraer
extravagancy: extravagancia, gasto excesivo, gastos excesivos
exult: regocijarse, exultar, exultas, exulto, exulte, exultan, exulta, exulten, exultáis, exultad, exultamos
eye: ojo, el ojo, ojear, mirar
fabian: fabianista
fair: justo, rubio, mercado, feria,

verbena, bazar, equitativo, hermoso
fairly: bastante, con justicia
faith: fe, la fe
fall: caer, os caéis, cáedos, se caen, se
cae, te caes, caígase, cáete, caíganse,
me caigo, nos caemos
falls: se cae, decrece, derriba
false: falso
fame: fama, hambre, conocimientos,
la fama, gloria
familiar: conocido
fancies: extravagante
fancy: figurarse, de fantasía,
imaginación
fantastically: fantásticamente
fare: tarifa, pasaje
farewell: adiós, despedida
fashion: moda
fat: gordo, grasa, grueso, manteca
fatal: mortal
fate: destino, suerte, sino, hado
fault: culpa, defecto, avería, falla,
falta, fallo, error, imperfección
faults: desperfecto, fallas
favour: favor, favorecer
fear: temer, miedo, temor, angustia,
recelar
fearful: temeroso, medroso,
angustioso
feast: banquete, fiesta
feature: característica, facción,
función, rasgo
feed: alimentar, alimentad,
alimenten, alimente, alimentas,
alimentan, alimentáis, alimenta,
alimentamos, alimento, dar de
comer
feelingly: con sentimiento
feet: los pies, pies
feign: fingir, fingen, finjo, finjan,
finja, fingís, fingimos, finges, finge,
fingid, aparentar
feigned: fingido, aparentado
feigning: fingiendo, aparentando
fell: talar, derribar
fellow: compañero, hombre, socio,
tipo, becario
fence: reja, valla, cerca, vallado,
obstrucción, la cerca, cercado
fencer: esgrimidor, floretista
fencing: esgrima
fertile: fértil, fecundo
fervour: celo
fetch: traer, traemos, traed, trae,
traéis, traes, traigo, traigan, traen,
traiga, coger
fiction: ficción
field: campo, el campo, zona, cancha
fiend: demonio
fight: luchar, pelear, lucha, combate,
pelea, batallar, riña, combatir
fighter: luchador, combatiente

filed: archivado
finder: descubridor
finds: funda, funde
fine: multa, fino, multar, excelente,
bonito, delgado, bien, estupendo,
bueno
fingers: los dedos
finished: acabado, terminado, listo,
concluido
fire: fuego, incendio, despedir,
disparar, el fuego, tirar, animar,
incitar, lumbre, hacer fuego,
encender
fit: adaptar, acomodar, ajustar,
apoplejía, ajuste, caber, ataque, en
forma, encajar
five-fold: quíntuplo
fixed: fijo, fijado, reparado
flatter: adular, adula, adulo, adulen,
adule, adulas, adulan, adulamos,
aduláis, adulad, halagar
flatterer: lisonjero, adulador
flax: lino
flea: pulga, la pulga
fleet: flota, parque
flesh: carne, pulpa
flint: pedernal
flock: bandada, rebaño, manada
flood: diluvio, inundación, enterrar,
pleamar, inundar
flower: flor, la flor, florecer
fly: volar, voláis, vuelen, vuele,
vuelas, volamos, vuela, volad,
vuelan, vuelo, mosca
foamy: espumoso, espumante
fog: niebla, bruma, neblina, la neblina
follow: seguir, seguid, sigues, siguen,
sigue, sigo, sigan, seguís, seguimos,
siga, venir después
followed: seguido
follower: seguidor
follows: sigue
folly: tontería
fond: aficionado
food: comida, alimento, comestibles,
alimentos, plato
fool: engañar, necio, tonto
foolery: tontería
fooling: engañar
foolish: zote, tonto, necio, bobo
foot: pie, pata, el pie, pujamen
forbear: antepasado
forbid: prohibir, prohibid, prohiban,
prohibo, prohibimos, prohibes,
prohiben, prohíbe, prohibís, prohíba
force: fuerza, forzar, obligar, virtud
forehead: frente, la frente
foreknowledge: presciencia
forgive: perdonar, perdona,
perdonad, perdono, perdonen,
perdonas, perdonan, perdonamos,
perdonáis, perdone

forgot: olvidado, pret de forget
forgotten: olvidado
formal: formal
formed: formó, formado
forms: formas, Formularios
forswear: abjurar, abjuráis, abjuro,
abjuren, abjure, abjuras, abjuramos,
abjurad, abjura, abjuran
forth: adelante
fortified: fortificado
fortune: suerte, fortuna
forty: cuarenta
foul: falta, asqueroso, sucio
fourteen: catorce
fox: zorro, el zorro
frail: frágil
frailty: debilidad, flaqueza, cosa
débil, fragilidad
fraught: cargado
freedom: libertad
freely: libremente
frenzy: frenesí
fresh: fresco
friend: amigo, amiga, el amigo
friends: amigos, los amigos
fright: espanto, susto, miedo,
angustia, terror
front: frente, fachada, delantero, el
frente, frontón, delantera
frown: ceño, fruncir el entrecejo,
fruncir el ceño
fruitless: infructuoso
fulsome: de mal gusto
function: función, funcionar, cargo,
oficio
furious: torcido, furioso, furibundo
furnish: amueblar, amueblas,
amueblen, amueblo, amueble,
amueblamos, amuebláis, amuebla,
amueblan, amueblad, suministrar
fury: furia, furor
fustian: fustán
gabble: charla
gagged: amordazado
gait: paso
gall: bilis, hiel, agalla
garde: guarda
garden: jardín, el jardín
garments: ornamentos
gate: puerta, paso, verja, compuerta,
barrera
generous: generoso, dadivoso
genius: genio, ingenio
gentle: dulce, suave, manso, apacible
gentleman: caballero, señor,
gentilhombre
gentlemen: señores
gentleness: apacibilidad, suavidad
gentlewoman: dama
gently: suavemente
giant: gigante
giddily: mareadamente, frívolamente

giddy: mareado
gift: regalo, donación, el regalo, don, talento
gifts: regalos
gilt: dorado
gin: ginebra, la ginebra
ginger: jengibre
gives: da
giving: dando
glad: alegre, contento
glass: vidrio, vaso, cristal, copa, el vidrio
glorious: glorioso, famoso
glove: guante, el guante
god: Dios
godliness: piedad
gods: paraíso, gallinero
goes: va, marcha
gold: oro, el oro, de oro
golden: dorado, áureo, de oro
gone: ido, marchado
gossip: cotillear, cotilleo, chismear, chismes, los chismes, chismorreo
governs: gobierna, capitanea, rige, reprime
gown: vestido, toga
grace: gracia, garbo, honrar
graces: Gracias
gracious: cortés
grain: grano, cereal, veta, fibra
grand: magnífico, grande, grandioso
grant: subvención, concesión, beca, conceder, subsidio, otorgar, otorgamiento, donación, ceder
grapple: agarrar, asir, coger
grave: tumba, grave, crítico, sepulcro
gravity: gravedad
greatness: grandeza
greek: griego
green: verde
grew: creció, pret de grow, crecida
grey: gris, pardo
grief: pesar, dolor
grieves: aflige, apena
grizzle: color gris, gimoteado, gimotear
gross: bruto, asqueroso, grueso, doce docenas
grossly: groseramente
grossness: grosería
ground: suelo, terreno, tierra, molido, masa, conexión a tierra, el suelo, fondo, fundamento
grounds: terreno
grow: crecer, crecen, crezco, crece, creced, crecemos, crezcan, crecéis, creces, crezca, cultivar
grown: crecido, aumentado, adulto
grows: crece, aumenta
guard: guardia, guardar, vigilar, cobrador, guarda, revisor, defender, proteger, amparar

guilt: culpa
guiltless: inocente
gull: gaviota
gust: ráfaga, racha
ha: ah, decir ah, ja
habit: costumbre, hábito, resabio, mala costumbre
habits: hábitos
haggard: ojeroso, macilento, demacrado
hair: pelo, cabello, el pelo, vello
hale: sano
halting: parar, detenerse, hacer alto, renqueante, parada, interrupción, interrumpir, claudicante, vacilante, alto, detener
handmaid: sirvienta, criada, peón
hands: las manos
hang: colgar
hanged: colgar, ahorcado, continuar, caída, colgó
hanging: ahorcamiento, pendiente
hangs: continúa, cuelga
hap: destino, pase, tener suerte
haply: posiblemente
happy: feliz, alegre, contento
hard: duro, difícil, tieso
hard-hearted: corazón duro, duro, duro de corazón, empedernido, insensible
hardly: apenas
hardy: robusto, fuerte, resistente, audaz
hare: liebre
harm: daño, dañar, perjudicar a, detrimento, dañar a, perjuicio, mal
hart: venado, de Ciervo, Ser Un Ciervo, ciervo
hast: haya
haste: prisa, precipitación
hate: odiar, odio, aborrecer, detestar
havoc: estrago, destrucción
headstrong: terco, cabezudo, caprichoso, impetuoso, obstinado, testarudo, testarudo tozudo, voluntarioso, ingobernable
healths: sanidad
hear: oír, oigan, oyes, oyen, oye, oís, oigo, oíd, oímos, oiga
heard: oído
heart: corazón, cogollo
hearts: corazones, copas
heat: calor, calentar, el calor, hornada, carga de fusión
heathen: pagano
heaven: cielo
heavens: cielo, cielos
heels: taco, tacón
held: tuvo lugar, sostuvo
hell: infierno
hence: de aquí a, por tanto
henceforth: de aquí en adelante

heresy: herejía
hermit: ermitaño
herrings: arenque
herself: sí, ella misma, se, sí misma
hey: eh, hola
hid: escondió, pret de hide
hide: ocultar, oculto, oculta, oculte, ocultas, ocultan, ocultamos, ocultáis, ocultad, oculten, piel
hideous: horroroso, abominable, horrible
hie: ir caminando, apresurar, caminar, correr, pasear, ir con pasos, ir paseando, ir volando
higher: superior
highest: sumo, el más alto, suma, máximo, sumamente, alto, máxima
history: historia, la historia
hit: golpear, acertar, golpe, pegar, llamar, éxito
hither: acá
hob: hornillo, fresa-madre, fresamatriz, hornilla, quemador, punzón de acuñación, placa, cubierta
hoist: montacargas, enarbolar, izar, polipasto
hold: tener, sujetar, continuar, retención, sostener, contener, mantener, retenido, presa, bodega
hollow: hueco, cavidad, hondonada, vacuo
holy: santo, sagrado
homage: homenaje
honest: honrado, sincero, honesto
honesty: honestidad, honradez
honour: honor, homenaje
honourable: honorable
hope: esperanza, esperar, espera, espere, esperen, esperas, esperan, esperamos, esperáis, esperad, espero
hopes: espera
horrible: temeroso, abominable, lúgubre, horroroso, horrible
horribly: horriblemente
horrid: hórrido
horse: caballo, el caballo, potro, cabio
hot: caliente, picante, caluroso
hour: hora, la hora
hours: horas, las horas
housekeeper: ama de casa, ama de llaves
houses: casas
howling: aullido, lamentarse, clamoroso, aullador, alarido, aullar, lamento, gritar, rugir, grito, dar alaridos
hull: casco, cáscara
humble: humilde, humillar
humour: humor
hungry: hambriento
hunt: cazar, cazo, caza, cazáis, cazas,

cazamos, cazad, cacen, cace, cazan, acosar
hunter: cazador
hurling: lanzar
hurt: doler, herir, dañar, herida, lastimar
husband: marido, esposo, el esposo
hyperbolical: hiperbólico
icicle: carámbano
i'd: Hago
idiot: idiota, bobo, estúpido
idle: ocioso, haraganear, perezoso, inactivo, en reposo
idleness: ociosidad
idol: ídolo
ignorance: ignorancia
ignorant: ignorante
ill: enfermo, malo, doliente
image: imagen, grabado, retrato, reproducción
imagination: imaginación
imitate: imitar, imite, imito, imitamos, imitas, imitáis, imitan, imitad, imita, imiten
impetuosity: irreflexión, impetuosidad
implacable: cosa implacable
impossible: imposible
improbable: inverosímil, improbable
incensed: encolerizado, indignado, inciensado
incites: incita
inconstant: inconstante, voluble
increasing: creciente
incredulous: incrédulo
indeed: verdaderamente, en efecto, de veras, en realidad, efectivamente
india: India
indies: indias
indifferent: indiferente
indignation: indignación
induced: inducido
inevitable: inevitable
infection: infección
infirmity: enfermedad, debilidad
ingrate: desagradecido, ingrato, desleal
ingratitude: ingratitud
inhabit: habitar, habite, habitan, habito, habitas, habitamos, habitáis, habitad, habita, habiten
injunction: requerimiento, interdicto
injuries: las lesiones
injury: lesión, herida, daño
ink: tinta, la tinta, entintar
inner: interior, interno, interna
innocence: inocencia, la inocencia
instance: instancia, ejemplo, ejemplar
instant: momento, instante, momentáneo, instantáneo
intent: intento, intención, propósito
interim: interino

intimate: íntimo, cómodo, intimo
inure: habituar
invention: invención, invento
inventoried: inventariado
invisible: invisible
iron: hierro, planchar, plancha, de hierro, el hierro, fierro
item: artículo, elemento, partida, ítem, rubro
iv: IV - intravenoso
jade: fatigar, cansar, jade
jaws: mordazas
jealous: celoso
jealousy: celos
jest: bromear, broma
jester: bromista
jesting: chistes, dichos, en broma, chistoso, chanzas, bromas, bromeando, burlón, guasón
jests: bromas
jets: azabaches, chorros
jewel: joya, la joya
jezebel: Jezabel
jig: giga
jocund: jocundo
joinder: reunión, acumulación, acumulación de acciones, comunidad, asociación
jolly: alegre, jovial
jot: pizca
jove: Júpiter
judgment: juicio, fallo, sentencia, criterio
justly: justamente
keeps: guarda, vigila, conserva, preserva
kept: guardado, vigilado, conservado, preservado
kill: matar
kin: parientes
kindly: amablemente, bondadosamente, amable
kindness: amabilidad, la bondad
king: rey, el rey
kinsman: pariente
kiss: besar, beso, besarse
kisses: besos
knave: bribón
knavery: bribonada
knight: caballero, caballo
knot: nudo, correlimos gordo, lazo
knowledge: conocimiento, saber
knows: sabe, conoce
labelled: etiquetado, marcado
lack: falta, carencia, escasez, faltar, carecer de, carecer
lacks: le falta
lad: muchacho, chico
ladies: damas, señoras
lady: dama, señora
ladyship: señora, señoría
laid: puesto, colocado, recostado,

acostado
lamb: cordero, carne de cordero, el cordero, borrego, oveja
languages: las lenguas
lapsed: decrépito
lasting: continuo, duradero
late: tarde, tardío, tardo
lately: últimamente
laudable: digno de loor
laugh: reír, reírse, risa, carcajada
laughter: risa, la risa, carcajada
lay: poner, colocar, coloque, colocamos, pongan, ponga, pones, ponen, ponemos, ponéis, poned
lead: plomo, guiar, guía, conducir, guiáis, guiamos, guían, guías, guíe, guíen, guío
lean: apoyarse, fino, magro, enjuto, apoyar, delgado
leap: saltar, salto, brincar, el salto
learned: aprendido, estudiado, docto, erudito, sabio
leasing: arrendamiento, alquiler, arriendo
least: menos, mínimo, menor
leave: salir, sal, sale, salís, salimos, salgo, salgan, salga, sales, salen, saled
leaves: sale, deja, hojas, las hojas
leaving: saliendo, dejando
lechery: libertinaje, lascivia
led: guiado, conducido, dirigido
leg: pierna, la pierna, pata, tramo
legion: legión
legitimate: legítimo
legs: las piernas
lend: prestar, presto, preste, presten, prestas, prestan, prestamos, prestáis, prestad, presta
lenten: cuaresmal
lest: para que no, a no ser que, con el fin de, no sea que, si es necesario
lethargy: letargo
lets: deja, alquila
let's: permítanos
letter: carta, letra, la carta
letters: letras
licence: licencia, permiso
lids: cubiertas
lie: mentir, mentira, yacer, estar tendido, embuste, echarse
lief: con placer
light: luz, claro, ligero, encender, alumbrar, débil, liviano, la luz, radiación visible, lámpara, iluminar
lighter: encendedor, mechero, gabarra
lights: luces
liking: afición, gusto
limbs: extremidades
limed: calcinado, Encalado
limits: límites

lines: partida de matrimonio, destino, pauta, especificado de líneas, líneas, papel

lion: león

lips: labios, los labios

list: lista, listar, la lista, listado, minuta

live: vivir, viven, vive, vivo, vivan, vivís, vivimos, vives, viva, vivid, habitar

lively: animado, vivo, alegre

liver: hígado

lives: Vive, habita

living: viviendo, habitando, vivo, viviente

loath: renuente

lodge: alojar, hospedar, la casa del guarda

lodging: alojamiento

longer: más, más tiempo

longing: anhelo, anhelante

looks: mira

lord: señor, caballero

lordship: señoría

lose: perder, pierda, pierdo, perdéis, perdemos, pierdan, pierde, pierden, pierdes, perded, adelgazar

lost: perdido, adelgazado

loud: alto, fuerte, ruidoso, chillón

loved: amado, estimado, querido, considerado

lover: querido, amante, novio

lovers: amantes

loves: amor

low: bajo, depresión

lowly: humilde

loyal: fiel, leal

lubber: palurdo

lullaby: arrullo, canción de cuna

lunatic: lunático

lustrous: lustroso

lying: mentiroso

mad: loco, enojado, chiflado, majara, majareta, demente, enfadado

madman: loco

madmen: locos

madness: locura, demencia, chifladura

madonna: Madona

mads: loco

maid: criada, sirvienta, doncella, la criada

maiden: doncella, soltera

maidenhead: virginidad, himen

makes: hace, comete, confecciona

malice: malicia

malignancy: malignidad

manhood: hombría

mankind: humanidad

manner: manera

manners: modales, educación

map: mapa, tarjeta, plano, el mapa,

correspondencia, plan

maria: María

mark: señal, seña, marca, nota, marcar, sellar, signo, timbrar, señalar, marcos, marco

markets: salidas

marriage: matrimonio, casamiento, enlace

married: casado, casada, se casado, conyugal

marry: casarse, casar, cásese, se casan, se casa, nos casamos, me caso, te casas, cásense, cásate, cásados

martial: marcial

marvel: maravilla, asombrarse

mary: María

masculine: masculino, varonil

mast: mástil

master: maestro, amo, dueño, patrón, principal, magister

match: fósforo, cerilla, correspondencia, partido, coincidir, hacer juego con, emparejar

matter: materia, asunto, particular, caso, importar

meanest: signifique

meaning: intención, significado, sentido, significación

measure: medida, medir

meddle: entrometerse

meditate: meditar, medite, meditamos, medito, mediten, meditan, meditáis, meditad, medita, meditas

meet: encontrar, encontrad, encuentro, encuentren, encuentre, encuentras, encuentran, encontramos, encontráis, encuentra, quedar

melancholy: melancolía, melancólico

mellifluous: melifluo

mend: remendar, enmendar, reparar, zurcir

mended: Mejorado

mercury: Mercurio, azogue

mercy: misericordia, compasión

mere: mero

merry: alegre

message: mensaje, recado, noticias, publicación, noticia, el mensaje

messenger: mensajero, embajador, ordenanza

met: encontrado, hallado

metaphor: metáfora, lenguaje figurado

method: método, procedimiento

mettle: temple

midnight: medianoche, media noche, la medianoche

midsummer: canícula

midwife: comadrona, partera

milk: leche, ordeñar, la leche

mine: mina, mío, minar

minion: favorito

ministers: asiste, atiende, auxilía, oficia

mint: menta, hierbabuena, ceca

minute: minuto, el minuto, minuta, menudo

minx: bribona

miracle: milagro

mirth: alegría

miscarry: abortar, aborte, aborto, abortas, aborten, abortan, abortamos, abortáis, abortad, aborta

mistake: error, equivocación, yerro, la falta

mistaken: malo, equivocado

mistress: señora

mitigation: mitigación

mockery: burla

mocks: ridiculiza, trisca, befa, desbarata, escarnece, mofa, remeda

moderate: moderado, módico, moderar

modest: modesto

modesty: modestia, pudor

mole: topo, lunar, mol

mollification: apaciguamiento, molificación, tranquilización

monster: monstruo

month: mes, el mes

mood: humor, el humor, estado de ánimo, capricho

moon: luna, la luna

moreover: además, demás

mores: moralidad, costumbres, tradiciones

morrow: día siguiente

mortal: mortal

motion: movimiento, moción, petición

motions: movimientos

motley: abigarramiento, abigarrado, multicolor

mountains: sierra, monta a

mourn: deplorar, deploro, deplora, deplorad, deploráis, deploramos, deploran, deploras, deplore, deploren, llorar

mouse: ratón, laucha

mouth: boca, desembocadura, la boca

move: mover, conmover, moverse, mudar, mudanza, movimiento, trasladar, traslado, mudarse, jugada

murder: asesinar, asesinato, homicidio, el asesinato

murderer: asesino

music: música

mute: mudo, muda, sordina

mutton: carnero, carne de carnero

mutual: mutuo, mutua

myself: yo mismo

nails: clavos

naked: desnudo
named: denominado
names: nombres, Michael
nap: siesta, la siesta, echar la siesta
natural: natural
nature: naturaleza, índole, carácter
nay: más aún, más bien, voto
  negativo, voto en contra, no,
  negativa, mejor dicho
near: cerca, próximo, cerca de,
  cercano, entrante, casi
necessity: necesidad
neck: cuello, el cuello, garganta,
  pescuezo, cerviz
needs: necesidades
ne'er: nunca
negatives: negativos
negligence: negligencia, descuido
negotiate: negociar, negocias,
  negocien, negocia, negocian,
  negociamos, negociáis, negociad,
  negocie, negocio
neither: tampoco, ninguno, nadie, ni
nephew: sobrino, el sobrino
nettle: ortiga
newly: nuevamente, recién,
  recientemente
news: noticias, noticia, nueva, las
  noticias
nicely: agradablemente
niece: sobrina, la sobrina
niggardly: mezquino, ávido, cicatero,
  ávidamente, tacaño, avariento
nightingales: ruiseñores
nightly: nocturno
nine: nueve
noah: Noé
nob: personaje, pez gordo, majo,
  golpear a la cabeza, currutaco,
  cholla, cabeza
noble: hidalgo, noble
nobly: con nobleza, noblemente,
  hidalgamente, nobiliariamente,
  noble, prócermente, generosamente,
  personaje
non: in, fattening, des, no
none: ninguno, nadie, nada
nonpareil: sin igual, cosa sin par,
  persona sin pareja, sin par, persona
  sin par
nor: ni, tampoco
nose: nariz, la nariz, proa
notable: señalado, memorable,
  excelente, personaje, notabilidad,
  insigne
note: nota, apuntar, billete, anotar,
  apunte, anotación, notar
notorious: notorio, fragante, infamo
notoriously: notoriamente
notwithstanding: sin embargo, a
  pesar de, no obstante
nought: cero, nada

numbered: foliado, numerado,
  contado
numbers: números
nuncio: nuncio apostólico
o: oxígeno
oath: juramento
oaths: juramentos
obedient: obediente, dócil
obey: obedecer, obedecemos,
  obedezco, obedezcan, obedecen,
  obedecéis, obedeced, obedece,
  obedeces, obedezca
obscure: oscuro, disimular,
  disimulan, disimulas, disimulo,
  disimule, disimula, disimuláis,
  disimulamos, disimulad, disimulen
observe: observar, observa, observen,
  observe, observas, observan,
  observad, observáis, observo,
  observamos, hacer
obstacle: obstáculo, impedimento
obstruction: obstrucción, obstáculo
occasion: motivo, ocasión, lugar,
  oportunidad
occurrence: ocurrencia, suceso,
  acaecimiento, aparición,
  acontecimiento
o'er: sobre
offence: delito, escándalo, injuria
offend: ofender, ofendo, ofendan,
  ofende, ofended, ofendéis,
  ofendemos, ofenden, ofendes,
  ofenda, injuriar
offended: ofendido, injuriado,
  ultrajado, insultado, delinquido
offerings: productos
officers: oficialidad, personal
  directivo, Mesa
oft: a menudo, mucho, con
  frecuencia, muchas veces
olive: aceituna, oliva, la aceituna
ones: unos
opened: abierto
opinion: opinión, dictamen, juicio,
  parecer
opportunity: acontecimiento,
  oportunidad, ocasión
opposite: enfrente de, opuesto,
  contra, enfrente, contrario, frente a,
  frontero
orb: orbe
orbed: redondo, esférico
orchard: huerto, huerta
ordinary: ordinario, común
organ: órgano
other's: otro
otherwise: de otra manera, de lo
  contrario
ought: haber que, deba, deber, haber
  de
ounce: onza
ourselves: nosotros mismos

outside: afuera, fuera de, fuera,
  exterior, externo
outward: exterior
overture: proposición
overweening: altranero, altivo,
  arrogante, presuntuoso
owe: deber, adeudar
oxen: buey
pace: paso
pacified: apaciguado, pacificado
pack: paquete, empacar, embalar,
  empaquetar, manada, envolver
paid: pagado
pains: dolores del parto, esfuerzos,
  desvelos
pair: par, pareja, emparejar
palace: palacio
pale: pálido, palidecer, descolorido
paltry: vil, mezquino, ínfimo,
  despreciable, ruin, miserable
pang: punzada
pants: pantalón, pantalones
paper: papel, documento, el papel,
  papel pintado, ponencia, tapizar,
  periódico
pardon: perdón, perdonar, indulto,
  indultar
parentage: linaje
parson: sacerdote, cura, párroco
partake: compartir, compartan,
  comparto, compartís, compartimos,
  compartid, compartes, comparte,
  comparta, comparten
particle: partícula
partly: en parte, parcialmente
parts: talento, regiones, piezas, partes
pass: pasar, adelantar, paso, pase,
  desfiladero, entregar, pasada,
  aprobar, alargar, paso de montaña,
  llegar
passage: paso, pasillo, pasaje
passed: pasado
passing: paso
passion: pasión
pastime: pasatiempo
patched: remendado
patience: paciencia
patient: paciente
payment: pago, retribución, abono
pays: paga
peace: paz, la paz
pearl: perla, la perla
pedant: pedante
peevish: malhumorado
peevishly: tercamente,
  enojadizamente, obstinadamente,
  quejándose, con mal humor
pen: pluma, la pluma, corral, un
  bolígrafo
penance: penitencia
penned: escrito
pension: pensión

pepper: pimienta, la pimienta, pimiento
perceive: percibir, perciben, percibes, percibe, perciban, percibid, percibimos, percibís, percibo, perciba
perchance: quizás, tal vez
perdition: perdición
perfection: perfección
peril: peligro
perpend: perpiaño, pesar, considerar, meditar
personage: personaje
perspective: perspectiva
persuaded: convencido, persuadido
persuades: convence, persuade
persuasion: persuasión
peruse: lean, examina, leo, lees, leen, leemos, leéis, leed, lee, examino, examinen
perverseness: obstinación, perversidad
phoenix: fénix
phrygia: Frigia
physic: medicamento, remedio
picture: imagen, cuadro, grabado, pintura, retrato, el cuadro, reproducción, ilustración, foto
piece: pieza, pedazo, parte, trozo, tela
pirate: pirata
pistol: pistola
pitch: paso, pez, grado de inclinación, tono, cabeceo, diapasón, altura, brea, pendiente
pity: dolerse por, piedad, compadecer a, lástima, compasión
plague: plaga, peste, atormentar
plain: llanura, llano, claro, evidente, liso, plano
plainly: simplemente
plaintiff: demandante, querellante
plant: planta, plantar, cultivar, fábrica, instalación
play: jugar, jueguen, juega, juegan, juegue, jugad, jugáis, jugamos, juegas, juego, tocar
played: jugado, tocado
plays: juega, toca
please: por favor, agradar, gustar, complacer, haz el favor, contentar, haz favor
pleased: contento
pleasure: placer, agrado, gusto, complacencia, el gusto
plot: parcela, trama, argumento, complot, gráfico, solar, trazar
pluck: arrancar, tirón, cortar, desplumar
plumes: plumas
pocket: bolsillo, el bolsillo, bolsa, casilla
poetical: poético

points: puntos, aguja
poison: veneno, envenenar, intoxicar
politic: sagaz
politician: político, hombre político
pollution: contaminación, polución
poor: pobre, malo, deplorable, indigente, miserable
portend: presagiar
possess: poseer, poseen, posees, poseo, posean, poseéis, posee, poseed, poseemos, posea, tener
possessed: poseído
possibly: posiblemente, quizás, tal vez
post: poste, correo, empleo, cargo, puesto, oficio, apostar, posta, función, fijar, estaca
postscript: posdata, postdata
potent: potente, poderoso
pound: libra, la libra
practice: ejercicio, practicar, emplear, práctica, ejercer
practising: ejercicio, ejercicios, entrenamiento, práctica, practicante, practicar, que ejerce
prague: Praga
praise: alabar, alabanza, elogio, elogiar
pranks: bromas
prattle: cháchara, balbuceo, charlar, parlotear, parloteo, balbucear
pray: rezar, rezáis, rezas, rezamos, rezad, reza, recen, rece, rezan, rezo, rogar
prayers: ruegos, rezos, oraciones
prays: reza, ruega, ora
pregnant: embarazada, en estado, encinta, preñada
preparation: preparación, preparado, preparativo
prepare: preparar, preparas, prepare, prepara, preparad, preparáis, preparan, preparo, preparen, preparamos, prepararse
prerogative: prerrogativa
presage: agüero
presence: presencia
present: presente, actual, presentar, regalo, contemporáneo, ofrecer, reproducir, retratar
presently: por ahora
pretty: bonito, lindo, majo, amable, guapo, bastante, guapa
prevail: prevalecer, prevalecemos, prevalece, prevaleced, prevalecéis, prevalezco, prevaleces, prevalezca, prevalezcan, prevalecen
prevents: impide, previene
prey: presa
price: precio, el precio, costo
priest: sacerdote, cura, preste
princess: princesa

prison: prisión, cárcel, presidio, encierro
private: privado, soldado raso
prized: apreciado
probation: libertad condicional
proceed: proceder, actuar
prodigal: pródigo
profanation: profanación
profit: beneficio, provecho, ganancia, aprovecharse, ganar, lucro, rendimiento
profound: profundo
promise: prometer, prometéis, prometemos, prometen, prometo, promete, prometan, prometa, prometes, prometed, promesa
promised: prometido
prompt: indicador, aviso
prompted: interactiva, incitado
proof: prueba, demostración, probanza
proper: conveniente, preciso, correcto, apropiado, propio, debido
propertied: adinerado, propietario, hacendado
prospect: perspectiva
protect: proteger, protegéis, protejo, protejan, proteges, protegemos, proteged, protégé, protegen, proteja, guardar
protection: protección, amparo, defensa
protest: protestar, protesta
proud: orgulloso
prove: probar, probad, prueban, pruebas, pruebo, probamos, probáis, prueben, prueba, pruebe, verificar
proves: prueba, verifica
provident: previsor, providente, prudente
prudent: prudente
publish: publicar, publicáis, publiquen, publico, publicas, publican, publicad, publica, publicamos, publique, editar
purchase: compra, comprar, adquisición, procurarse, la compra, adquirir
pure: puro, limpio
puritan: puritano
purpose: fin, objeto, finalidad, propósito
purposely: intencionalmente, deliberadamente, a propósito
purse: portamonedas, monedero, colecta, bolsa, bolso, la bolsa, cartera
pursue: perseguir, perseguid, persiguen, persigue, persigo, persigan, persiga, perseguís, perseguimos, persigues
pursuit: persecución, acosamiento
putting: poniendo, metiendo,

Twelfth Night

colocando
puzzled: perplejo, desconcertado
pythagoras: Pitágoras
quaffing: zampar
quality: calidad, ralea, cualidad, la calidad
quantity: cantidad, la cantidad, magnitud, cuantidad
quarrel: disputar, reñir, riña, pelear
quarreller: pendenciero
quarrelling: disputas, peleón, pelear
queen: reina, la reina, dama
quenching: extinción, temple, apagado, extinción sin conmutación
quick: rápido, pronto
quickly: rápidamente, de prisa, aprisa, pronto
quiet: quieto, silencio, tranquilo, calmar, silencioso, sosegar, callado
quieter: más silencioso que
quirk: ocurrencia, rareza, mediacaña, chifladura, rasgo, moldurera, juntera, cimacio, capricho, escapatoria, peculiaridad
quits: abandona, en paz
radiant: resplandeciente, radiante, brillante
rage: rabia, furia, furor, ira
rail: carril, riel, pasamanos, barandilla, baranda
railing: barandilla, balaustrada, pasamano, baranda
rain: llover, lluvia, la lluvia
range: alcance, gama, rango, intervalo, ámbito, margen, recorrido
rank: rango, fila, turno, línea, clasificar
rapier: estoque
rare: raro
rascal: bribón
rascally: pícaro
rave: delirar, deliras, deliro, delire, deliran, deliramos, deliráis, delirad, delira, deliren
reading: leyendo, lectura, la lectura
reads: lee, estudia, indica
ready: listo, preparado, propenso, disponible
reap: cosechar, cosechamos, cosechen, cosecho, cosecháis, cosechad, cosechas, cosechan, cosecha, coseche, segar
reason: motivo, causa, razón, lugar, razonar
reasons: razona
receive: recibir, reciben, recibís, recibimos, recibes, recibe, reciban, recibid, reciba, recibo, tomar
recollected: recordado, acordado
recommended: recomendado, ensalzado, encarecido
recompense: recompensa

record: registro, registrar, récord, disco, expediente, grabar, inscribir, acta, certificar, ficha
recover: recuperar, sanar, recupere, sanad, recuperad, recuperáis, recuperamos, recuperan, recuperas, recuperen, recupero
recreation: recreación, recreo
red: rojo, tinto, encarnado
redeem: amortizar, redimir, rescatar, redima, redimimos, redimid, redimes, redimen, redime, rediman, redimo
regard: mirar, considerar, mira, miran, miráis, miro, miramos, mirad, miras, mire, miren
reins: riñones, rienda, riendas
relieve: aliviar, alivie, alivias, aliviad, alivio, alivien, aliviamos, aliviáis, alivian, alivia, relevar
religious: religioso
relish: paladear, condimento, saborear
remain: quedarse, restar, permanecer, restas, resto, reste, restan, restamos, restáis, restad, resta
remedy: curar, remedio, recurso, medio, remediar
remember: recordar, recuerde, recuerdo, recuerdan, recuerdas, recuerden, recordamos, recordad, recordáis, recuerda, acordarse de
remembrance: recuerdo
remorse: remordimiento
renown: hambre, renombre, conocimientos
represented: representado
reproof: reparo, censura, reprobación
reprove: reprobar, reprobad, reprueba, repruebo, reprueben, repruebe, reprueban, reprobamos, reprobáis, repruebas, reprender
reproves: reprueba
request: petición, pedir, solicitar, solicitud, demandar, solicitación, requerimiento, ruego, rogar, demanda
requite: reembolse, compensar, recompensar, pagar
rescue: salvar, rescate, rescatar, socorro, salvamento
resemble: parecerse, asemejarse, parecerse a
resembled: Parecido
reserve: reservar, reserva, pedir
resolute: resuelto
resolved: resuelto
respect: respetar, respeto, estima, estimación
rest: descansar, descanso, resto, detrito, desechos, reposar, reposo
restore: restaurar, restablecer,

restaure, restaurad, restablezca, restableces, restablecen, restablecemos, restablecéis, restableced, restablece
retention: retención, conservación
return: volver, devolver, regresar, retorno, devolución, rendimiento, vuelta
returned: devuelto
returns: devolver, reembolso, ganancias, devoluciones, cheques y letras devueltos, retorno, rendimiento, remuneración, regreso, ingresos, volver
revels: jarana, jolgorio, fiestas
revenge: venganza, revancha
reverberate: reverberar, reverbere, reverbero, reverbera, reverberen, reverberas, reverberan, reverberamos, reverberáis, reverberad
reverend: reverendo, clérigo
revolve: girar, gira, gire, giro, revolver, giramos, giren, giran, giráis, girad, giras
rich: rico
rid: librar, libro, librad, librado, libráis, libramos, libran, libras, libre, libren, libra
riddle: enigma, acertijo, adivinanza
ride: montar, conducir, paseo, cabalgar, cabalgata
ridiculous: ridículo
rightly: debidamente
ring: anillo, el anillo, llamar, aro, anilla, argolla, tocar la campanilla, sonar, sortija, corro
ripe: maduro
robin: petirrojo
rogue: pícaro
rough: áspero, crudo, desigual, bronco, brusco, grosero
roughly: ásperamente, aproximadamente, bruscamente
rouse: animar, instigar, espolear, incitar, despertar, estimular, espoleen, espoleo, espolead, espoleamos, espolean
royal: real
rub: frotar, refregar, friccionar
rubious: de color rubí
rude: grosero, rudo, insolente, descortés
rudely: grosero, groseramente, bastamente, rudamente
rudeness: rudeza
ruffian: rufián
rule: regla, gobernar, la regla, norma, fallar, refrenar, dominio, subyugar, reprimir, regir, contener
ruled: reglado
runs: corre

sack: saco, despedir, bolso
sacrifice: sacrificio, sacrificar, ofrecer,
  presentar
sad: triste, afligido
safety: seguridad
sage: salvia, sabio
sail: vela, navegar, la vela
sailed: navegado
sailor: marinero, navegante, el
  marinero, marino
sailors: marinería
saint: santo, santa, san
sake: motivo, fin, bien, causa
salt: sal, la sal, salar, salado
sanctity: santidad
sat: pret y pp de sit, sáb, servicio de
  administración tributaria, sentado,
  sábado, soplado, asentado,
  empollado, se sentado, sentido
satan: Satanás, Satán
satisfaction: satisfacción
satisfy: complacer, complacen,
  complazca, complazcan, complaces,
  complazco, complacéis, complace,
  complaced, complacemos, satisfacer
saucy: descarado
savage: fiero, salvaje
save: guardar, guarda, guardan,
  guardáis, guardamos, guardas,
  guarde, guardo, guardad, guarden,
  salvar
saved: guardado, salvado, ahorrado
savours: sabores
saws: serrar
saying: diciendo, dicho, decir, refrán
sayings: dichos
scab: costra, esquirol, roña
scabbard: vaina
scarce: escaso
scene: escena, escenario
scent: olor, perfume, aroma
schedules: programas
scholar: erudito, estudiante, escolar
scorn: desdén, desdeñar
scoundrels: sinvergüenzas
scout: explorador, explorar
screws: tornillos
scruple: escrúpulo
scurvy: escorbuto
sea: mar, el mar
seal: foca, sello, sellar, precinto,
  precintar
sebastian: Sebastián
secret: secreto, el secreto, arcano,
  clandestino
seek: buscar, busque, busca, buscan,
  buscamos, busquen, buscas, buscáis,
  buscad, busco
seeking: buscando
seem: parecer, parezca, parecen,
  parezcan, pareces, parezco,
  parecemos, parecéis, parece, pareced

sees: Ve, serra
self: mismo
self-love: narcisismo, egolatría,
  egoísmo
semblance: semejanza
send: enviar, envío, envía, envíe,
  enviad, enviáis, enviamos, envían,
  envías, envíen, mandar
sends: envía, manda, despacha
senseless: insensato
senses: juicio, los sentidos, sentido
sent: enviado, mandado, despachado
sentence: frase, condenar, sentencia,
  oración, la frase, pena, punición,
  condena
separate: separado, separar, apartar,
  aparte, particular, dividir, separarse,
  segregar, independiente, compartir
sepulchre: mausoleo, sepulcro,
  sepultura, tumba
sequel: continuación
servant: criado, criada, sirviente,
  servidor
servants: servicio
serve: servir, sirva, sirvo, servimos,
  servid, servís, sirvan, sirve, sirven,
  sirves
served: servido
serves: sirve
seven: siete
severs: separa
sex: sexo, el sexo, tener sexo
shackles: grilletes
shadow: sombra, sombreado
shake: sacudir, sacuda, sacudimos,
  sacudís, sacudid, sacudes, sacuden,
  sacude, sacudan, sacudo, sacudida
shallow: poco profundo, somero, de
  poca profundidad, superficial
shalt: irá, verbo auxiliar inglés para
  especificar futuro
shame: vergüenza, verguenza, pudor,
  oprobio, avergonzar
shameful: vergonzoso
shape: forma, formar, figura,
  amoldar, horma, la forma, perfil,
  conformar
shapes: las formas, formas, aspectos
share: compartir, acción, parte,
  dividir, ración, cuota, lote
sharp: agudo, afilado, sostenido,
  justamente, acre, cortante, áspero
sharply: bruscamente
sheet: hoja, lámina, sábana, libra,
  escota, folio, placa, chapa, plancha,
  sabana
shine: brillar, brillo, lucir
shines: brilla
ship: barco, enviar, enviad, envía,
  envíen, envíe, envías, envían,
  enviamos, enviáis, envío
shortly: brevemente

showed: mostrado, pret de show
shown: mostrado
shows: muestra
shrew: arpía, musaraña
shrewdly: astutamente,
  perspicazmente, con perspicacia,
  sagazmente, mañosamente
shrewishly: regañonamente,
  regañónmente
shrill: chillón
shroud: mortaja, obenque, protector,
  protector de contacto
shuffled: barajado
shut: cerrar, cerrado
sick: enfermo
sicken: enfermar
sides: costados, Lados
sight: vista, aspecto, mira, avistar
silence: silencio, acallar, hacer callar,
  el silencio
silly: tonto, necio, absurdo, bobo
simple: sencillo, simple
simply: simplemente, sencillamente
simulation: simulación
sin: pecado, pecar
sinews: tendones, recursos
sing: cantar, cantan, cantas, canten,
  cantamos, cantáis, canta, cantad,
  canto, cante
singing: cantando, canto
singularity: singularidad
sinister: siniestro
sinner: pecador
sir: señor
sister: hermana, la hermana, cuñada
sit: sentarse, estar sentado, sentar
sits: asienta, siente, sopla, empolla, se
  sienta
sitting: sesión, sentada
sixpence: seis peniques
skilful: hábil, experto
skill: destreza, habilidad, arte,
  agilidad
skills: competencia
skipping: saltar, salto a la comba
skittish: caprichoso, frívolo, nervioso,
  asustadizo
skull: cráneo, calavera
slain: matado
slander: calumniar, calumnia,
  infamar, difamación
sleep: dormir, duerme, duermes,
  dormimos, duermen, duermo,
  dormís, dormid, duerma, duerman,
  sueño
sleeping: durmiendo, durmiente
slew: cambio rápido de orientación,
  girar, giro sobre el eje, giro veloz,
  montón, pret de slay, torcer, torcerse
  a
slip: deslizamiento, resbalar, desliz,
  deslizar, combinación

slough: pantano, Abismo, cenagal, Costra, fangal, Deshacerse Por, Desprenderse De, Mudar, desprenderse, Mudar La Piel

slow: lento

smell: oler, olor, apestar, oler mal, olfatear, olfato

smile: sonrisa, sonreír, la sonrisa, sonreírse

smiling: sonriente

smoke: fumar, fumo, fume, fumas, fuman, fumamos, fumáis, fumad, fuma, fumen, humo

smooth: liso, plano, alisar, suavizar, suave

snatched: arrebatado

soft: blando, suave, tierno, dulce

soldier: soldado, el soldado

solemn: solemne

solicit: solicitar, solicita, solicitad, solicito, soliciten, solicitas, solicitan, solicitamos, solicitáis, solicite

sometime: algún día

somewhere: en alguna parte

son: hijo, el hijo

song: canción, canto

sonnet: soneto

soon: pronto, luego

sooner: más pronto

sooth: verdad, realidad

sorry: afligido, arrepentido, pesaroso, siento, triste

sot: beodo, borrachín, borracho

sought: buscado

soul: alma, espíritu, ánimo

soundly: sanamente, solventemente, sólidamente, razonablemente, profundamente, firmemente, vigorosamente

sovereign: soberano

sowed: sembrado

spare: sobrante, ahorrar, recambio, perdonar

speak: hablar, hablamos, hablo, hablas, habláis, hablad, hablen, habla, hablan, hable

speaking: hablando, parlante

speaks: habla

speech: discurso, habla, lenguaje, oración, conversación, dialecto, idioma

speedy: rápido

spend: gastar, gastáis, gastas, gasten, gastad, gasta, gastamos, gastan, gasto, gaste, pasar

spheres: esferos

spin: giro, girar, hilar

spirit: espíritu

spirits: alcohol

spite: rencor

spleen: bazo

spoke: decir, radio, rayo, raya,

radioactivo, rayo de rueda, hablar, pret de speak, expresar

sport: deporte

sportful: alegre

spur: espolear, espuela, espolón, alimentación en derivación, línea en derivación, estimular

squash: aplastar, calabaza

squeak: rechinar

stable: cuadra, establo, estable, fijo, caballeriza

stage: escenario, fase, etapa, escena, plataforma, estrado, organizar

stainless: inoxidable

stand: estar de pie, puesto, levantarse, granero, posición, cabina, soporte, base, estante, caseta, pararse

standing: permanente, posición

stands: tenderetes, jaulas

star: estrella, la estrella, astro

stark: severo

stars: estrellas

started: comenzado, encaminado

stay: quedarse, quedar, queden, quede, quedas, quedan, quedamos, quedáis, quedad, queda, quedo

stayed: quedado, permanecido

steel: acero, ballena, el acero, acerar

step: paso, escalón, peldaño

steward: camarero, administrador, mayordomo

stir: conmover, revolver, remover, agitar

stitches: puntos de sutura, los puntos de sutura

stock: acciones, existencias, existencia, almacenar, acción, mango, proveer, reserva, ganado, valores

stockings: las medias

stone: piedra, la piedra, cálculo

stood: pret y pp de stand

stooping: inclinar, inclinarse, rebajamiento, rebajar, rebajarse, cargado de espaldas, agachado, agacharse, inclinación, humillarse, encorvado

stoup: pila de agua bendita

stout: obstinado

straight: derecho, recto, directamente, recta

strain: colar, esfuerzo, deformación, cepa, tensión, torcedura

strange: extraño, raro, ajeno

strangeness: extrañeza

stranger: forastero, extraño, desconocido

strangle: estrangular, estranguláis, estrangulen, estrangulamos, estrangulan, estrangulo, estrangula, estrangulas, estrangulad, estrangule

straps: abrazaderas, cintas

street: calle, la calle

streets: calles, las calles

strength: fuerza, resistencia, virtud, potencia, fortaleza

strike: huelga, golpear, llamar, declararse en huelga, acertar, paro, golpe

strip: tira, raya, faja, desnudarse, franja, desmontar, banda

strive: esforzarse

stroke: acariciar, caricia, apoplejía, carrera, golpe, derrame cerebral, recorrido

strong: fuerte, intenso, marcado

struck: pret y pp de strike, golpeado

stubborn: terco, testarudo, obstinado

stuck: punzar, picar, atrancarse

student: estudiante, alumno, el estudiante

studied: estudiado

stuff: rellenar, cosas, material, llenar

subtle: sutil

suburbs: las afueras

suffer: sufrir, sufres, sufro, sufrís, sufrid, sufren, sufre, sufran, sufrimos, sufra, padecer

suffering: sufriendo, padeciendo, sufrimiento

suffers: sufre, padece

suit: traje, convenir, el traje, pleito

suited: demanda, conveniente, traje, satisfacer, preparado, pleito, idóneo, ajustarse a, adecuado, acomodado, conjunto

summer: verano, el verano, estival

sun: sol, el sol

supplied: suministrado

supporter: partidario, hincha, seguidor

suppose: suponer, suponéis, supongo, supon, suponed, suponemos, suponen, supones, supongan, supone, suponga

sure: seguro, cierto

surely: seguramente, ciertamente

surfeit: superabundancia, empacho, exceso, hartar, hartura, saciar, saciedad

surgeon: cirujano, el cirujano

surly: bronco, brusco, hosco

sustain: sostener, sosten, sostengan, sostiene, sostenemos, sostenéis, sostened, sostienes, sostienen, sostengo, sostenga

swabber: mozo de la limpieza

swaggering: pavoneándose, fanfarrón

sway: oscilación, vaivén

swear: jurar, jura, jurad, juráis, juramos, juran, juras, juren, juro, jure, maldecir

swears: jura
sweet: dulce, caramelo, postre
sweetheart: novio, querido
swiftness: ligereza, prontitud, rapidez
sword: espada
sworn: jurado
syllogism: silogismo
taffeta: tafetán, tafeta
tailor: sastre, costurera
taint: deterioración, putrefacción, mancha
tainted: perdido, contaminado, corrompido, echado a perder, fraudulenta, infecto, manchado, pasado, viciado
tainting: Manchar
takes: toma, desempeña
talents: talentos
tales: cuentos
talk: hablar, hablas, hablan, hablad, habláis, hablamos, hablo, hable, hablen, habla, charla
talking: hablando, parlante, charlando, hablar
tall: alto
tang: rabera, sabor, regusto, lengüeta, extremidad, espiga, dejo, chaveta, sabor picante, poner una espiga a
tarry: quedarse atrás, alquitranado
tartar: tártaro, sarro
taste: gusto, saborear, sabor, probar, catar
taunt: insultar, insulto, insultas, insulten, insulta, insulte, insultamos, insultad, insultan, insultáis, mofarse
taurus: Tauro
taxation: tributación, fiscalidad
teaching: enseñando, enseñanza, instruyendo, desacostumbrando
tear: lágrima, desgarrar, rajar, romper, rasgar, desgarro
tears: desgarra, rasga
tempt: tentar, tentad, tiento, tienten, tientas, tientan, tentamos, tentáis, tienta, tiente
tend: cuidar, cuidas, cuidan, cuido, cuide, cuida, cuidáis, cuidamos, cuidad, cuiden, tender
tended: cuidado, Tendido
tender: tierno, oferta, dulce, subasta, proposición, ofrecer, destajo, licitación, presentar, reproducir, retratar
terms: condiciones, condición
terrible: terrible
terror: terror
text: texto
thank: agradecer, agradezco, agradeces, agradezcan, agradece, agradezca, agradecemos, agradeced, agradecen, agradecéis, dar gracias

thanked: agradecido
thankful: agradecido
thanks: gracias, agradece
thee: ustedes, te, vosotros, usted, tú
theme: tema
thereby: en consecuencia de esto, por lo tanto
therein: en eso, adjunto
thereto: a eso
thief: ladrón
thighs: muslos
thine: tuyo, tuyos, tuyas, tuya, tus
thinks: piensa, reflexiona
thirteen: trece
thou: tú, usted, vosotros, ustedes, vos
thoughts: pensamientos
thousand: mil
thousands: miles
thread: hilo, rosca, hebra, el hilo
threw: pret de throw, Tiró, tiro
thrice: tres veces
thriftless: gastoso, malgastador
throat: garganta, la garganta
throw: lanzar, echar, tirar, tirada, arrojar, lanzamiento
thrown: tirado, pp de throw
thrust: empujar, empuje, empujón
thunder: trueno, tronar, el trueno
thy: tu
thyself: ti, tú mismo, ti mismo, tú misma, te, ti misma
tickled: Cosquilleó
tickling: cosquillas
tiger: tigre, el tigre
till: caja, hasta que, hasta, a que
tinkers: arregla, remienda, manosea, estropea, compone, caldereros
tiny: diminuto
tired: cansado
to-day: hoy
toe: dedo del pie, dedo de pie, el dedo del pie
to-morrow: mañana
tongue: lengua, la lengua, lengüeta
tongues: lenguas
touch: tocar, toque, tacto, palpar, contacto, rozar
toward: hacia, a
town: ciudad, pueblo, población, el pueblo
trade: comercio, oficio, negocio, intercambiar
transgresses: transgrede
transparent: transparente
trappings: captura, arreos, galas, jaeces, adornos
travel: viajar, viaje, viajo, viaja, viajas, viajan, viajamos, viajen, viajad, viajáis, conducir
travelled: viaje, moverse, viajado, viajar, viajar por, camino
treasure: tesoro, atesorar

trial: ensayo, juicio, prueba
trick: engañar, truco, resabio, mala costumbre
trip: viaje, disparo, excursión, el viaje
triplex: triple
tripping: desconexión
troth: fidelidad, fe
trouble: molestar, prueba, inconveniente, incomodar, molestia, perturbación, problema, dificultad, avería, esfuerzo
troubled: molestar, de enfermedad, agitado, problema, desventurado, apurado, molestarse, dificultad, no sabroso, pasado difícilmente, pena
trout: trucha
true: verdadero, cierto
truly: verdaderamente, de veras, en realidad, en efecto, realmente
trunks: traje de baño, bañador, mampara encerradora de la escotilla, pantaloneta, pantalón de baño
trust: confiar, fideicomiso, confianza, fiduciario
truth: verdad, veras, la verdad
tuck: alforza
tune: melodía, acomodar, adaptar
turn: girar, gira, giro, giráis, giramos, giran, giras, gire, giren, girad, vuelta
turned: girado, vuelto, trastornado
turning: girando, volviendo, trastornando
tut: eso no, vamos, pche, hacer un gesto de desaprobación, gesto de desaprobación, qué horror, Vaya
twanged: Vibrado
twelfth: duodécimo
twelvemonth: mes doce
twill: tela cruzada o asargada
tyrannous: tiránico, tirano
tyrant: tirano
uncivil: descortés, incivil
uncle: tío
uncourteous: descortés
underneath: abajo, debajo, debajo de, en el fondo
understand: entender, entiendes, entienda, entiendan, entendemos, entendéis, entended, entienden, entiendo, entiende, comprender
undertake: emprender, emprenda, emprendes, emprended, emprendo, emprendes, emprendéis, emprendan, emprende, emprendemos, encargarse de
undertaker: enterrador
undo: deshacer, deshaga, deshagan, deshago, deshaces, deshacen, deshacemos, deshacéis, deshaced, deshace, deshaz
unfilled: vacío

unfold: desplegar, despliegue, desplegáis, desplegamos, despliega, despliegan, despliegas, desplieguen, desplegad, despliego, desdoblar
unfriended: hostil
ungird: Desciña, desceñir, desceño, desceñís, desceñimos, desceñid, desceñes, desceñen, desceñe, desceña, desceñan
ungracious: descortés, poco gracioso
unjust: injusto
unkind: brusco, bronco
unknown: desconocido, incógnita
unless: a menos que, a no ser que
unmatchable: incomparable
unsafe: inseguro, peligroso
unsound: enfermo
unsuitable: inadecuado
untangle: desenredar, desenmarañe, desenredáis, desenredo, desenreden, desenrede, desenredas, desenredamos, desenredad, desenreda, desenredan
unthought: desaconsejado
unto: hacia
upbraid: regañar
upbraids: reprende, reconviene, regaña
upshot: resultado
usage: uso, costumbre, usanza, utilización
uses: usa, utiliza
usurp: usurpar, usurpe, usurpo, usurpa, usurpad, usurpáis, usurpamos, usurpan, usurpas, usurpen
utensil: utensilio
utters: pronuncía
v: foulardar, excitar, velocidad, v, operar, aumentar la torsión, impregnar, aplicar torsión suplementaria, accionar
vain: vano, hueco, vanidoso
vainness: vanidad
valentine: Enamorado, nota amorosa, novia, -via, novio, Tarjeta Amorosa, Valentín
valiant: bravo, valiente
validity: validez, vigencia
valour: valor
veil: velo
veiled: rebozado, velado
velvet: terciopelo, el terciopelo
venerable: venerado
venom: veneno
vent: abertura, respiradero, desahogar
verse: verso, estrofa, copla, versículo
vessel: vaso, embarcación, barco, estuche, recipiente, vasija, olla, buque, jarro, caja
vex: vejar

vice: vicio, virtud, tornillo de banco
viewing: inspección, visita, ver la televisión, ver la tele, ver, programación, de los espectadores, censura, programas
vile: vil
villain: bribón, malo
villainously: ruinmente, villanamente, malvadamente, malamente, vilmente
vinegar: vinagre, el vinagre
viola: la viola
virago: arpía
virtue: virtud
virtuous: virtuoso
visage: visaje, semblante, rostro, gesto
visit: visitar, visita, visitad, visiten, visitan, visitas, visito, visitamos, visitáis, visite
visited: visitado
vouchsafed: Concedido
vow: voto
vows: promesas solemnes
vox: voz
voyage: viaje
vulcan: Vulcano
vulgar: chabacano, cursi, grosero, cutre, corriente, vulgo, vulgar, ramplón, ordinario, ordinaria, común
walk: andar, andamos, ando, anden, ande, andas, andáis, andad, anda, andan, caminar
walks: anda, camina
wanton: petulante, lascivo
wardrobe: armario, guardarropa, armario ropero, ropero, vestuario
ware: mercancía
warrant: garantía, orden, orden por escrito, certificado, autorizar, autorización
wash: lavar, lave, lavo, lava, lavad, laváis, lavamos, lavas, laven, lavan, lavarse
waste: desechos, desperdicio, residuo, residuos, detrito, gastar, acabar, desperdicios, derrochar, gasto, desecho
watch: reloj, mirar, observar, reloj de pulsera, ver, contemplar, el reloj, prestar atención, vigilar, guardia, guardar
waters: aguas
watery: acuoso, aguado
wavering: vacilando, vacilación, duda, vacilante
waves: olas
waxen: ceroso
waylay: acechar, aceche, acechan, acecho, acechen, acechas, acecháis, acechamos, acecha, acechad

ways: maneras
weak: débil, flojo
wear: llevar, desgaste, usar, tener puesto, vestir, uso, llevar puesto
wears: lleva, usa
weary: cansado, fatigado
weather: tiempo, el tiempo, clima
weave: tejer, tejido
weaver: tejedor
weeds: malas hierbas, hierbajos
weep: llorar, llore, lloren, llora, lloro, lloras, lloran, lloramos, lloráis, llorad
welcome: dar la bienvenida, bienvenida, bienvenido, acoger, grato, agradable, acogida, acogen, acojan, acojo, acoges
we'll: Haremos
wench: muchacha
whatsoever: lo que, en absoluto, todo lo que, cualquier cosa, cualquier
whence: de dónde
wherefore: por qué, por eso, por consiguiente
wherein: en qué
whereof: de que, de lo cual, cuyo, del cual
whet: afilar, afile, afilen, afilas, afilan, afiláis, afilad, afila, afilo, afilamos
whilst: mientras
whirligig: molinete, movimiento confuso, tiovivo
whisper: cuchichear, cuchicheo, susurrar, susurro, murmurar
whither: adónde, adonde
whom: quien, quién, que
whose: cuyo, cuya
wide: ancho, amplio, vasto, lejos
wife: esposa, mujer, la esposa
willing: dispuesto, deseoso
willow: sauce
wilt: marchitarse, marchitar
wind: viento, serpentear, el viento, enrollar, devanar
windows: ventanas, ojal
windy: ventoso
wine: vino, el vino
wing: ala, el ala, guardabarros, la ala
wink: guiño, pestañeo, parpadeo, guiñar
wins: gana
wisdom: sabiduría, sapiencia
wise: sabio, sensato, guisa
wisely: sabiamente
wish: desear, deseo, voluntad, querer, tener, gana
wished: deseado
wishes: anhelar, anhelo, ansiar, desear, deseo, deseos, querer, votos
wit: ingenio
witchcraft: brujería
withal: además

wittily: chistoso, ingeniosamente,
   graciosamente
witty: ingenioso
wolf: lobo, el lobo
womb: útero, matriz
wonder: preguntarse, maravilla,
   asombrarse, prodigio, preguntar
wonderful: maravilloso
woo: cortejar, corteje, cortejamos,
   cortejo, cortejen, cortejan, cortejáis,
   cortejad, corteja, cortejas
woodcock: becada
wooer: pretendiente, cortejador
woos: corteja
word: palabra, la palabra, vocablo,
   término, formular
worm: gusano, lombriz, el gusano
worse: peor
worth: valor
worthy: digno
wrangle: disputa, disputar, reñir
wrath: ira
wreck: naufragio, desbaratar
wren: reyezuelo, chochín
writ: escritura, orden, escrito, orden
   por escrito
write: escribir, escriba, escriban,
   escribo, escribís, escribimos,
   escribid, escribes, escribe, escriben
wrong: malo, mal, falso, incorrecto,
   entuerto, agravio, impropio, erróneo
wronged: explotado
ye: usted, vosotros, ustedes, vosotras,
   tú, los, lo, las, la, el, vos
yellow: amarillo
yeoman: hacendado
yesterday: ayer
yield: ceder, cedemos, cedes, cedo,
   ceden, cedéis, ceded, cede, ceda,
   cedan, rendimiento
yonder: allí, ahí, aquel
younger: menor
youngest: más joven
yours: vuestro, suyo, el tuyo
yourself: tú mismo, se
yourselves: ustedes mismos
youth: juventud, joven, jóvenes,
   adolescencia
zanies: Estrafalario